Football Fandom in Italy and Beyond

Football fans are passionate and devoted followers. They are also creators and dissenters, performers and producers. This volume analyzes football fandom through the media that fans use to construct fandom itself. Media is the lifeblood of modern life; it is the canvas on which ideas are spread, communities are formed and identities are expressed. Today's fan has an unprecedented variety of tools in which to express their passion, to commune with others and to *become* a fan in front of local, regional and global audiences.

The football stadium has always been rife with symbolism. Colourful scarves and communal songs and chants evoke and display local pride and distinguish *us* from *them*. The Italian football stadium has a particularly rich history as a place of collective celebration, mourning, support and political dissent. Over time, Italian fans have integrated print, radio and television into their rituals of fandom while modern digital media allows fans to publicise their identities to global audiences. This volume addresses the beauty and humour as well as the fear and anger that are conveyed in the spectrum of media as fans attempt to assert themselves as material and spiritual 'owners' of the club of their affection. This book was originally published as a special issue of the journal *Soccer & Society*.

Matthew Guschwan has written extensively about Italian football fans. He lives in Bloomington, Indiana, where he occasionally lectures about fandom and media culture.

Sport in the Global Society – Contemporary Perspectives

Series Editor: Boria Majumdar, *University of Central Lancashire, UK*

The social, cultural (including media) and political study of sport is an expanding area of scholarship and related research. While this area has been well served by the *Sport in the Global Society* series, the surge in quality scholarship over the last few years has necessitated the creation of *Sport in the Global Society: Contemporary Perspectives*. The series will publish the work of leading scholars in fields as diverse as sociology, cultural studies, media studies, gender studies, cultural geography and history, political science and political economy. If the social and cultural study of sport is to receive the scholarly attention and readership it warrants, a cross-disciplinary series dedicated to taking sport beyond the narrow confines of physical education and sport science academic domains is necessary. *Sport in the Global Society: Contemporary Perspectives* will answer this need.

DIY Football
Edited by David Kennedy and Peter Kennedy

A Social and Political History of Everton and Liverpool Football Clubs
The split, 1878–1914
Authored by David Kennedy

Football Fandom in Italy and Beyond
Community through media and performance
Authored by Matthew Guschwan

Numbers and Narratives
Sport, history and economics
Edited by Wray Vamplew

Sex Integration in Sport and Physical Culture
Promises and pitfalls
Edited by Alex Channon, Katherine Dashper, Thomas Fletcher and Robert Lake

A Social and Cultural History of Sport in Ireland
Edited by David Hassan and Richard McElligott

Football and Health Improvement: an Emergent Field
Edited by Daniel Parnell and Andy Pringle

A Social and Cultural History of Sport in Ireland
Edited by Richard McElligatt and David Hassam

The Containment of Soccer in Australia
Fencing Off the World Game
Edited by Christopher J. Hallinan and John E. Hughson

The History of Motor Sport
A case study analysis
Edited by David Hassan

The Making of Sporting Cultures
Authored by John E. Hughson

Football Fandom in Italy and Beyond

Community through Media and Performance

Matthew Guschwan

LONDON AND NEW YORK

First published 2017 by Routledge

2 Park Square, Milton Park, Abingdon, Oxfordshire OX14 4RN
52 Vanderbilt Avenue, New York, NY 10017

Routledge is an imprint of the Taylor & Francis Group, an informa business

First issued in paperback 2018

Copyright © 2017 Taylor & Francis

All rights reserved. No part of this book may be reprinted or reproduced or utilised in any form or by any electronic, mechanical, or other means, now known or hereafter invented, including photocopying and recording, or in any information storage or retrieval system, without permission in writing from the publishers.

Notice:
Product or corporate names may be trademarks or registered trademarks, and are used only for identification and explanation without intent to infringe.

British Library Cataloguing in Publication Data
A catalogue record for this book is available from the British Library

ISBN 13: 978-1-138-70182-3 (hbk)
ISBN 13: 978-0-367-13927-8 (pbk)

Typeset in TimesNewRomanPS
by diacriTech, Chennai

Publisher's Note
The publisher accepts responsibility for any inconsistencies that may have arisen during the conversion of this book from journal articles to book chapters, namely the possible inclusion of journal terminology.

Disclaimer
Every effort has been made to contact copyright holders for their permission to reprint material in this book. The publishers would be grateful to hear from any copyright holder who is not here acknowledged and will undertake to rectify any errors or omissions in future editions of this book.

Contents

	Citation Information	ix
1	Introduction	1
2	Fandom face to face	8
3	Performance in the stands	24
4	Print media: circulating fandom	51
5	Broadcast media: live and in-person	66
6	New media: online fandom	85
7	The football brand dilemma	106
8	Fan politics: dissent and control at the stadium	122
9	Conclusion	137
	Index	141

Citation Information

The chapters in this book were originally published in *Soccer & Society*, volume 17, issue 3 (May 2016). When citing this material, please use the original page numbering for each article, as follows:

Chapter 1
Introduction
Matthew Guschwan
Soccer & Society, volume 17, issue 3 (May 2016) pp. 267–273

Chapter 2
Fandom face to face
Matthew Guschwan
Soccer & Society, volume 17, issue 3 (May 2016) pp. 274–289

Chapter 3
Performance in the stands
Matthew Guschwan
Soccer & Society, volume 17, issue 3 (May 2016) pp. 290–316

Chapter 4
Print media: circulating fandom
Matthew Guschwan
Soccer & Society, volume 17, issue 3 (May 2016) pp. 317–331

Chapter 5
Broadcast media: live and in-person
Matthew Guschwan
Soccer & Society, volume 17, issue 3 (May 2016) pp. 332–350

Chapter 6
New media: online fandom
Matthew Guschwan
Soccer & Society, volume 17, issue 3 (May 2016) pp. 351–371

CITATION INFORMATION

Chapter 7
The football brand dilemma
Matthew Guschwan
Soccer & Society, volume 17, issue 3 (May 2016) pp. 372–387

Chapter 8
Fan politics: dissent and control at the stadium
Matthew Guschwan
Soccer & Society, volume 17, issue 3 (May 2016) pp. 388–402

Chapter 9
Conclusion
Matthew Guschwan
Soccer & Society, volume 17, issue 3 (May 2016) pp. 403–406

For any permission-related enquiries please visit:
http://www.tandfonline.com/page/help/permissions

Introduction

The central premise of this volume is that football fandom is essentially a social project.[1] As a social project, fandom is about people who gather together to talk, to share stories, compare ideas, test hypotheses, exchange information, do business, and basically, to be together to create meaningful bonds and to share the human experience. Therefore, I start this volume not at the stadium but in the spaces where smaller groups can gather to be 'hang out'. In these meetings, smaller groups of people gather and develop relationships and a sense of intimacy. They compare notes and they compete for status, they define roles and they participate in a social formation larger than themselves. They form communities that can help build proud individual identities, and they build vibrant communities that can become strong and change the world in small ways, both positively and negatively. Starting from face-to-face interactions, this analysis branches out to media that extend fandom beyond geographical boundaries. Media extends the communicative and social capabilities of the fans. It allows for the broadcast of a message to many and/or it allows for the transcendence of space – where that be a few hundred feet or across continents. Instead of focusing on how media can replace or displace the in-person meeting, this volume focuses on how the fans use media to facilitate in-person sociality and, in some cases, reinvigorate a connection to place.

It is not in the scope of this work to explain why, exactly, man is a social animal. That is the terrain of social psychologists and philosophers, and sociologists. A rudimentary evolutionary explanation might find that survival just tends to be easier in groups, especially when people trust each other, and cooperate. Trust has to start somewhere, and perhaps football provides a context in which trust can develop in low-stakes situations. Maybe football acts in place of gossip or perhaps, football is a substitute for war – an arena in which we get to act out primal aggressions. Football is a little bit of all of this and more, but the basis of this volume considers that people like to be brought together, and that football is a good alibi for which to gather – even if it is to argue and fight. In social life, much of the meaning of the world is created. We are, in Aristotle's estimation, social animals.

Football has become good at capitalizing on human desires, and giving them structure, and generating meaning from a game in which two sides of 11 individuals, disregard their most useful physical gift of opposable thumbs and coordinate their actions to kick a ball over an arbitrary line into a netted goal. An absurdly simple game from a certain standpoint. Yet, its simplicity provides for countless variations, endless physical training, lifelong analysis, serious research, massive public interest and lest we forget, great sums of capital and the attendant competition for fame and fortune.

The game itself is secondary in my approach, to what I contend is the heart of football: fandom. Fans are often connected to game from playing it, but the career of most fans is much longer than their active playing career. Fans support the game from local levels to the greatest of world spectacles. This volume is focused on fandom of the highest levels of football – primarily men's professional football in Europe with occasional references to other locations. The top European football leagues employ most of the top players and generate as much fan interest as any leagues in the world. Countless fans and fan clubs support European teams from the major capitals to provincial towns. Fandom incorporates local customs while fans also steal ideas from fans around the world. Fandom gives people a time, a place, a format – a context with which to express their personal pride in the team, pride in their community and to assert their presence in the world. Football stokes passions and gives them a time and place to be expressed. The football fan gathers with other fans who endorse his or her fandom. They are the ones able to affirm or to reject the 'authenticity' of one's fandom. This happens at the stadium, yes, but it also happens in the small gatherings of fans. The small group is a good place with which to test ideas and to confer with others on how to best *become* a fan. If identity is a constant state of *becoming*, rather than a simple state of *being*, one will need guidance along the way to ensure one's appropriate fan-ness so as not to stray too far.

Methods and constraints

My methodology is a hybrid of anthropologically informed ethnography and media studies inspired textual analysis. My graduate work was heavily interdisciplinary as it integrated Performance Studies, Media Studies, Anthropology and Rhetorical Studies. Each of these disciplines informs my approach as I write an ethnography of media. My first step towards this volume came in 1998 when I was studying in Rome. I went with a group of Americans to see Lazio play in an early round of the Italian Cup. I remember little of the game on the field, but I have vivid memories of seeing the gigantic banners that the Lazio fans displayed as a way of celebrating the previous season's triumphs. I remember the incessant chants, the coordinated move-ments and the overall kinetic energy emanating from the north end of an otherwise sparsely populated stadium. A few years later, I would go to graduate school to study Italian cinema, but Fellini turned out to be no match for my fascination with the Italian football stadium. I had made several smaller trips to Italy including a stint during the 2002 World Cup when I made a short documentary, *In Search of Tottigol*,[2] with a friend during Italy's ill-fated tournament.

My first substantial stay dedicated to research was carried out during the 2005–2006 season where I stayed within walking distance of Rome's Olympic Stadium for 10 months. The ideal location was also a mile or two from St. Peter's Square. As I would joke, I went to the St. Peter's to cheer, and to the stadium to pray. In my extended time, I was able to develop strong relationships with several types of fans ranging from the old-timers to the hardcore youth. I stood in the north end with some moderate fans, and I travelled on the bus of right wing fans in order to confront the devout communist fans on their home turf. I conducted some formal interviews, but mainly relied on informal interviews with my 'subjects'. I wrote fieldnotes daily, though rarely at the stadium or in the immediate presence of others. In the spirit of participant-observation, I participated in as much as I could, recording my experiences with audio, photography, a touch of video and lots and lots of written notes. During my stay, I read everything I could get my hands on, participated in online forums, monitored TV and radio broadcasts, and never turned down an invitation to dine with fans, or watch a game on TV. I believe it is this breadth of fandom that sets my research apart from others. I gained a strong sense of Roman fandom as I acquired better *Roman* language skills that were not included in my Italian studies in school. To some degree, I 'went native' in becoming just a little bit Roman. I should also point out that my identity as a white male of mixed European descent opened (or at least did not close) opportunities to engage in the fan culture. No doubt that a female researcher or one with darker skin would have a different experience with some of the fans that I encountered. In the years since my extended stay, I have returned to Rome to renew contacts and deepen relationships. Returning to a place and seeing old friends and acquaintances is extremely rewarding personally, but also for the research. The bonds of trust deepen over time, and even in absence. On my return trips, I could see things with a new perspective as well as ask richer questions of my subjects. The most compelling advantage of extended fieldwork is that the researcher is able to develop a deep understanding of the local culture. It does not generally provide as much breadth or generate large amounts of survey or other data suited for comparative analysis. The portions of this volume that deal with fan cultures outside of Rome are generally informed by library and online research.

I collected newspapers and magazines obsessively in order to get a well-informed view on the role of mass media in fandom. In addition to reading widely in the popular press, I made note of how various media were circulated around the city. For example, I knew what papers I could expect at the local cafe and so I could be ready to engage with other patrons. Football is a way for strangers to initiate conversations, and as I found, for an American to gain access to a deeper level of Italian culture than I would have otherwise attained. My training made me aware of the political economy of media and also sensitive to the ways in which media represented power relations among various groups in the society. This research inevitably draws from the greatest repository of sport fan studies that the sociology of sport has provided.

As an American, I find the organized fan club to be the heart of fandom. Simultaneously, I find the comparative lack of fan clubs in the USA to be, on the one hand, peculiar. American fans are, in their own way, hardcore. They spend lots of time and money watching sports and support media empires built on sport, yet this fandom is almost always done privately – in one's home, a bar, or communally at the stadium. With the exception of college football and basketball, there seems to be very little in the way of organized fandom. Mostly, Americans support their teams as strangers. Why are there no neighbourhood fan clubs? In Italy, I was and am an outsider, and though I made strides towards becoming an insider, my perspective is unshakably comparative as I ponder the energy and organization of the European football experience.

Media criticism

I consider communication starting with the local, small scale of face-to-face communication I define media as anything used by fans to express ideas. The essential media of human communication is the voice and the body. We use them as media to conduct face-to-face interactions in intimate and in large-scale, stadium settings. This grounding in media as personal and human acts as a corrective to any critique that might blame, 'the media' for the problems with the game of football. 'The media' is not, in my view, a monolithic distant alienating force, though certainly some mass media corporations make decisions that seem that way. Instead, this book attempts to list and analyze the wide variety of media that fans consume and produce in order to build their own sense of fandom. In some contexts, fans are active producers of media that express their devotion to the team. In some contexts, fans are held hostage to the force of decisions made by disconnected mass broadcast media companies. But, even the coldest, most distant media company ultimately must respond to the behaviours of its audiences. If fans can act in a coordinated manner, they have some power to shape the media landscape. In some contexts, fans act as consumer activists who can organize and publicize their grievances using various media to publicize their grievances and goals. Of course, the power asymmetries between the individual fan and the media institutions make it a challenge to effect change.

Organized fan groups make a difference. The effect of fan groups can be seen everywhere from the stadium boycotts in Italy, to the resurrection of a club in greater London to the organization of protests of fans in Cairo and in Turkey. Fans have used their communicative and organizational expertise to organize protestors in their attempts to effect real political change. Some regimes look to the stadiums as a place of catharsis where people can vent their frustrations and energies in a controlled environment. But they overlook the real bonds that form between and among large numbers of people who see each other every week. United by a common cause, and aided by pre-existing social structures found in the stadium, citizens can resist authority, and demand change.

According to Richard Giulianotti, 'No other form of popular culture engenders football's huge and participatory passion among its devotees'.[3] While this may be true presently, it should not be taken for granted. Football as big business is a threat. The influx of global capital diminishes the relative importance of the local fan. Global media extends the brand, but it is unclear what the benefits are for the local fan. The powerful rituals that draw fans together within the stadium and ultimately draw fans (and researchers) to the stadium are threatened by forces that would sterilize the stadium for the sake of profits. The prevailing formula for economic success seems to recruit and train docile, seated consumers who are able to pay thousands of pounds for the privilege of entry in the football shopping experience. Fans stake their identity on their team and they tend to be loyal, but their loyalty demands a voice in the team, and a team that they can be proud of. If the team is to represent them, it must reflect their values.

Contemporary football fandom may be based in consumer society that requires material outlays in order to participate, but football means so much to so many because it offers moments of transcendence – moments of identity – moments of community or 'communitas'[4] wherein one can forget about differences, and give oneself to the energy of the group. Most often this happens in the stadium, but its roots are in the streets of Manchester and Barcelona, Munich and Milan, Liverpool and Rome. The daily newspapers, television, radio and internet keep football in the air even when the stadiums are empty on Monday afternoon. Mediated communication is vital to the project of becoming a fan not because it allows for fandom in isolation, but because it provides the basis of knowledge for connection between strangers and provides the fuel for relationships. In this volume, I systematically focus on fans as communicators rather than as consumers. I am concerned with the ways in which they consumer, produce and circulate media. I am concerned with the ways that they appropriate ideas for use in the social rhythms of their daily lives.

The arguments will unfold in the following order:

Chapter 1 – Fandom Face-to-Face – This chapter focuses on the contexts away from the stadium where fans congregate, organize, develop and learn to perform their fandom. I define the concept of performance and show how it applies to fandom. I describe how, in small- to medium-scale face-to-face settings, fan are able to form bonds and validate each others' fandom. For some, fandom is an extension of playing as in Holland where one might play in the amateur ranks of one of the famous professional teams. In Italy, organized fandom follows from a history of neighbourhood social clubs. I describe the Roma Club Testaccio as the epicentre of Roma fandom, and how it serves to educate fans in Roman-ness. Hardcore fan clubs support the team home and away, and I describe one of my own intense experiences travelling on the bus with some of the most notorious hardcore fans in Italy. Italians can also visit the grounds at which their beloved team practices and where they can catch a glimpse of the players up close, and connect with other devotees. As these snapshots demonstrate, the social meetings of fans away from the football stadium are where fandom takes shape.

Chapter 2 – At the Stadium – This chapter focuses on the football stadium and all of the communicative acts that happen therein. Building on the definition of performance outlined in Chapter 1, this chapter lists the ways in which fans communicate in the stadium in order to accomplish their performance of fandom. Every fan brings their voice and body to the stadium as communicative means. Others bring small banners, while many groups bring huge visual symbols, and pointed messages on banners that can stretch for fifty meters. The performance of the fans at the stadium builds on the bonds formed outside the stadium. The passion that goes into everyday fandom sustains the energy that ignites in the stadium.

Chapter 3 – Print Media – This chapter catalogues the variety of printed material that circulates among fans. In addition to the traditional newspapers available at newsstands, free papers are given away at the stadium. The images of football players are an essential part of the fan experience as they are posted on the walls of fan clubs. Mass distributed print media is social media. It educates fans, it fuels conversations between strangers and it is used by fans to decorate their clubhouse walls. Smaller scale, fan-produced media is used to proclaim and solidify an identity and to recruit new members. Though print media may seem outdated, it is still an essential social media, as evidenced by the uses and reuses of print by football fans.

Chapter 4 – Broadcast Media – Radio broadcasts of brought fans into the drama of the football match in real time for the first time. The indelible impact of radio shaped the development of football fandom in the early to middle twentieth century. While television is now the biggest financial supporter of top level football, owners used to worry that TV would diminish gate receipts. Mass media are often suspected of contributing to social alienation, this chapter shows how fans use television broadcasts to create social events. This chapter discusses various viewing contexts such as pubs and fan clubhouses in order to illustrate, yet again, how media is used by fans to create social bonds.

Chapter 5 – Online Media – Online media is a boon to fandom. It provides mountains of information for the devout follower, while it also provides the opportunity to create and share content. The internet allows fans to transcend geographical barriers to form communities that could not otherwise exist. One particular group of A.S. Roma fans shows how fans can use the 'placeless' internet to invigorate a connection to place. They use their website in conjunction with meeting at the stadium and at other places in real life. The website provides the glue to their geographically dispersed set of Romans. The web is another tool that serves the social needs of fans.

Chapter 6 – Branding – Brands symbolize our market-dominated, globalizing world. Football brands are particularly well suited for an economy of attention where branded goods are worth more because of their connection to abstract ideas. Football is media friendly, and, in its current incantations, corporate friendly. While football teams are bound to particular places such as Manchester or Madrid, they garner massive global TV audiences that dwarf the in-stadium crowd. The ambivalent relationship between a football team and a place is a hallmark of our times. Football teams are community goods – they draw from people to give them value and meaning, but what people and where? What happens when fans attempt to go from symbolic to real owners of a team? The mutiny of a group of Lazio fans serves as an illustration of the tension between the performance of fandom and the market-logics of branding.

Chapter 7 – Politics – This essay delves into the theoretical and practical dimensions of political expression at the stadium. While previous chapters are organized around the form of media, this essay considers the breadth of media put to use to convey political sentiments. While the notion of sport as apolitical has surface appeal, the stadium has always been political, and provided that sport continues to aggregate tens of thousands of fans in an enclosed space, there is little hope of eliminating politics. The stadium offers the chance for average citizens to gain a voice and, I argue, the stadium is an important part of the Public Sphere. The chapter considers how the stadium is used for dissent in several contexts. In Italy, the stadium has long been a site of political expression while more recently, in Cairo and Istanbul, football fandom has provided the tools to directly confront the state.

The volume will conclude with some remarks on the tensions that will likely structure the coming decades of fandom, and suggestions for further research. Overall, the aim of this volume is to show how fans communicate in order to perform identities, build communities and *become* fans. This volume is unique in its focus on communication and its systematic analysis of the media and the contexts of its production and consumption. We live in an era of enormous media expansion. While exploring the territory of the global media-sphere, this volume returns again and again to the notion of the fan as a social animal whose desire for togetherness and pride is structured through fandom. These desires persist through changes to the game and to our daily lives. This volume is dedicated to the expression and performance of these desires.

Notes
1. I'll use football to mean what Americans like myself call soccer.
2. Guschwan, *In Search of Tottigol* can be found on Youtube.
3. Giulianotti, *Football: A Sociology of the Global Game*, 1999.

4. Anthropologist Victor Turner coined the term to describe intense moments of togetherness marked by liberation from everyday social status and anxiety.

References

Giulianotti, R. *Football: A Sociology of the Global Game*. Malden, MA: Blackwell, 1999.
In Search of Tottigol. Online Video directed by Matthew Guschwan. Bloomington, IN: Gnomesonice Productions, 2002.
Turner, V. *From Ritual to Theater: The Human Seriousness of Play*. New York: PAJ, 1982.

Fandom face to face

This essay focuses on the contexts away from the stadium where fans congregate, organise, develop and learn to perform their fandom. I define the concept of performance and show how it applies to fandom. I describe how, in small to medium scale, face-to-face settings, fans are able to form bonds and validate each others' fandom. For some, fandom is an extension of playing the game as in Holland, where one might play in the amateur ranks of one of the famous professional teams. In Italy, organised fandom follows from a history of neighbourhood social clubs. I describe the Roma Club Testaccio as the epicentre of Roma fandom, and how it serves to educate fans in Roman-ness. Hardcore fan clubs support the team home and away, and I describe one of my own intense experiences travelling on the bus with some of the most notorious hardcore fans in Italy. Italians can also visit the grounds at which their beloved team practices and where they can catch a glimpse of the players up close, and connect with other devotees. As these snapshots demonstrate, the social gatherings of fans away from the football stadium are where fandom takes shape.

'Il calcio è la cosa più importante delle cose non importanti' – Arrigo Sacchi

(Football is the most important of the things that are not important.)

Fandom is a social activity. My approach to fandom focuses on the social aspects of fandom rather than upon individual consumption or any other aspect of fandom that focuses on the individual's choices in preference to the social contexts and social bonds that shape fandom. I am far more invested in the bond between fans than in the bond between the individual fan and their object of attention. In my view, the camaraderie with other fans creates the context in which fandom is meaningful and, ultimately, sustainable. As an obvious example, the bonds between fans allow for the incredible organisation and pageantry that takes place at the football stadium. I maintain that this is what sets apart the football stadium in the bastions of football culture in Europe and South America from professional sports in the USA. The urge to be with others and to be part of something bigger than one's self is what motivates football fandom.

Fandom is performative. Fans express their identities and they connect with other fans through ritualised communication that I term performance. People *become fans* through performances – through the learned and behaviour actions that make one feel like a fan, and, crucially, allow others to recognise that fandom. I will discuss the concept of performance in more depth below, but one of the fundamental features of performance is that it requires an audience. To be a fan, one must perform their fandom in front of those most able to judge the effectiveness of that performance: namely, other fans. Most people can relate to being the brand new person at school, at a job, at a club or in some sort of social situation, and feeling anxious as to whether they can or will fit in. Over time and through repeated interaction, we adapt our persona to the social group in order to achieve our social goals – perhaps we want to achieve acceptance, or we might reject the social group, or we might try to change the group in some way to suit our needs. The key is that one must learn the codes and nuances of the group in order to communicate most effectively. So a key component of fandom is learning. This volume will go into great depth in regard to the media that fans use to educate themselves in the ways of fandom, but certainly one of the most effective and enduring modes of education is the face-to-face interaction that requires the least technologically advanced media – the voice, face and the entire communicative apparatus of the human body.

The stadium is the place where much of the energy, passion and identity is expressed, but it is the meetings between fans in everyday life outside of the stadium that undergird the 'atmosphere' of the stadium and makes what happens in the stands every week possible, meaningful and comprehensible. Therefore, I start this volume with a collection of snapshots of contexts in which fans organise and meet face to face to share and develop their fandom. The co-presence of fans allows for direct communication without telecommunication devices. The traditions of fandom vary by time and place, and I must rely heavily on my personal experiences, so this chapter is clearly not comprehensive; however, I intend to tease out wider themes of fandom and how it evolves in social contexts from my limited examples. Before getting to the contexts of face-to-face fan education, I will sketch out a fuller explanation of performance as it relates to fandom.

Fandom as performance

Performance is a broad concept that is most closely associated with the theatre. The metaphor of actors/performers on stage, enacting and improvising a script in view of a requisite audience has been adopted and applied to several academic disciplines including linguistics, folklore, anthropology and sociology amongst other disciplines.[1] The framework of performance employed here is rooted in the multidisciplinary work of Richard Bauman,[2] who conceives of performance as a frame of understanding wherein a performer calls attention to himself or herself, thus taking responsibility for a set of communicative acts. Performance is 'an aesthetically marked and heightened mode of communication, framed in a special way and put on display for an audience',[3] or, more bluntly, performance is 'A mode of communicative display, in which the performer signals to an audience, in effect, "Hey, look at me! I'm on! Watch how skillfully and effectively I express myself"'.[4] Performances are worth considering not only in terms of the aesthetic pleasure of the audience, but because performance is carefully considered communication. Performers prepare extensively and performances are carefully assessed by audiences for, amongst other criteria, their emotional power and for the authenticity in representing people and place, thoughts and feelings, etc.[5] As social and communicative events, performances must be understood in relation to the time and place in which they occur and in relation to the audiences they are presented to.[6]

Fandom is accomplished through everyday performances[7] that bring to the fore a fans' passionate attachment to a team. By wearing a team scarf, singing at the stadium, arguing in a clubhouse or through modes of writing, these fans, communicate, in effect, 'Look at me. Notice how passionately I support my team'. Fans' declarations of identity take shape most vitally within the spaces of fandom. The individual fan or performer is held accountable to the spoken and *unspoken* standards of fandom that develop within a fan community. A fan's authenticity may only be ratified by insiders – by other authentic fans. One of the underlying functions of a fan culture, if not the essential function, is to create the context in which fandom is accepted, understood and encouraged, as well as disciplined, contained and critiqued. This book discusses, with ethnographic detail, the ways that fandom takes shape through performance in specific contexts. In some of the literature on football, the performance of fandom is assumed to follow sociological facts – a team might represent a social class, or a geographic entity and the people who identify themselves with the given class or location will naturally and inevitably follow the sociological clues, and attach themselves appropriately. The perspective of this book is that fandom – and most prominently the fandom that I engaged with in Rome – takes its particular shape through everyday social life, and through social and historical lessons that are learned in spaces and places beyond the bimonthly congregations at the stadium. While one might learn how to act appropriately as a fan at the stadium, the spaces away from the stadium teach powerful lessons that reach further in one's life than the occasional excursion to the stadium. This chapter pays particular attention to the spaces of two contrasting fan clubs that not only provide a place to socialise, but in their artful construction also enact identities.

The training ground

For the Dutch, their fandom can be a direct extension of their participation in the game. As Simon Kuper describes,[8] 'every Dutch boy belonged to a football club'. These neighbourhood clubs field teams of every age and from the modest skill levels all the way up to the highest levels of professional football. Even Amsterdam's most famous club, Ajax, originated as a normal, local club. For a kid growing up and watching his heroes play on at the local club, fandom must seem like less of a choice than an indoctrination. Of course, fans in other parts of the world do not have the same opportunity to play for a famous club, even at the lower levels. Italy, in particular, seems more like a nation of fans and critics than a nation of players, though it is expected that a young boy will try the game out and get some coaching along the way. One way that fans can interact with the team they love is to travel to the site where their team trains. Football fans in Rome have the opportunity to watch their teams practice on a regular basis. While not every practice is open to the public, many are.

The organised fan groups that I describe below are fans of *Associazione Sportiva* Roma, (aka A.S. Roma, or hereafter, Roma),[9] and *Societa Sportiva* Lazio (aka S.S. Lazio, or herafter, Lazio). Both Roma and Lazio are professional football team based in Rome that play in Italy's highest tier of competition, *Serie A*. Roma was formed in 1927 through the merging of three smaller teams.[10] Roma's primary rival, Lazio, takes its name from the region of Italy of which Rome is the capital. Lazio was founded in 1900. The rivalry between the two teams is a primary obsession for both fan cultures. Historically, Roma represented the working class and leftist politics, while Lazio represented the aristocratic right. The link between fans' political affiliation and team affiliation has never been absolute, though Lazio's fan base retains a reputation for conservative politics.[11]

I travelled to Formello to see Lazio and to Trigoria to see Roma. At Lazio's training ground, I watched the team scrimmage against a lower level team – I simply showed up and walked into the stands adjoining the field without a ticket. Roma fans often arrive at the team's training ground at Trigoria. On a trip I made out there, I was not able to enter the grounds, but I did gather with a reporter and another few fans to watch through a chain link fence as the team trained. The reporter took notes on the condition of players. His presence is indicative of the huge desire for information that fills up the usual media outlets as well as a daily paper devoted to A.S. Roma and the countless radio programs that fill the afternoon airwaves. I struck up a conversation with another fan and I was able to secure a ride to the subway station. Neither of these training grounds is located in the city centre, and travelling to both via public transportation turned out to be a remarkable journey through hilly country hills. On my way to Formello, the bus driver was a Lazio fan who insisted on playing his audio recordings from the stadium. I was happy to listen, but this meant that I had to stand at the front of the bus as he scrolled through his cell phone while paying little attention to the winding road that we were travelling. The bus ride to Trigoria goes down roads populated with provocatively dressed women spaced evenly between bus stops. Presumably, these women were not necessarily avid Roma fans. Watching practice up close contributes to a more intimate relationship between fans and the team than simply viewing them from afar in the stadium or on TV. If I were more persistent, I probably could have gotten autographs. Instead, I witnessed an injured Scandinavian player set out on a country jog and I saw a highly compensated French defender speak to a mysterious woman in a trenchcoat through his car window.

The intimacy between fans and players is not always a happy intimacy. At times, the training grounds become sites of protest for disgruntled fans. They may verbally harass players as they come and go, or demand to speak to the captain. When things really get bad, they might throw eggs or rotten vegetables at the expensive cars of their idols. Roman fans are effective at pressuring their teams into some form of accountability through these face-to-face interactions.

On the road

The Italian Ultràs are notorious in Italy and abroad for their outrageous displays and their fits of violence against each other and, in more recent times, against the police. Ultràs groups originated in the 1960s, a time of political instability and violence in Italy. Perhaps inevitably, the ultràs were aligned with radical political movements on both the far left and the far right. In more recent times, the xenophobia and racism of right wing fans has garnered more attention in the popular press. The Lazio ultràs are the most notorious of these groups for their anti-Semitic and pro-fascist displays at the stadium. I will return to this subject later, but what I want to emphasise in this chapter is their organisation from a purely social standpoint. The Roman ultràs maintained clubhouses in the city that are sites of leisure, sites of organisational meetings and the sites of fan-related work. For example, this is the members go to play ping-pong and it is also where they paint the banners that will show up at the stadium. Another primary function of these clubs is to organise travel to away matches. This requires scheduling a bus, collecting money and procuring the tickets. In more recent times, this also requires notifying the police of their travel. Supporting the team at away matches is an important ritual for these fans and it is a mark of dedication to do so. On the bus, one learns the gossip and the social hierarchy of the members, and one cannot help but learn the fan songs that are sung over and over at random intervals. It is also, as one might imagine, a raucous event as 50 or so young men and a few women cram themselves into buses for weekend trips throughout Italy. I went on a few of these voyages.

Excerpt from personal fieldnotes:

GianPaolo:	*Sei communista?*	Are you communist?
Me:	*Io? Non, e tu?*	Me? No, and you?
GianPaolo:	*Fascista.*	Fascist. (pointing to statue of Benito Mussolini on the shelf behind me)

San Lorenzo is the bohemian university district of Rome. It has vibrant bookshops and cafés and it is where one might go for a night of jazz music or a poetry reading or even a Marxist March. It is a bastion of communism with walls that bear some of the most beautiful graffiti in town. In short, it is not the neighbourhood where one would expect to find hardcore, right-wing, neo-fascist soccer fans who are often accused of racism and intolerance. Nevertheless, Roma's 'Boys' have made a home – on Via degli Equi in the heart of San Lorenzo.

I was introduced to the Boys by Valerio Marchi,[12] an author, jazz enthusiast, and, more generally, a larger than life presence who ran a red framed bookshop filled with counterculture books and jazz posters. His shop was a place where you could pick up a flyer for a rave or a funk show along with hard to find books. When I met him, Valerio was about 50-year old with grey hair, a broad chest, tattooed arms and a thick Roman accent that comes through a rich rough baritone that, combined with the speed in which he spoke, made it difficult for me to understand half of what he was saying. I was entranced by his energy. Valerio had a strong interest in the ultràs and in rebellious youth culture more generally and had written books about them.[13] After I asked him if he could introduce me to some *ultràs*, he walked across the street to the Boys' headquarters and left me to mind the shop. After gaining their permission, he sent me over to introduce myself. I was 'greeted' by a young woman with a cast on her left arm and a teenage boy with hostile body language. I was told to return in an hour or so to meet the guy in charge.

I returned to meet Gianpaolo, a imposing man with short hair, prominent tattoos and double-sided axe on a necklace. The ensemble was completed, or rather contradicted, by a business-like collared shirt. Gianpaolo was seated at a desk. Above him on the wall, hung a Boys' scarf inscribed with '1972', their founding year which makes them one of Roma's oldest fan clubs. In the centre of the wall, there was a large picture of a man holding a red flare in the midst of the stadium crowd, the red light illuminating his face. It read, 'Paolo Vive'. I later learned that the picture was for Paolo Zappavigna, the well-known leader of the Boys who had died months earlier in a motorcycle accident. I told Gianpaolo that I was an American student and that I wanted to learn more about the ultràs. I asked if I could do an interview, he said 'no, we are a closed society'. I asked if I could hang out at the clubs' meetings, and he said 'what meetings?'[14] I kept the conversation go as best I could, but with my non-native Italian language skills and his curt responses, it was a very uncomfortable session. I changed topics and we talked about American basketball and the NBA. He said that he liked Tim Duncan, the African American star of the San Antonio Spurs. I thought this strange since these Ultràs are supposed to be racists, but I did not pursue this line of questioning.[15] After a few more uncomfortable pauses, on a lark, I asked if I could travel with the Boys to Roma's away game at Livorno. To my surprise, he said, 'si' and told me it would cost 50 Euros for the bus and the match ticket. Then he asked me if I was a communist. I knew enough to say 'non'.

Sometimes, I try to imagine what it would be like if, say, Chicago Cubs were known to reliably support radical politics or if young New York Yankee fans were coerced to vote republican. These ideas seem so far fetched, yet, in Italy, it's almost natural that politics and soccer are entangled on various levels. One of the visible effects of this entanglement is that the soccer stadium is an outlet for the expression of political sentiments.[16] As a result, soccer matches can become even more heated. The lovely beachfront city of Livorno is a stronghold of the communist party. Neither fans nor players are shy about this. The team wears red uniforms and one of the team's all time best players, Cristiano Lucarelli, is an outspoken communist.[17] For years, he refused more lucrative offers to play for other teams in order to stay at his hometown team. He would celebrate goals with a closed fist salute to his adoring fans and wear Che Guevara t-shirts.[18]

The Boys, on the other hand, are right-wingers. Though historically Roma fans were leftist, the Boys are part of a radical right wing movement that has been growing in Roma's ranks since the 1990s. These neo-fascists embrace the double-sided axe as a symbol, they wear a lot of black, they chant 'duce' while flashing the fascist salute at the stadium, and they have a statue depicting Mussolini with muskets in their headquarters. At the stadium, they bring their own megaphone to orchestrate *their* cheers in *their* section. For the Boys, the Livorno match is the perfect opportunity for a political confrontation with the despised communists. In previous years, this match has been marred by violence and is considered by journalists and the police as a match to be weary of.

Nevertheless, when Gianpaolo said I could join the group to go to the match, I jumped at the chance, and made plans to return the next day with money to reserve a spot. After this meeting, I went back to Valerio's shop and told him the news. He said, in no uncertain terms, 'Don't go'. He said I should go to the game if I wanted, but by myself. 'Do not go with the Boys. It will have nothing to do with soccer'. Despite Valerio's warning, I returned the next day with money and photo ID that was a new requirement to obtain a soccer ticket. Gianpaolo gladly took my money and put my name on the handwritten list. I asked him if he himself would be going. He said no, he cannot go to the stadium. He had been legally banned from the stadium for a matter of years as the result of something that happened at the Derby. I did not ask more questions. I was told to show up at Piazzale delle Provincie, a 10 minute walk from where I was staying at Piazza Bologna, at 11am on game day for the trip to Livorno.

On the day of the game, after leaving the apartment a few minutes late, I hurried to get to the appointed spot. I figured the trip to Livorno should take about 3 h, and the game was in 4 h, so, we had an hour to spare, but I did not want to slow anything down. When I arrived, I thought I had missed the bus. I saw people milling about, but no bus and no organisation. As I looked around, I saw plenty of guys with shaved heads, black t-shirts, pilot glasses, tattoos and one girl with a Roma scarf on. They don't look friendly, and I don't talk to anybody, but I identified my fellow travellers. After about 45 min, several more fans arrived. At about 10 min to noon, two buses arrived. I was secretly panicking thinking that leaving this late, we would be cutting it close to game time. It was past noon when we actually board the buses and it was a slow process. I got on the bus and took my chances by sitting next to a guy in his mid-20s who was wearing a Keith Haring t-shirt. He turned out to be a good guy who I will call Carlo. Once it seemed that everyone was on board, we waited. A car drove up and out popped two more guys. It was probably 12:20 when we started moving and by this point, I was sure we'd miss a good chunk of the first half, unless the driver planned to speed recklessly, which made me wonder which would be worse: arriving late or arriving motion-sick from a hurtling bus.

I was rooting for green lights with the anxious hope of a person running late as we navigated the constricted urban streets. When we arrived on the highway, I thought the worst of the delays was over. Instead, I learned my next lesson in Italian football. After passing the highway tollbooths by 1 pm, we pulled over on the side of the road. We join another bus, a bunch of Carabinieri, the Italian state police dressed in their sharp navy blue uniforms and black boots. A couple of them are leaning on their vehicle smoking cigarettes. There are several inside their vans engrossed in books. Nowhere do I see the slightest hint that anybody is in a hurry. The biggest sign of concern on our bus is that some of guys put out their hash-cigarettes, and then file off the bus to urinate in the weeds on the side of the road. They smoked regular cigarettes, stood around, chatting with the carabinieri and stretched out their legs. Time slowed down in an anxiety-heightening way. I was already on edge since I was travelling with strangers against Valerio's advice, and so I was almost expected something bad to happen. I imagined I might get threatened, or intimidated, or worse and so the stop on the side of the road was hardly welcomed by me.

Next lesson: we will be travelling in a caravan escorted, or rather, chaperoned, by several police vehicles. We are not honoured dignitaries being whisked to our destination. No, we (as I am now, for better or worse, included in this group) are being escorted rather deliberately because we represent a threat to public safety. This fixture – Roma against Livorno – has been designated a risky match by the police and the soccer league, and the media and who knows who else. We, as potential menaces to society, cannot be trusted to drive 200 miles up the road to attend a soccer match in peace. We need police chaperones to be sure that we do not rob the roadside oases – the Italian Autogrills along the way. Without the patriarchal state intervention, we might have organised a fight in the parking lots in one of these roadside oases. This has happened before – as police grew more effective at stamping out violence in the stadium, rival fan groups organised *scontri* (brawls) outside of the stadium, sometimes along the roadways. Even if we had not planned it, we might have scuffled with rival fans going to or returning from another match. This, too, has happened, with fatal consequences on at least two occasions.[19]

It finally struck me that there was no way that this game was starting at 3 pm – or more precisely, we might hardly make it out of Rome by 3 pm, and thereby miss the entire match. I had assumed that this would be a normal 3 pm start, but instead, this is going to be a *posticipo*, a night game with an 8:30 pm kickoff. I'm not sure how I missed this, and so a rush of adrenaline and shortened breath accompanied this realisation because I was not prepared for this at all. Gradually, I calmed down since I had brought a light jacket so as not to freeze, and I brought enough money for food, so I would not starve. After waiting an hour or so for another bus to join the convoy, we were on our way again. Our police escort ensured that we would not exceed, or even approach, the speed limit during the entire journey. I have no doubt that every car filled with Roma fans going to the game passed us along the way.

At about 4 pm, I asked new acquaintance, Carlo, how long would it take to get there. He shrugged and said about 4 h in total. I figured that we would get to the stadium *hours* before the 8:30 kickoff. We drove awhile until we reached the first Autogrill, the ubiquitous food and gas oases along the Italian tollways. These establishments are well known to any road traveller in Italy. They have good *panini*, decent espresso, snacks and a beer cooler that, on Sundays, is protected by a large 'bouncer' dressed in all-black and outfitted with a radio earpiece. His arms were folded, and he projected an overall dour impression. His job for the day was to make sure that all of my companions and others like them have a receipt *before* reaching their paws into the beer cooler. Apparently, petty theft has occurred at the old Autogrill.

The Autogrill plays a prominent role in the life of the Ultra, especially when one's mother or girlfriend has not packed enough sandwiches. The Autogrill parking lot has also become a place for ultràs to organise fights. In the old days, ultràs went to the stadium to pick fights, but in the last few years, ultràs have found the parking lot of the Autogrill a convenient place to park the car, grab a sandwich and beat the crap out of any fan wearing the wrong colour. This is part of the explanation of why the police escort the fan buses throughout the journey instead of just at the departure and arrival. Anyhow, our stop at the Autogrill is mostly eventless, but just takes a looong time. Even these oversized facilities designed for busloads of people have trouble serving five busloads of hungry, rambunctious young men. After everyone has missed the return time to the bus by five minutes, we file back onto the bus, there is a quick headcount, and we get back on the road. At about an hour from kickoff time, the petite blonde girl sitting in the front row went up and down the aisle distributing tickets. The tickets were printed on white paper backing with a red, heart-like shape scripted on them. In reference to the dainty design, Carlo says to me, 'Fucking Communists', and I had to admit that the tickets looked more suited for a Valentine's dance than a soccer match, much less one with ideologically and potentially physically clashing fans.

As we approached the exit for Livorno around 8 pm, there was light rain falling, and a collective gasp amongst us who have not brought adequate rain gear for the trip. It was close to game time, but it seemed okay as we can see the lights emanating from the stadium off in the distance. The problem was that our new police escort, who took over at the Livorno exit, took us *away* from the stadium, not *toward* it. Apparently, we had been rerouted so as not to approach the city centre. For a while, we drive along Mediterranean, and I thought to myself, that this must be a great place to relax on a cosy beach, but at the moment, it was a cold, rainy night in mid-September and we were late for the game! We seemed to have been moving in every direction, but towards the lights for 10 min, when a sense of urgency really started to set in amongst my comrades in the bus. We were not near the stadium at kickoff time, but I knew we must be getting close when I saw a human chain of Carabinieri clad in anti-riot gear with helmets, long face-shields and batons held out. They were back up by a dozen navy blue armoured vehicles. They were shoulder to shoulder, blocking the streets to the right – the blackness of the sea to the left.

Are they protecting us from the thousands of home fans or are they worried that a few hundred of us barbarians will sack the town? As the bus came to a halt, I saw, just past the Carabinieri, a few of the Livorno fans trying to get close enough to yell something to us, but their message did not come through. I am almost trampled as I try to get off the bus. We all rushed to the gates, while some start chanting '*Duce, Duce*'[20] with their right arms extended in the Fascist salute. Amidst the chaos, it was not clear to whom this chant was directed. We, the visiting fans, were in a bad mood, but when the ticket taker handed back my ticket stub, I said, 'Grazie' and he said, 'Prego' without sarcasm or resentment. This small courtesy delighted as it so sharply contrasted with the rowdiness surrounding us. I suppose he, the ticket taker, was accustomed to this sort of chaotic scene, and was mildly appreciative of the small gesture of courtesy. The game was underway, as we filed in. I lost track of everyone that I recognised. I was by myself and it was cold, but I was thankful that it had stopped raining, as I was as unprepared as anybody.

The game itself? Perhaps the less said the better. Lots of defensive, sloppy play on a sloppy wet pitch made for few chances and no goals. By normal standards, this trip was a total disaster. A three-hour drive became an eight-hour ordeal to a cute little city on the Mediterranean, of which I saw nothing but an outdated stadium, bored Carabinieri, and scant glimpses of sea and rain in the dark distance. Yet, as an investigation of fandom, this trip was a revelation of the trials and tribulations of the Italian fan. The passion and commitment of these fans sustain the cheers, the songs and the focus despite a dreary match in even more dreary weather in a somehow even drearier stadium. The waves of cheers and shouts warm the body and enliven the soul. The barriers put in place by the police serve to strengthen our resolve. The weather just confirms that we, the faithful, are worthy of supporting this team and being part of a select group.

On the bus ride home, Carlo said, 'Tonight we won. We always win'. He meant the literal 'us,' the *fans*. How do fans *win*? To Carlo and other fans, the loudest, cleverest, boldest, brashest and bravest fans win.[21] Fans must use anything that they can get their hands on, and, more importantly, smuggle into the stadium past police pat-downs, to accomplish this goal. Megaphones, banners and flags are inspected and tolerated, but flares are expressly forbidden, yet, a few always make it inside. In addition to the external instruments, and but even more importantly, fans bring their voices, whistles, bodies and imaginations. The key ingredient is passion. What else could sustain 5000 cold, wet fans watch an early season game with little action and few shots on goal? This was a game between two teams that do not have much of a history despite relatively close proximity. As of 2003, Livorno had not featured in Italy's top league for over 50 years and so only rarely faced Roma post World War II. Rome's regional rivalry with Tuscany is mild compared to that with Campania to the South, and if there is a Tuscan rivalry, it is with Florence's Fiorentina. Despite these factors, we, the fans *brought* it. We sang. We cheered. Sometimes cheers come from great plays, other times as a way to try to prod the team. Some cheers serve to pass the time as defenders pass the ball amongst themselves. On this night, few could argue with Carlo's assessment – we did win. The bus ride home was much shorter as the police lost interest in us once we were an hour outside of Livorno. The bus still did stop a lot as many of these young me continued to drink and yell and scream as others tried to sleep. It was a long day turned night. By the time we returned to Rome's early morning sunlight, all on board were exhausted.

I had survived a day with some of Rome's most notorious fans and learned invaluable lessons about the conditions of fandom. While these fans profess neo-fascism and intolerance, they were kind enough to me. No doubt that there is a small element of the fandom that is sociopathic, fanatical and potentially violent, but overall, this collection of fans was just that – fans. They went to have a good time, escape the city, support the team, and be part of a group with a strong identity, and effective means of expressing it. This trip made me reflect on the conditions of modern life that make such an intense experience a rarity. As much as an uncomfortable busride inhibits freedom, it cultivates camaraderie. Perhaps our cultures need to adapt to provide a strong sense of togetherness and meaning and outlets to express that if we decide that football is not the only solution. In the US, college campuses do this effectively – alumni associations sell bumper stickers, sweatshirts and football tickets as adults look back at the time when they were fully connected to their community. Unfortunately, the American university experience is limited to a select group of people due to ever increasing costs.[22] Perhaps the ultràs represent the outsiders – a group of people that will always look for spaces and colleagues to rebel against a mainstream culture that they do not fit into. This question of inclusion and exclusion is central to social life. Football fandom is one answer.

Football fandom and food

Another ritualised site of communion that has a revered place in Italian culture is the dinner table. Italian football fans are no different. At organised banquets, fan clubs fuse their love of team with their love of dining together. The Core de Roma fangroup that is devoted to A.S. Roma brought their stadium sized banner to the banquet table. These dinners were organised on the periphery of the city and on weeknights in order to facilitate a good meal at a good price. The dinner itself was of many courses including traditional Roman dishes, such as *trippa* (tripe), and many subsequent courses of pasta and meat. All of the food was capped off with a specially decorated cake and the traditional espresso and after dinner drinks. One member of the fan group distributed specially made DVDs that celebrated Roma's 2001 championship season. Another banquet included footballs with the Roma logo on them. One dinner was organised to welcome the Roma Club from Malta that was in town to watch a game. The first banquet that I went to was the result of the group posting an open invitation on their website. I sent an email, and without much fuss, someone in the group had arranged to pick me up from the subway station in order to take me to the banquet. An Italian friend of mine had warned me not to go since they might be like the 'crazy' fans that are condemned in the popular media, but, they turned out to be a group of family oriented, gainfully employed people who shared a passion for A.S. Roma.

In meetings like this, away from the stadium, people learn to become fans. As an outsider, it was an education in how to speak the Roman dialect, and how to adopt the proper attitude – an attitude that is proud of Rome and defiant to the end. I did my best to fit in by, at first, listening. Later, I was gratified that I had been asked to bring along a banner that I had displayed at the stadium. For me, this was a sign that I had achieved a level of acceptance, and that I had somehow contributed to the fan culture. From a critical perspective, the exchange of opinions, jokes and arguments over dinner is an educative process. While all are there to have a good time, this is where the modes of fandom are taught and learned. Of course, friendships and relationships develop at these get together that are structured around fandom. In this way, the lines between fandom and daily life, and distinctions between fellow fans and friends disappear. Fandom and social life merge.

The clubhouse

Fandom, in Rome at least, comprises many aspects: it is the way one carries oneself, the knowledge one possesses, knowing how to talk, how to argue, how to respond to defeat with a combative attitude, knowing the history of the club, carrying a healthy scepticism of the mass media, not trusting the owners, expecting great things and preparing one for disaster. Many, if not most, of these traits, are shared by other fan cultures, no doubt. What makes Roman fans unique is their connection to the Eternal City. Their attitude in the stadium is conditioned by the difficulties of living in such a beautiful but chaotic city.

In Italy, football teams become important symbols of local identity. In Rome, constructing a civic identity is enriched by extraordinary cultural history, but complicated by the realities of contemporary life. Fandom provides the format with which to construct, organise, and perform a powerful sense of Roman-ness, or *Romanità*. While there is no single authentic way of being Roman, fans use culturally available resources to construct deeply felt, 'authentic' civic identities.[23] One reason why this fandom is worthy of study is because of the depth of feeling experienced by fans. They know fandom not as a casual hobby but as a lifestyle. This section describes fans expressing Romanità within the context of an organised fan club.

Regionalism in Italy

For Romans, football fandom becomes a vital way to express civic identity. After Italy was unified in 1861, the Marquis D'Azeglio famously said, 'We have made Italy, but now we must make Italians'.[24] His comment underscored the deep economic, linguistic, and cultural divisions amongst Italy's regions that have endured to the present day. Economic disparity between the relatively prosperous North and the struggling South has fuelled regional antipathy and vocal sentiment for northern secession, spearheaded by Umberto Bossi's xenophobic political party, the Northern League. In the early 1990s, Italian scholar Angela Zanotti wrote, 'Now, for the first time in the history of the Republic, there is an attempt to spell out the problems of the Italian state on the basis of [regional] ethnicity'.[25] She finds that the region-based cultural and ethnic differentiation echoes the colour-based racism found in other parts of Europe. Within this historical context, football has become a highly visible outlet for the expression of regional rivalry in contemporary Italy.

Roma wears city colours (golden-yellow and deep red), and the team's official logo is the Capitoline she-wolf that suckled Romulus and Remus, mythical founders of Rome. At the outset of every Roma home game, fans sing the anthem written by pop singer Antonello Venditti that features the lyrics, 'Roma, Roma, Roma, heart of this city, the one great love, that takes the breath away from so many'. This melodramatic song invigorates (and reflects upon) the emotional connection between fans and city. The team's appropriation of Roman symbols strengthens the bond with (and weakens the distinction between) Roma, the football team, and Rome, the city.

Roma fans are defined by rivalries with, or in the words of Gray,[26] the 'anti-fandom' of opposing teams and fans. Roma's primary rivalries with Lazio, Napoli, and Juventus are inflected by geography. Lazio is its crosstown rival, Napoli is the nearest big-city rival, and Juventus is Roma's powerful rival from the so-called 'cold, industrial north'. Roma fans construct their identity most strongly in opposition to Lazio and consider their team to be the one that represents the real people of the city, whereas Lazio is the team for 'country bumpkins' outside the city.

The Roma Club Testaccio

The administrative, 'dirty work' of fan culture occurs in the organised fan clubs away from the intensity of the stadium.[27] Organised football fan clubs have long been entrenched in the fabric of Italian social life.[28] In eras past, neighbourhood fan clubs were an essential link between professional teams and ticket buyers, a.k,a, fans. While fan groups are no longer the primary distributor of tickets, organised fan clubs remain a vital part of local social life for many Italians. Anthropologist Keith Basso laments anthropologists' disattention to, 'the elaborate arrays of conceptual and expressive instruments – ideas, beliefs, stories, songs – with which community members produce and display coherent understandings of [the physical environment].'[29] Basso's words underscore the understanding that 'meaning of place' is the product of a social process rather than of the predetermined effect of an indisputable essence. This article highlights the process in which fans understand, display and reconfigure the significance of their neighbourhood.

The Roma Club Testaccio is a traditional fan club that supports A.S. Roma. Their clubhouse is situated in Testaccio, a working-class neighbourhood located a few miles south of the historic centre of Rome. This fan club, founded in 1968 with 15 members, has grown to more than 250 *soci* [dues paying members] as of 2010. Members tend to be male *Testaccini* [Testaccio residents] over 40 years old who speak with Roman accents. The long-serving president of the club, Sergio Rosi, is a sprightly man in his late 60s. The Roma Club Testaccio is a space for Roman men to perform their version of Roman masculinity.[30] The social life of the club consists of gathering at the clubhouse every evening after work to play cards or just to socialise. Similar to the 'male spaces' in other Mediterranean contexts, the Roma Club Testaccio is a gendered space where men use foul language, tell bawdy jokes, and play cards in a competitive atmosphere of masculine showmanship. At the club, the men seem to feel liberated from the demands and restrictions of home and work life.

Testaccio stands as a vestige of traditional, working class Rome. It is both a residential and commercial neighbourhood and is one of 22 central *rioni* [neighbourhoods] of modern Rome. Testaccio is the site of the *Monte di Cocci* [Hill of Amphorae], composed of broken clay jars discarded by ancient Romans. At the outset of the twentieth century, Testaccio housed the city's stockyards that supplied the cheap pig intestines and ox tail that inspired distinctive Roman recipes. In recent decades, Testaccio has come to signify nostalgia for a simple life of manual labour and neighbourhood sociability. The local news website[31] calls Testaccio, 'The heart of the old Rome' and 'Perhaps the last surviving neighbourhood of the old Rome.'

Testaccio has mythic significance for A.S. Roma fans. In 1929, the team began playing and training in the *Campo Testaccio* [Testaccio Field], nestled in the middle of the neighbourhood. In the 1940s, A.S. Roma moved to the other side of town, but Testaccio is still revered as the place where A.S. Roma was founded and as the spawning ground of authentic Roma fans. The largest national newspaper,

Il Corriere della Sera, has referred to the Roma Club Testaccio as the 'Most Roma-crazed place that there is'.[32] The mayor of Rome recognised the club as 'A historic place that has represented for almost 40 years an important social place to congregate'.[33] For members of the Roma Club Testaccio, the image of Testaccio as a bastion of traditional Roman life and as the origin of the football team is intertwined.

Becoming Roman everyday

A vital resource for the performance of Roman identity is Roman dialect (Romanesco). Few have articulated the bond between language and social identity as forcefully as Anzaldúa: 'Ethnic identity is twin skin to linguistic identity – I am my language'.[34] The power of language to express regional identity is embraced by Italians despite national education efforts that mandate standardised Italian and the power of national television to homogenise speech. As language scholar Kenneth Pratt noted 'However functional, rich and persistent their dialect, [Italians] have been taught that their way is divisive and déclassé'.[35] Roman dialect is alternately called *Romano*, (Roman) which has neutral connotations, *Romanesco*, which is associated with nineteenth century Roman poets Belli and Trilussa, or *Romanaccio*, a term that implies vulgar or corrupted Roman language. I prefer to use Romanesco here, as it implies a sense of artistry that is found in the colourful dialogue between Testaccini. In spite of – or perhaps more accurately because of – the notion that Roman dialect is considered 'low', vulgar or inappropriate, Roma fans embrace Roman dialect as a resource for the performance of Romanità. Romanesco has distinctive pronunciation, phrasing, and unique vocabulary. For example, users may cut off the end of a word: Rather than say or write *arrivederci*, one might use *arrivedé*, or use *ragà* instead of *ragazzo* [boy]. Roman speakers tend to talk quickly and accompany their words with demonstrative hand gestures.

The Roma Club Testaccio provides the setting for the linguistic performance of Romanità through Romanesco. As previously mentioned, an essential part of the social life of the club is for members to gather in the evenings for card playing and masculine socialisation. Typically, club members tell stories and jokes and compete for attention by speaking passionately in an argumentative tone of Romanesco. These conversations are performances in which members may gain or lose status with every turn. Bauman names this power the 'emergent quality of performance'[36] wherein, through a display of communicative skill, a performer may gain status and thereby alter the social structure of the group. The documentary, *Core de Roma* [Heart of Rome],[37] captures a sample of this banter. In one scene, a few members of the club are gathered around a table, playing cards. One of the members relates an anecdote about Testaccio, saying that the neighbourhood used to be filled with 'thieves and bandits'. A second member, Giorgio, questions the storyteller, 'When?' and then asserts, 'You come from the mountains of Abruzzo'. Giorgio then accuses the storyteller of being a thief himself, saying, 'Look at the way you play cards'. This playful confrontation is met with laughs from the other members who witness this assertion of dominance. Giorgio's performance is marked by his use of Romanesco and his general combativeness. He is the club vice president and has, no doubt, utilised his performance skills to gain a position of authority within the club's hierarchy. Surrounded by images of Rome and Roma, these fans perform Romanità every evening.

Conclusion

This volume is concerned with communication and media – and how fans construct identities through communicative rituals – through performance. I start with the relatively small, face-to-face contexts outside of the stadium in order to emphasise the ways in which fandom encompasses a lifestyle that must learned in daily life. The process of learning the proper attitudes is a social process that requires time and repetition. The concept of performance helps us to see the ways in which a fan must express their fandom in full view of other fans in order to realise their fandom – to become a fan.

This chapter has provided several snapshots of the 'classrooms' of fandom. The training ground offers the opportunity to not only see the players up close, but to connect with others fans who are dedicated. Busrides to the far flung stadium cannot help but to foster intimacy. Being in close proximity with other fans for hours on end breaks down social barriers and fosters trust as fans must share the basic burdens of eating, drinking, and, as I learned, smoking. Though I am not much of a smoker, I brought packs of cigarettes to give away on these journeys as a way to make friends. I figured each cigarette to be worth at least a moment of acknowledgement and courteous conversation. The Roma Club Testaccio is the atheneum of old-school fandom. From the photos on the walls to the lively Romanesco spoken nightly, Testaccio is the place to learn to become an authentic Romanista, as well as an authentic Roman. The lessons learned in these smaller spaces inform the expressions of fandom in the stadium, online and in every form of media available. Further chapters will extend to different forms of communication and media, but they will return to these questions of how fans share information, learn attitudes and express passions with the goal of performing fandom and becoming part of a larger community.

Disclosure statement

No potential conflict of interest was reported by the author.

Notes

1. Cf. Schechner, *Performance Studies*.
2. Bauman, 'Performance'.
3. Ibid., 41.
4. Bauman, *A World of Others' Words*, 9.
5. Bauman and Briggs, 'Poetics and Performance as Critical Perspectives', 61.
6. Bauman, 'Performance', 46.
7. Goffman, *The Presentation of Self in Everyday Life*.
8. Kuper, 'Holland, A Country of Clubs'.
9. *Roma* refers to the football team and *Rome* to the city.
10. http://www.asromaultras.it/storia.html.
11. The political dimensions of Italian calcio will not be adequately addressed here. See Chapter 7.
12. Sadly, Valerio died of a heart attack in 2006 not long after relocating to southern Italy.
13. Marchi published on the ultràs, and on right wing music scene, amongst other things. See references.
14. Remarkably, Alberto Testa was able to conduct lengthy interviews with leaders from this group. See Armstrong and Testa. One of the keys to Testa's success was his Italian mother who goaded the Ultràs into compliance.

15. It is worth mentioning that my own appearance is white Caucasian. I have no Italian heritage, and look blandly European, and I suppose, plausibly northern Italian.
16. Guschwan, 'Stadium as Public Sphere'.
17. In his biography, he proudly admits it.
18. See Doidge, 'The Birthplace of Italian Communism', for more on this subject.
19. During the 2007–2008 season, Matteo Bagnaresi was run over by a Juventus fan bus and Gabriele Sandri was shot and killed as he was in the back of a car of Lazio ultràs leaving the rest stop.
20. Fascist dictator, Benito Mussolini's nickname.
21. BBC, 'Lone Udinese Football Fan'.
22. I have to wonder if the money is going towards cultivating the rituals of community that might represent the true value of college, instead of brand new buildings, elite faculty and well-compensated administrators and coaches.
23. Ricatti, 'La Roma: Soccer and Identity in Rome'.
24. Doyle, *Nations Divided*, 39.
25. Zanotti, 'Undercurrents of Racism in Italy', 182.
26. Gray, 'New Audiences, New Textualities'.
27. One key advantage of fan clubhouses is that they are not subject to the surveillance of the stadium, and they allow for participation that does not require the purchase of game tickets or other elements of commodification.
28. Podaliri and Balestri, 'The Ultràs, Racism and Football Culture in Italy'.
29. Basso, *Wisdom Sits in Places*, 106.
30. In 2010, the club was forced to move a few blocks, but remains in Testaccio.
31. See http://www.testaccio.roma.it.
32. Menicucci and Stracca, 'A Testaccio, Dove il Cuore Batte solo per Totti'.
33. Menicucci, 'Testaccio non Perdera il suo Club'.
34. Anzualda, *Borderlands/la Frontera*, 59.
35. Pratt, 'The Dialect of Rome', 167.
36. Bauman, *Verbal Art as Performance*, 37.
37. *Core de Roma*, directed by Gwin Sannia, 2006.

References

Anzaldúa, G. *Borderlands/La Frontera: The New Mestiza*. San Francisco, CA: Spinsters/Aunt Lute, 1987.
Basso, K. *Wisdom Sits in Places: Landscape and Language among the Western Apache*. Albuquerque: University of New Mexico, 1996.
Bauman, R. *Verbal Art as Performance*. Prospect Heights, IL: Waveland Press, 1977.
Bauman, R. 'Performance'. In *Folklore, Cultural Performances, and Popular Entertainments*, ed. R. Bauman, 41–9. Oxford: Oxford University Press, 1992.
Bauman, R. *A World of Others' Words: Cross-cultural Perspectives on Intertextuality*. Malden, MA: Blackwell, 2004.
Bauman, R., and C. Briggs. 'Poetics and Performances as Critical Perspectives on Language and Social Life'. *Annual Review of Anthropology* 19 (1990): 59–88.
BBC. 'Lone Udinese Football Fan Wins Hearts in Italy'. *BBC Online*, December 12, 2012. www.bbc.com/news/world-Europe-20700529 (accessed April 7, 2015).
Core de Roma [Heart of Rome]. DVD. Directed by Gwyn Sannia. Rome: Oyibo Productions, 2006.
Doidge, M. '"The Birthplace of Italian Communism": Political Identity and Action amongst Livorno Fans'. *Soccer & Society* 14 (2013): 246–61.
Doyle, D. *Nations Divided: America, Italy, and the Southern Question*. Athens: University of Georgia, 2002.
Goffman, E. *The Presentation of Self in Everyday Life*. New York: Doubleday, 1959.
Gray, J. 'New Audiences, New Textualities: Anti-fans and Non-fans'. *International Journal of Cultural Studies* 6, no. 1 (2003): 64–81.
Guschwan, M. 'Stadium as Public Sphere'. *Sport in Society* 17, no. 7 (2014): 884–900.
Kuper, S. 'Holland, a Country of Clubs'. In *The Global Game*, ed. J. Turnbull, T. Satterlee, and A. Raab, 42–4. Lincoln: University of Nebraska Press, 2008.

Marchi, V. *La Sindrome di Andy Capp: Culture di Strada e Conflitto Giovanile* [Andy Capp Syndrome: Streets Cultures and Juvenile Conflict]. Rimini: NdA Press, 2004.

Marchi, V. *Il Derby del Bambino Morto: Violenza e Ordine Pubblic nel Calcio* [The Derby of the Dead Child: Violence and Public Order in Football]. Rome: DeriveApprodi, 2005.

Menicucci, E. 'Testaccio Non Perdera Il Suo Club'. [Testaccio will not lose its club.] *Corriere Della Sera*, December 28, 2006, 7.

Menicucci, E., and R. Stracca. 'A Testaccio, Dove il Cuore Batte solo per Totti'. [In Testaccio, where the heart longs only for Totti.] *Corriere Della Sera*, June 27, 2006, 6.

Podaliri, C., and C. Balestri. 'The Ultràs, Racism and Football Culture in Italy'. In *Fanatics!: Power, Identity and Fandom in Football*, ed. A. Brown, 88–100. London: Routledge, 1998.

Pratt, K.J. 'The Dialect of Rome'. *Italica* 43, no. 2 (1966): 167–79.

Ricatti, F. 'La Roma: Soccer and Identity in Rome'. *Annali d'Italianistica* 28 (2010): 217–36.

Schechner, R. *Performance Studies: An Introduction*. New York: Routledge, 2002.

Testa, A., and G. Armstrong. *Football, Fascism and Fandom: The UltraS of Italian Football*. London: Black Publishers, 2010.

Zanotti, A. 'Undercurrents of Racism in Italy'. *International Journal of Politics, Culture and Society* 7, no. 2 (1993): 173–88.

Performance in the stands

> This essay focuses on the football stadium and all the communicative acts that happen therein. Building on the definition of performance, this essay lists the ways in which fans communicate in the stadium in order to perform fandom. Every fan brings their voice and body to the stadium as communicative means. Others bring small banners, while many groups bring huge visual symbols and pointed messages on banners that can stretch for 50 meters. The performance of the fans at the stadium builds on the bonds formed outside the stadium. The passion that goes into everyday fandom sustains the energy that ignites in the stadium.

The stadium is the centre of football fandom. It is the physical and symbolic home of the fan and it provides a space for the expression of all types of fandom. Hardcore fans command one end of the stadium, while other organized fan clubs stake their bit of space along the sides or corner. The stadium accommodates the 'casual' fans and the tourists along with the wealthy and glamorous who occupy the expensive seats. The range of fans from the casual to the hardcore is not always harmonious. Fans sing and chant and post banners that express sentiments of all sorts. They use their clothes and their bodies and anything else at hand to perform fandom.

While there are moments when the entire crowd seems to act as one; much of the time is spent differentiating from other groups and other individuals and contesting owners, players and other fans. In this sense, the stadium is not so different from much of social life. In argument and agreement, we see communication and relationship building and tearing down. The stadium is an incredibly rich site of communication involving, above all, the visual and auditory faculties, but also, the touch, scent and taste. At times, there is even an intense spirit of unity that builds from and transcends of the usual senses. The ostensible attraction of the stadium is, of course, the match on the field, but the spectacle that occurs at the stadium is so rich and so layered that it is a performance worthy of analysis itself. This chapter offers an extended analysis of the Roman football stadium. It shares many similarities with stadiums throughout Europe and South America, though every place has its own eccentricities.

At the match

The football stadium is a focal point of Italian cultural and social life every Sunday during the football season, from September through May. Every week, tens of thousands of fans pack the stadiums in cities throughout Italy. As all sport fans do, they watch, they cheer, they shout, they meet friends and do what they can to support and encourage their local team. Italian football fans do much more than that. When football fans in many parts of the world go to the stadium, they go not just as witnesses to a spectacle – they go to participate in the event. Fan choruses echo throughout the stadium. Team scarves turn the stands into a sea of colour. Banners praise the home team and mock the visitors. At every game, fans compete to be the loudest, cleverest and most passionate supporters and to defend the honour of their team against their rivals. Fans feel accountable for the success or failure of the game. In short, these fans in the stands perform as much as the players on the field.

The Italian football stadium in particular is a venue of heightened emotions and intense experiences. Fans follow rituals and superstitions in order to prepare themselves psychologically and physically for the intensity of the event. Italian fans are nicknamed *tifosi*, a term that links their passion to the madness of typhoid fever. Fans must be ready to shout, to exalt, to curse, to jump up and down and to hug strangers. They arrive at the stadium hours before kick-off. Superstition binds them to routine. They consume licit and illicit substances. Fans make an emotional investment in their team that is either rewarded or exploited based on the result of the particular game. Sometimes this energy is directed towards joyous celebration; sometimes, it dissipates as smouldering anger and frustration. Fans know that they are vulnerable to a metaphorical punch in the stomach if their team fails. They risk part of their identity at every game.

The stadium atmosphere magnifies these shows of emotion and puts them on display for the immediate public as well as the larger media audience. Countless journalists and photographers bring the football event into homes via TV, radio and print media. Media makes the events at the football stadium a national spectacle, and moreover, a national and international social phenomenon. Rather than being set apart as a space for escapist leisure and innocuous demonstration, Italian football stadiums have long reflected the anger, joy and grief of everyday life. The stadium is a place to meet with friends and cheer, but also to remember the dead or to protest against perceived injustices. The passion, beauty, humour and elegance of Italian life are performed and intensified by the fans singing choruses, waving flags and staging demonstrations. Demonstrations at the stadium address issues beyond the scope of football. As Historian Paul Ginsborg wrote of his experience at Italian football matches, 'Sunday afternoon at the stadium was sometimes a political, as much as a sentimental, education of a pretty disturbing sort'.[1] The fans use the stadium as a forum to display the beauty and passion of Italian life as well as the ugliest, antisocial aspects of contemporary Italian life: xenophobia, racism, violence and pointed intolerance.

This chapter describes the visible, audible and occasionally visceral dimensions of the performance of fans at the football match, the centrepiece of fan culture. The chapter focuses on the various modes of expression and participation available to fans. These include the use of voice to sing songs and chant curses, the use of simple media like flags and banners and the use of bodies to gesture and mark space. These expressive means effectively coordinate fans, ridicule rivals, support their team, and, through mass media, address people, audiences and issues outside of the stadium. Fundamental to this study is the notion that fans are active participants in the football match event and that their activities go beyond simply 'adding atmosphere' to the football game. Fans are active agents and their activities are creative endeavours. This book and this chapter, in particular, invert convention in the sense that the actual football becomes the backdrop, rather than the focus, of this investigation into fans and fan culture.

This section focuses primarily on football fans in Rome, Italy, the home of two teams, *Associazione Sportiva Roma* (Sporting Association Roma, known as A.S. Roma or Roma) and *Società Sportiva Lazio* (Sporting Society Lazio, known as S.S. Lazio or Lazio). For both sets of Roman fans, the rivalry between these two teams is a fundamental part of fan identity, and the biannual derby games between the teams are the grandest displays of fan activity. In a sense, this chapter serves as a field guide to the stadium experience.

Football matches as cultural performances

The concept of cultural performance provides a framework for thinking about the significance of fan activity at the stadium. Borrowing from the work of performance studies scholars Milton Singer and Richard Bauman, I define cultural performances/special events that are staged by members of a particular social group.[2] Cultural performances often involve skilled performers and are marked by society as events *to be looked at* and interpreted by audiences. In this frequently quoted passage, Singer sets forth an early conception of cultural performances.

> Indians, and perhaps all peoples, think of their culture as encapsulated in such discrete performances, which they can exhibit to outsiders as well as to themselves. For the outsider these can conveniently be taken as the most concrete observable units of the cultural structure, for each performance has a definitely limited time span, a beginning and end, an organized program of activity, a set of performers, an audience, and a place and occasion of performance.[3]

Singer's notion of cultural performance helps us to understand football matches as rich reflections of culture. Viewing Italian football matches as cultural performances emphasizes the ways in which fans' performance inside the stadium reflects and affects modern Italian society. Bauman argues that cultural performances are compelling subjects of study because they have the following attributes[4]: (1) they are artful or at least have an aesthetic aspect; (2) they are reflexive. Cultural performances represent and comment upon the values and ideas of the society that stages the performance; (3) cultural performances do social 'work' and accomplish social goals; and (4) cultural performances combine the traditional and the emergent. They repeat well-known ideas and themes while creating a space for the expression of new, *emerging* ideas that may contest older ideas. Cultural performances provide a structured outlet for people to channel their creative energies and to confirm and contest the values of their society. In the words of MacAloon, cultural performances are,

> More than entertainment, more than didactic or persuasive formulations, and more than cathartic indulgences. They are occasions in which as a culture or society we reflect upon and define ourselves, dramatize our collective myths and history, present ourselves with alternatives, and eventually change in some ways while remaining the same in others.[5]

This chapter highlights the ways in which the Italian football, through its artful, reflexive and performative aspects, serves to accomplish multiple social ends. The cultural performances that occur in Italian stadiums every week are not simply spontaneous, superfluous events that last for two hours a week. When understood as cultural performances, we see that football matches are tied to the long history of Italian culture and the immediate conditions of contemporary life.

The fan performances at football matches are inspired, in part, from other cultural performances. For instance, the Palio, a tradition-laden horse race in Siena, functions as a long-standing source of *and* expression of civic identity. In the Palio, each neighbourhood in Siena sponsors a horse to compete in a raucous race held on a makeshift track in the town's central piazza. The centuries old race pits neighbourhood against neighbourhood in a nexus of traditional rivalries. As Alan Dundes and Alessandro Falassi illustrate in their landmark study, *La Terra in Piazza* (Turf in the Plaza), the Palio permeates Sienese culture year round and forms the basis for a vibrant civic identity. In large, urban centres, the football match might provide an analogous platform for the expression and cultivation of civic identity in the urban lifestyle of modern Rome. Differences in scale and in funding aside, each of these cultural performances are community building. The notion that a football team might represent a people, an identity or a movement is not unique to Rome or to Italy. For example, Jimmy Burns' book, *Barça*,[6] shows how Football Club Barcelona became the symbol of Catalan nationalism during the repressive Francoiste regime. In other contexts, football teams represent religious, class and other cultural divides. The literature about how a football team can represent a people or an idea is nothing new. The bulk of this chapter demonstrates, in ethnographic detail, how culturally significant ideas, emotions and sentiments are communicated in the context of the major Italian football stadium.

The setting – the Olympic stadium

The *Stadio Olimpico* (Olympic Stadium) is the home stadium of both A.S. Roma and S.S. Lazio. The stadium was originally constructed for the 1960 summer Olympics Games and is located on *Viale dei Gladiatori*, (Pathway of the Gladiators) in the north-west corner of the city, miles away from the original Coliseum. The stadium sits adjacent to the Olympic tennis and swimming facilities. A roof was added to the stadium for the World Cup in 1990 and the seats were refurbished in 2012. The *Stadio Olimpico* structures the performance of the fans during the football match. The football match is segmented by ticket price. In 2005–2006, prices ranged from 15 euros for tickets in the *Curva Nord* (North Curved end) or *Curva Sud* (South Curve) to over 130 euros to sit in the *Tribune Monte Mario* (The Monte Mario grandstand). In over-simplified terms, the wealthy sit and watch in passive comfort in the *tribune*, the sideline grandstands, while the raucous youth and working-class fans stand and cheer in the *curva*, the cheap ends of the stadium.

The two *curva* have the cheapest tickets because they are located behind the goals and offer the worst view of the game. Despite the poor sight lines, the most rabid fans, called *ultràs*, make the *curva* their home territory. The A.S. Roma fans claim the *Curva Sud*, while the Lazio fans claim the *Curva Nord* as their symbolic territory. In the *curva*, the *ultràs* stand throughout the games, while their leaders use bullhorns and loudspeakers to initiate the songs that spread throughout the stadium. Standing in the *curva* is an intense experience with loud cheers, cramped spaces and always brewing energy. Though the view of the game is generally better from the *Tribune* sections, many of the most committed fans choose to sit in the curva, even if they can afford more expensive seats since it has far more fan energy.

The *distinti* sections, in the corners of the stadium, attract fans that want to avoid the raucous *curva* and cannot or will not pay for the expensive seats in the *tribuna*. The *distinti* seats have a slightly better view of the game than the *curva* and the people in these sections tend to sit down during the game. These sections generally have more women, children and families. Fans of the visiting team are always cordoned in the *distinti* corner of the stadium opposite the hometown *ultràs*. The visitors' section is contained by plexiglass walls buffered by 100s of empty seats on either side. Throughout Italy, the visitors' section is always surrounded by police in riot gear in order to reduce the chance for conflict between rival fans.

The various sections of the stadium are separated by 10-foot high, plexiglass walls. Though these walls are meant to be prohibitive barriers, some young and agile fans climb over them, especially to get into the *curva* section or to meet up with friends on the other side. As gametime approaches and the match begins, fans in the *curva* and *distinti* sections disregard the assignment of particular seats printed on their tickets and will sit in any seat or anywhere that space is available. At the important matches that attract large crowds, fans spill into the aisles, and many sit on the concrete steps for the entire game.

Timeline

The football match has a structured sequence of events that is consistently followed. On gameday, fans arrive at the stadium up to five hours before the match. They arrive via car, via bus and via the ever popular *motorino* (motor scooter). Hundreds of scooters align into vast rows outside the stadium before home games. Starting in 2005, stadiums have been required to maintain an outer barrier 500 m from the gates of the actual stadium that serves as a preliminary security checkpoint. Food and beverage trucks remain outside the fenced-in area. Within this barrier, ticket scalpers and merchandise vendors compete for territory. These vendors hope to attract some of the fans that arrive early to meet with friends and hang out in the stadium atmosphere. Many of the organized fans groups arrive hours before kick-off, so that they can get into the stadium to display their banner and reserve their space in the stands. Around and outside the stadium, vendors distribute a variety of free newspapers that contain the rosters, statistics, articles about the players and dozens of ads that presumably underwrite the production costs. These papers are especially popular on rainy days when fans use these papers to cover their wet seats inside the stadium. Other vendors sell the coffee-flavoured liquor, named Borgetti that is sold in small, one-shot, disposable plastic containers. Merchandise sellers hang their scarves, shirts and hats from lines tied around trees or set-up tables. There is no official merchandise shop inside the stadium, and surprisingly, there seems to be little regulation of the commerce that occurs around the stadium. The overall atmosphere outside the stadium before the game feels like a festival with a lot of commotion but without much structure or regulation.

Serie A matches are normally held on the weekend, though mid-week games have been added in recent years. The majority of Serie A matches are played at 3 pm on Sunday with the usual exception of two *anticipi* (early matches) – one on Saturday afternoon and the other on Saturday night – and one *posticipo* (late match). The Sunday night match usually showcases the biggest and most popular teams and the most important match-ups. For the 3 pm matches, many fans arrive at the stadium in the late morning, and make the match an all day affair. Two hours before kick-off, one would find 1000s of people milling around the stadium.

The *ultràs* are always the first fans to arrive at the stadium to claim their section of the stadium, the *curva*. These fans post their banners and start waving their flags up to four hours before kick-off. The fans in the rest of the stadium tend to start arriving an hour before kick-off. Fans of the opposing team usually arrive en masse via police escort, about 30 min before kick-off. Their arrival is typically met with boos and whistles of disapproval from the home fans, and especially from the *ultràs*.

Before the game, there is almost no ancillary entertainment such as cheerleaders, so the fans are left to socialize and watch the teams warm up. Little more than occasional spoken advertisements are broadcasted over the public address system. Fans entertain themselves by singing sporadic football songs or chatting with each other. Around 40 min before the match, players go back into the locker rooms before the 'show' begins. Roughly 10 min before the kick-off, the formal aspects of the match begin. The teams march onto the field, often holding the hands of children or wearing t-shirts over their jerseys that publicize the day's social campaign, whether an antiracism campaign or a pro-youth movement. After this mini-ceremony, the players run around and stretch, while the captains of each team meet with the referees in the centre circle of the playing field for a coin-toss to determine which goal each team will defend and which team will kick-off. During the coin-toss, the public address announcer gives the starting line-ups, first for the visitors and then the home team. At A.S. Roma games, the announcer will shout the number and first name of each Roma player and the home fans will reply by yelling out the last name. A few minutes before kick-off, the song 'Roma, Roma, Roma' is broadcasted over the loudspeaker, fans rise to their feet, stretch their scarves over their heads and sing along to this sentimental ballad.[7] Before games, Lazio fans rise, twirl their scarves and shout the lyrics to their rock'n'roll mantra, *Non Mollare Mai* (Never Back Down) or their ballad, the *Inno della Lazio* (the Lazio Anthem).

These ritualized songs prepare the fans for the match. They serve notice that the match is about to begin and they oblige the fans to 'warm up' their vocal chords and their bodies. In a more subtle interpretation, we may say that these songs 'frame' the football event/performance. Richard Bauman draws from Gregory Bateson's concept of framing to explicate the ways in which certain so-called 'meta-communicative acts' transmit information on how to interpret subsequent communicative acts within a frame.[8] In this case, the singing of the ballad 'Roma, Roma, Roma' is a meta-communicative act that signals the start of the football event 'frame', and thus, the communication that follows is to be interpreted in a specialized way. Within the frame of the football event, fans communicate differently than they do in everyday circumstances. They yell, shout and sing. They use exaggerated language and threats, and they interpret the messages of other fans within this context, which is to say, they understand the words not as literal, but as expressions of support for their team. Words that might initiate a fight on the street are to be interpreted as innocuous expressions of passion. The lyrics of the songs boast reflexively of the song's own power to alter the fans' perceptions and actions, as I will discuss in depth below.

Once the game on the field begins, most fans focus on the game and the players. The fans react to the action with cheers, sighs, screams and whistles. Throughout the game, fans sing songs that disparage the enemy and spur their team on. These songs are usually initiated by the leaders of the *ultràs* groups seated in the *curva*, though, at times, these songs are initiated spontaneously from other parts of the stadium. At half-time, the *ultràs* in the *curva* sit down to rest, while the fans in rest of the stadium stand up to stretch. The intermission is the time to use the restrooms or to buy refreshments at the concession stand. Concession stands sell bottled water, beer, soft drinks, pre-packaged ice cream, espresso, popcorn and other snacks. Eating food and drinking beer at the game is not an integral part of the experience as it is at many American sporting events, and the food on offer is not particularly enticing. During the game, vendors climb up and down the steep stairs around the stadium selling refreshments, but, they do not play as prominent a role as one might attribute to the hot dog vendors that are mythologized in American baseball. Cigarette smoking, on the other hand, is a widely practiced fan ritual. Though technically illegal, marijuana smoke is prominent in the stadium, and particularly in the *Curva Sud* of Roma and the *Curva Nord* of Lazio. Even though the stadium is essentially in the open air, my clothes would reek of cigarette smoke after an outing to the stadium.

To appreciate the complexity of a football match, a fan must pay close attention to the action on the field and learn to tolerate the disappointment that comes after a brilliant but unrewarded move. The myriad fakes, intricate footwork and fantastic skill displayed by players are applauded by the discerning fan, even when these moves do not lead to goals. Fans are obliged to watch the game intently since goals tend to come rarely and unpredictably. They know that if they turn around to speak to a nearby friend, they could miss the crucial moment of a one-goal match. There are no timeouts in football and there is no instant replay in Italian stadiums, so fans must have the stamina and concentration to watch for an uninterrupted 45 min half of football. The 15-min half-time of Italian league games is a time to relax from the intent focus of watching the game. Organized half-time entertainment is minimal and features, at most, a promotional display that inevitably involves a few provocatively dressed, female models holding up some sort of logo. After the 15-min break elapses and the second half begins, the crowd turns its attention to the game once again.

Fans are sophisticated audiences and connoisseurs who develop complex, if not always consistent or explicit, expectations for their team. For example, fans expect their team to work hard, never quit and acknowledge the fans. Of course, if they do none of these things and win, fans may be content. If they do all of these things and lose, some fans will accept the loss, and even praise the team for their efforts as knowing that luck usually has something to do with the match result. If their team loses and fails to display determination or respond to the crowd, the fans will respond with anger, or worse, indifference. At one A.S. Roma match, the visiting team dominated the game so thoroughly that all the Roma fans in the *curva sud* gave up watching the team and started pushing each other back and forth creating a mock mosh pit, just to stave off boredom. If their team fails to perform, even the *ultràs* may stop paying attention.

The performance of the referee is always scrutinized and his[9] decisions are the subject of intense debate and derision. In the stadium, fans will whistle at calls that go against their team. From the stands, they will shout out threats and curses against the referee's family. Every Sunday night on Italian television, football-oriented talk shows review controversial decisions made by referees. Unlike match referees, these talk-show pundits have the benefit of slow-motion and reverse angle replays, which they use ad nauseam. Monday's sporting newspapers grade the performance of referees after every game, for those who missed the TV shows.

The performance of players, and their extraordinary abilities, inspire applause, screaming, shouting and awe and inspiration from the fans. When the home team scores a goal, the home crowd erupts into a frenzy of noise and movement. Nearby strangers hug each other, everybody jumps up and down and a crush of screams and cries collects into a single roar. For those the least bit claustrophobic, it may feel like an earthquake as bodies convulse and the stands shake. Oftentimes, a player will run up to the wall closest the *ultràs* to celebrate with the fans. If the opposing team scores, the visitors' section of the stadium erupts in chaos, while the rest of the stadium curses under their breath. The *ultràs* swear and make crude gestures at the opposing fans.

At the conclusion of a home victory, Roma fans remain in the stadium to sing the emotional ballad, 'Grazie Roma', in celebration and gratitude. The song signifies the closure of the performance frame of the football event. After the song is over, fans file out of the stadium quickly, back into the circumstances of daily life. On their way home, they might be handed a flyer advertising anything from food, to clothing to political material. The merchandising vendors hawk their apparel to those who want to memorialize the day with a scarf or t-shirt. There are no sports bars and few restaurants in the immediate vicinity of Rome's Olympic stadium, so once people leave the match, they tend to leave the neighbourhood. For half an hour to an hour after the game, the roads around the stadium are congested, and the air fills with the exhaust of cars, buses and scooters. Many fans will honk their horns all the way home to celebrate a victory.

Symbols

Italian football matches are highly symbolic events wherein the team represents the local people against the outsiders of the other team. Colours are a fundamental signifier of team allegiance that serve to distinguish teams and their allied fans. Team colours are displayed on jerseys, scarves and countless other apparel and paraphernalia such as hats and jackets. Italian teams are nicknamed for their colours. For example, A.S. Roma is often called the *giallorossi* (yellow and reds) and Lazio, the *bianc'azzurri* (white and blues). A.S. Roma's official team colours are identical to the official colours of the city of Rome: deep-red and golden-yellow. The founders of the Lazio sporting society were inspired by Greek ideals of mind and body. S.S. Lazio's official colours are sky-blue and white, a colour scheme inspired by this Hellenic tradition.

Lazio's current imagery draws from both foreign and Roman traditions. Lazio's official insignia is the *aquila* (eagle), a symbol of ancient Rome that was used prominently by Mussolini and the fascist regime. Lazio's fan base is predominantly the right wing and some groups within Lazio's fan base identify themselves as far right, neo-Fascists. For these radicals, Mussolini's fascist eagle is both a sporting and a political symbol. Both Roma and Lazio fans borrow Roman imperial iconography such as gladiators and Roman soldiers to represent their team, but Lazio fans use many non-local signifiers to express their fandom. For example, Lazio's main *ultrà* group, the Irriducibili, have their own 'mascot', Mr. Enrich. Dressed in a blue shirt and black bowler cap, the Popeye-like cartoon-drawn figure, Mr. Enrich, is adapted from English hooligan culture. A popular t-shirt among Lazio fans depicts

Lazio player and fan idol, Paolo DiCanio, with the dubious samurai saying, 'There are only two ways to return from battle. With the head of your enemy, or without your own'. Lazio's fans draw from a broad range of cosmopolitan influences for their imagery, especially when compared to the strictly local content of A.S. Roma iconography.

The official symbol of A.S. Roma incorporates the she-wolf and the suckling Romulus and Remus, the mythical founders of Rome. An alternate nickname of the *giallorossi* is the *lupi* (wolves) in reference to the mythical mother of Rome. In Roma's *curva sud*, fans have displayed huge tapestries depicting the Coliseum and the Roman Forum. Fans display banners with the image of player and captain, Francesco Totti, dressed as a gladiator. The Roma fans invoke this imagery as a way of displaying their allegiance to Roma, the team, and their close identification with Roma, the city. A recurrent theme among Roma fans is their claim to be 'true Romans', while Lazio fans are considered to be country bumpkins from the outskirts of town. Roma fans are quick to point out that their symbolic home, the *curva sud* in the *Stadio Olimpico*, sits closer to the heart of the city than Lazio's *curva nord*, located 100 or so meters north on the opposite end of the stadium. A.S. Roma fans display Roman imagery to assert their connection to the city of Rome and its imperial history.

Scarves

The team scarf is the most widely used symbol of fan allegiance throughout Europe. Fans wear their scarves to the football match as a badge of identity rather than as protection from the weather. Fans wear scarves around their necks during the winter and around the waist in the warmer months. Wearing a team scarf in and around the stadium can lead to trouble with opposing fans. On 29 January 1995, a 24-year old man named Vincenzo Spagnolo was killed by a mob of A.C. Milan fans outside the Genoa stadium because he was wearing a Genoa scarf.[10]

Scarves are usually 3–5 feet long, 6–10 inches wide and display the team colours. The most common cotton scarves are woven like tapestries, depicting team symbols. A typical Roma scarf is red and yellow, contains the symbol of the she-wolf and the suckling Romulus and Remus, and reads, '*Forza Roma - Non si discute, si ama*' (Go Roma – One does not discuss, one loves). This credo emphasizes the fans' unconditional and irrational devotion to the team. A typical Lazio scarf is blue and white, has the symbol of the eagle and reads, '*Forza Lazio – La rinascita di un grande mito. La realta di una grande storia..*' (Go Lazio – The rebirth of a great legend, the reality of a grand History). This credo evokes the historical continuity of Lazio present and past. Fan groups often make their own special scarves as a badge of membership in a smaller group. These groups then distribute the scarves to members or sell them to raise funds. A few enterprising fan groups produce and sell their scarves and other materials at retail shops around Rome. While many of these scarves are a variation of the more common scarves discussed above, some of them depart from the official colours and use only the name of the group. For instance, the right-wing Roma *ultràs* group, the Boys, sold black scarves with *tri-colore* (green, white and red) trim, with the word, 'Boys' accompanied by white, double-edged axes, a symbol of their right-wing affiliation. The *Core de Roma* fan group's scarf for 2005–2006 reads, '*C'e Rode Er Culo*', which is a local and vulgar way of saying, 'I'm a bit agitated'.

Football scarf sales are a major part of the ancillary football economy. Official scarves are sold only at the official stores. Popular 'bootleg' scarves are easily available at stands encircling the stadium and in outdoor markets and souvenir shops throughout Rome. In the 2005–2006 season, scarves were sold for 8–10 euros apiece in the vicinity of the stadium. In the souvenir shops around Rome, scarves are sold for 5 or 6 euros, while at the outdoor market, fans can bargain for even lower prices. Surprisingly, there seems to be little regulation of this commerce around the stadium or is there strict enforcement of copyright as it applies to the teams' logos. This is changing under the new, American ownership that has unveiled a slightly modified logo and plan for global branding. Historically, unofficial and unauthorized merchandise is widely available around the stadium and throughout the city.

Clothing

Clothing is an important medium for fans to visually express their allegiance. Official team jerseys are popular among fans and in recent years, have become fashion statements. The construction of the jerseys has developed from heavy cotton and polyester to lighter elastic and mesh-like materials. The designs and fit of the jerseys have also evolved to reflect fashion. For example, the classic collar that used to be on every football jersey had disappeared, though it has made a comeback in recent years. These jerseys often have the name and number of the fan's favourite player. Teams enter into lucrative contracts with global sportswear companies such as Nike and Adidas that pay for the right to produce and sell the official jerseys. The name and logo of a team sponsor invariably dominates the front of these jerseys. This 'advertising space' is another stream of income for the team. Telecom providers, airlines, consumer product brands, insurance companies and in recent years, online wagering companies are just of a few of the companies that have paid millions of dollars to sponsor Italian football teams.

Every year, teams release at least three official jerseys – one to be worn at home matches, another for away matches and one alternate for good measure. Typically, the team colours and insignia remain constant, but the jerseys are redesigned with new styles, and new sponsors, thus compelling fans to purchase a new jersey every year. Officially licensed jerseys generally cost between 60 and 100 euros. The high price of the jerseys makes them profitable for the jersey makers, sellers and, ultimately, for the team that sells the right to make and sell them. Jersey sales constitute a significant portion of all merchandising sales for a team. Unofficial, 'bootleg' team jerseys can be purchased for around 10 euros and are widely available in Rome. Though they are easily distinguished from the official ones and the team does not collect royalties from their sale, these jerseys enable fans to show their support for the team.

In addition to jerseys and scarves, fans wear both officially licensed and unofficial t-shirts with the colours and symbols of the team. Fan groups create their own t-shirts for themselves and to sell, similar to the way that scarves are produced and sold. Clothing accessories, such as American-style baseball hats, have grown in popularity and are common at Italian stadiums. They often bear similar messages as the t-shirts and act as another marker of fan identity.

The clothing and hairstyles of the fans vary widely from group to group. Some favour black t-shirts, shaved heads and tattoos for a 'tough' look. Other groups are more likely to have long hair and wear red, Che Guevara t-shirts. In general, younger fans tend to follow the prevailing trends of youth culture. They follow the fashions on the street and often wear jeans and running shoes to the games. For example, the large, mirrored, aviator-style sunglasses were very popular among the *ultràs* in the mid-2000s. In the stadium, fans use their clothing to demonstrate their allegiance to the team and also allegiance to the various sub-groups within the stadium.

Gestures

The arms and hands of the fans offer another convenient, and typically Italian, medium for expression. Hand and body gestures have rich and culturally significant meanings in various regions and cities in Italy. At the stadium, fans use gestures to express an array of emotions and ideas. Adam Kendon calls on those who would interpret gestures to consider what the gesture 'Affords its users as a means of communication, and consider in detail the circumstances of its use' and secondly, to consider, 'The prevailing norms by which conduct of co-presence is governed'.[11] Gestures used at the football stadium as borrowing from the rich array of Italian gesture, however, are also modified in accordance with the context of the football stadium. For instance, due to the large dimensions of a football stadium, big, demonstrative gestures are needed to communicate a message across large distances.

Clapping is one of the most universal forms of signalling approval and is widely used at the Italian stadium. One of the most common gestures is to thrust one's right arm above shoulder-level with the palm turned up for a few seconds. This gesture functions like an exclamation point adding emphasis to any aggressive verbal insult. Loosely translated, they mean something like 'What are you talking about?', 'C'mon, you must be kidding' or 'Listen to this'. Another common gesture starts with the gesturer raising, cupping both hands together then pushing and pulling the hands into/away from the body. This means something along the lines of 'Who? me?'. Shrugging one's shoulders and raising the palms in front of their chest is another classic Italian gesture that signifies disbelief. For vulgar gestures, a male fan might move his two hands in a chopping motion toward his groin or grab his groin as a provocation. The 'horns' gesture, in which the gesturer raises his hand in mid-air while extending the index and the little finger, insults its target by proclaiming that their romantic partner has cuckolded them. Football fans occasionally use the most infamous Italian gesture: the left hand grabs the right arm at the elbow while the right forearm is raised near vertical. This gesture might be translated, 'Fuck Off!' All of these gestures are commonly used in Italy, but may be exaggerated for performance in the context of the stadium.

Smaller gestures used in the stadium are performed more for personal expression than to communicate to the opposing fans. For examples, fans will often put their hands together in a prayer-like position and shake them back and forth. This gesture would seem to be a modification of catholic prayer, though with less overtly religious overtones. The gesture means something like, 'Oh my gosh, I cannot believe what just happened'. In all, gestures give the fans another resource, however crude or sophisticated, with which to express emotions and communicate within the stadium.

Banners

Banners are prominent means of direct fan communication within the stadium. Banners appear in every section of the stadium, though they tend to be most heavily concentrated in the *curva* and *distinti* sections, moderately concentrated in the *tribuna tevere* and uncommon in the elite *Tribuna Monte Mario* section. There are no strict rules for the creation and display of these banners, but there are consistent patterns and de facto guidelines. They commonly use similar fonts that can be legible from significant distances. Three primary categories of banners are evident: fan club banners that are regularly and consistently hung on the walls of the stadium, large 'message' banners that are temporarily held up by a row of fans and banners created and displayed by individuals. The first category, the fan club banner, asserts the name of the fan club. For example, the banner for the fan club from the Prati neighbourhood of Rome would read 'Roma Club Prati'. These banners are usually professionally made of vinyl or thick fabric, so that can be reused for several years. Banners are generally taped above the nearest stadium entrance in the vicinity of the group. These banners mark the spot where the fan club habitually congregates at home games. Fans also display these banners when they go to away games, posting the banner on any available surface in the visitors' section. Posting a banner is a big commitment since many of these banners are too large to be carried by one person. In most cases, they require two or three people to hang them up and take them down.

At A.S. Roma games, the club banners of the *ultrà* groups in the *curva sud* appear in the same place every game, season after season. At a typical A.S. Roma game, the banners read, from left to right (as viewed from the field), *Ultràs, Fedayn, Ultràs Romani* and *Boys*. Along the bottom wall of the curva are the signs of some of the smaller groups including *Tradizione Distinzione, Giovenizza* and the 'Irish Clan'. This arrangement seems to be the result of an ad hoc agreement made by the fan clubs rather than the result of any formalized rules. These groups are now mostly autonomous, though the entire curve was linked together during the 1980s under the umbrella group, the Commando *Ultràs* Curva Sud, (C.U.C.S).[12] The *ultràs* groups arrive hours before the match to ensure that they mark their spot for their banners and for their group. In typical Italian fashion, the job of arranging and handling the banners is accomplished without any orderly process and without any particular official supervision. One of the fans takes leadership in hanging the banners on the bottom level and relies on the help of bystanders to secure them. On several occasions, I was asked by one of these fan leaders to assist in mounting tape and securing a banner.

The second category of banners consists of those made for a one-time display at a particular game. These banners can be dozens of meters long and can stretch over an entire grandstand of the stadium. This type of banner is made from long sheets of paper, or several smaller sheets of paper, glued or taped together. I saw one banner that was written on the backside of dozens of glued-together political posters that litter Italian streets around election time. Banners are usually text-only messages painted with large black, block letters. Displaying these banners takes the coordination of a row of fans. Usually, a few fan leaders will give orders to the row of fans who are to unfurl and raise the banner at the specified moment during the game, hold it up for a minute and then upon a signal, drop the banner to the ground, left to be trampled. The fans holding up the banner may have no idea what the message of the banner is since they can only see the blank back of the banner in front of them. Similarly, the people sitting behind the banner cannot see what is written on these banners and the people sitting directly in front of the banner may not be able to read the entire message or they might be so engrossed in the game that they never turn around to look. The messages on these banners are directed to the rest of the stadium and to the photographers, camera operators and journalists down on the field level. These stadium banners draw attention from the larger sphere of popular culture as newspapers and websites frequently publish pictures of stadium banners. A Sunday evening television programme called, '*Striscia la Notizia*' (Slither of the News)[13] showcases the most entertaining banners of the weekend.

The major themes of banners found at the stadium are as follows:

(1) Anniversary/Memorial: Fans from organized groups or individuals display banners at the stadium to mark important events such as an anniversary of a triumph, or the occasion of the death of a fan. Topics can be serious, comedic, tragic or sentimental.
(2) Political: Fans display banners that comment on current political issues or promote extremist political slogans.
(3) Rivalry: Banners are often made to poke fun at the adversary, especially at the derby games or at games against other traditional rivals.
(4) Protest: Fans use the stadium as a forum to protest against police, journalists and team owners or other authority figures.

Anniversary/memorial banners

Banners are often made to recognize anniversaries or milestones. For example, an unidentified group of Roma fans displayed a banner on the city of Rome's supposed birthday that read '2759 Years of History, congratulations Mamma Rome'. Many *ultrà* groups display banners in tribute to fallen comrades. The *ultrà* group, the *Boys*, displays the banner reading, *Paolo Vive* (Paolo Lives), above their members at every home game in honour of their leader, Paolo Zappavigna, who died in a motorcycle accident in the summer of 2005. In a similar vein, the Brigata Roberto Rulli banner has been displayed in the Curva Sud in remembrance of the Fedayn *ultrà* group leader, who died early in the 1990s.[14]

The death of legendary Roma fan Luisa Petrucci in 2005 was another loss for the A.S. Roma fan community. Luisa was famous for displaying her red and yellow umbrella in the *curva sud* at every Roma game during most of her life and she was loved for her hospitality to the *ultràs*. After her death, several *ultràs* groups displayed banners in her honour. The *ultràs* group, the Boys, displayed a banner that read, 'You have left alone for the last away game … but upon arrival you will find many friends … and together with them you will always sing Forza Roma! Ciao Luisa!'[15] Another banner read, 'The sky now has another star … Ciao Luisa'. This banner was met by a standing ovation throughout the stadium. The rituals of mourning in the stadium are common and are, perhaps, a reflection of the dominant Catholic-Italian culture that provides for public mourning.

Political banners

Some banners are displayed to provoke different responses from those for the somber remembrances. In recent years, extreme right-wing symbols and banners have appeared in both Roma and Lazio sections of the stadium. Lazio fans have a history of showing racist banners at the stadium. In 2001, they displayed a banner in honour of the deceased Serbian war criminal, Arkan.[16] After widespread public condemnation, and under the threat of punishment from the league, the Lazio fans curtailed their open displays of radical right-wing material. More recently, right-wing and racist material has begun to show up in the Roma fan sections. On 29 January 2006, Nazi flags and banners referencing the Holocaust were displayed in the *curva sud* during an A.S. Roma game.[17] This incident was in the news for weeks as the police investigated the perpetrators of this act. No established Roma fan group claimed responsibility for these banners. On the contrary, fan groups reacted to this event by bring their own banners to the stadium that disavowed the offending messages by asserting their allegiance to Roma above all else.[18]

In response to the appearance of Nazi and neo-Fascist banners, police started to check the content of banners at the entry gates in February 2006. In 2007, the authorities began requiring that fans send a fax describing the entire contents of their banners days ahead of time. This control has significantly diminished the number of banners in the stadium and has also curtailed the spontaneity of fans who have entertained Italy with their clever banners. This clampdown may signal the end of an era in the Italian stadium. As authorities try to eliminate the antisocial manifestations in the stadium, they risk eliminating the expression of playfulness and joy that make the game so special.

Rivalry banners are a staple of Italian fan culture. In the typical Roman derby, fans spend half of their time insulting the other team and the remainder supporting their own. Banners are a primary medium for this rhetorical battle. At the derby on 26 February 2006, in which A.S. Roma star, Francesco Totti, was unable to play because of a serious injury suffered weeks earlier, a group of Lazio fans displayed a large 'handicapped' symbol. A Roma fan banner contained a message of support for Totti reading, 'With faith and love, we wait for you Francesco'.[19] During a derby, Roma fans posted the Italian rhyme, 'Better a year in jail than a Lazio fan for an evening'.[20] A less poetic message directed at the Lazio fans read, '*Che Dio ve furmini*' (May God strike you with lightning). The banter between the two sides is a staple of the media coverage of this game.

Protest banners

The primary Lazio fan club of the early 2000s, the Irriducibili, spent the bulk of the 2005–2006 season protesting against the Lazio ownership. They displayed dozens of banners for the Roma–Lazio derby that read, '*Lotito Vattene*' and '*Mezzaroma Vatene*' which mean roughly, 'Go away Lotito' and 'Go away Mezzaroma'. Lotito and Mezzaroma are the primary owners of the Lazio club. Even though Lotito rescued the club from the financial debts of its previous owners, the Irriducibili turned on him for what they perceived as his lack of pride in the club and his willingness to sell the team's best players in order to balance the financial books. This display demonstrated the remarkable unity and organization of this Lazio fan club. During this particular derby game, the Lazio owners were a more important target for the Lazio fans than were Roma and Roma fans. The Roma fans reacted to these protests with indifference or mild bemusement as they displayed little interest in the inner chaos of S.S. Lazio.

The third category of fan-created banners is comprised of those banners created and displayed by individuals. Oftentimes, these are made of an old bedsheet or a large piece of paper, two plastic poles and spray paint. These signs might depict an image or contain a textual message. The image of Roman actor and Roma fan,

Alberto Sordi, is a mainstay of these types of banners. Francesco Totti is another common image. At the 26 February 2006 derby game, I displayed a banner that thanked Real Madrid for buying the talented but disruptive player, Antonio Cassano because Roma had run off a string of victories after his departure. The banner read, '*Real Madrid: Grazie per portare via la spazzatura*' (Real Madrid: Thanks for taking out the trash). The next day, the banner appeared in the online version of a major newspaper.[21] This example demonstrates how easy it is to gain an audience for a message brought into the stadium.

The banners described above are the most prominent fan-produced visual media in the stadium. In addition, there are always the official advertising banners placed adjacent to the field at the *Stadio Olimpico*. These banners generate money for the club and the stadium management. It is worth noting that overt advertisement for products is not a common practice by the fans. Instead, fans use banners to promote ideas, pledge allegiance to the club and show off their style.

The voice

The voice is the most common instrument of fan expression at the stadium. Fans blurt out everything from choruses with pretty melodies to indistinguishable vocalizations and curse words. The action of the game acts as the cue to such noises. When the home team comes close to scoring a goal, the fans let out a collective sigh of disappointment. When they do score, an intense burst of noise that sounds something like 'yeah' and rings throughout the stadium for seconds. The individual sounds or syllables are impossible to distinguish from the collective roar. The stadium, and in particular, the *curva*, is a loud place, even if the game is moving at a slow pace. I would usually leave the stadium with slight ringing in my ears.

If the opposition scores a goal, the majority of home fans say little beyond muttering angrily under their breath. The visiting fans, who are always cordoned together in a corner of the stadium, rejoice with their own exasperated shouts of joy, though their celebrations can seem muffled from the other side of the cavernous stadium. When things are not going well, fans direct their frustration at the opposing team and the referee. Whistling is a sign of disapproval that fans aim at the referee after a dubious decision or at an opposing player after a dangerous play. Fans yell out cries of encouragement such as '*Daje!*' which is Roman slang for 'Come on!'. Fans will yell out suggestions to the players, (which of course will never reach the ears of the players) such as '*tira*' (shoot) '*attenzione*' or '*ochio*' (watch out). After a poor decision, a fan might ask rhetorically, '*Che fai?*' (what are you doing?). When the game becomes more intense, cursing in the stadium escalates in scale of offense. Of the more benign are phrases such as *porca puttana* (dirty whore), *bastardo* (bastard), *arbitro di merda* (Shitty referee) or *pezzo di merda* (piece of crap). A favourite curse of Romans is *mortacce tua*, which, roughly translated, means, 'Curse your dead ancestors'. Outside the stadium, this particular curse is a grave insult not to be used lightly. Inside the stadium, it is a common expression. Another popular phrase is *vaffanculo* which can be translated 'fuck off'. These phrases originate in everyday Italian life, but also used with particular frequency and liberality in the stadium. As discussed previously, the raucous environment of the stadium – the 'football frame' – neutralizes the phrases which, in other circumstances, would be considered offensive and injurious.

In addition to the individual curses, prominent in the stadium are the semi-organized chants that arise. One of the most common is the chant the calls the opponent a 'piece of crap'. For instance, Roma fans might shout at the Livorno fans, '*Li-vor-ne-se, pez-zo di mer-da*'. This chant is easily adaptable to target any four-syllable name, whether that of an individual or a group of fans. Fans sometimes chant in unison, *Va-fan-cu-lo!* (Piss off!) at the opposing fans, the opposing players or at the referee.

Songs

Fan-generated *cori* (choruses or songs) display complexity and reflexivity as well vulgarity and crudity. In stadiums throughout Italy, fans sing throughout the match. Older, well-known songs are sung from memory, while new songs are created and altered spontaneously. Fan groups disseminate these songs in printed song sheets or through sheer repetition. An A.S. Roma fan, nicknamed Galopeira, has become famous for writing songs about A.S. Roma. He regularly appears on radio shows and his songs are distributed online. The aim of these songs is generally to encourage their own team and degrade rivals. These songs use Roman dialect, emphasizing the fans' pride in their home city. Many of these songs borrow the melody from well-known tunes and insert new lyrics. For example, the following ode to Francesco Totti is sung to the melody of the traditional Cuban song, *Guantanamera*.[22]

Un Capitano,	One Captain
C'e solo un capitano	There's only one captain
Un capitano	One Captain
C'e solo un capitano	There's only one captain.

The song references Totti's official designation as captain of the team, while it implicitly praises Totti as the irreplaceable leader of the team. For Roma fans, Totti is in a unique figure in the history of the team as he grew up in Rome as a Roma fan and he became one of the best Italian players of his generation. The song's uplifting rhythm and lyrical simplicity express the joy of the fans and their adoration of Totti.

The following song sung by Lazio fans invokes the importance of the *curva nord* as their 'turf'.

C'e solo la nord	There's only the north
C'e solo la nord	There's only the north
Gli ultràs della Lazio	The *ultràs* of Lazio
Non mollano mai	Don't ever back down
C'e solo la Lazio	There's only Lazio
Sosteniam la Lazio	We support Lazio
La Lazio alé	Lazio alé

This song vocalizes the Lazio supporters' pride in the *curva nord*, the physical and symbolic home of Lazio fans. The lyrics, 'There's only the north' dismisses the other side of the stadium, the *curva sud*, the territory of the rival Roma fans. The song goes on to boast one of the key points of pride for the Lazio *ultràs* – that they 'Don't ever back down'. This phrase alludes to one of the primary Lazio choruses,

'*Non mollare mai*' (Never back down), a song that has become a credo of the Lazio faithful.

In addition to the fan-created songs, A.S. Roma has an official singer/songwriter, the pop star Antonello Venditti. Just before kick-off at every A.S. Roma home match, fans rise upon hearing the first notes of Venditti's anthem, 'Roma, Roma, Roma' played over the stadium's sound system. As discussed earlier, this song 'frames' the event to emphasize the new set of rules that are to be followed. In the case of a Roma home game, the new 'rules' of the social situation allow for heightened emotions and for amplified expressive behaviour including the shouts, gestures and singing discussed above.

Antonello Venditti's 'Roma, Roma' is incredibly powerful because it reminds the fans of the beauty and grandeur of Rome, invoking their pride in place and spurring a sense of commonality and belonging for the fans. The song posits the football club as an extension of the city. In this way, it raises the stakes of the game because the song ties the fate of the city to the fate of the football club. All of this is wrapped in a pretty melody.

Roma, Roma by Antonello Venditti

Roma Roma Roma	(Roma the football club)
core de 'sta Città	Heart of this city
unico grande amore	The only great love
de tanta e tanta gente	Of the many, many people
che fai sospirà.	That takes your breath away.
Roma Roma Roma	Roma Roma Roma
lasciace cantà,	Let us song
da 'sta voce nasce un coro	From this voice is born a chorus
so' centomila voci	A hundred thousand voices
c'hai fatto innamorà	You have made us fall in love.
Roma Roma bella	Roma, beautiful Roma
t'ho dipinta io,	I have painted you
gialla come er sole	Yellow like the sun
rossa come er core mio Roma	Red like my heart
Roma Roma Roma	Roma Roma Roma
nun te fa incantà	Don't be fooled
tu sei nata grande	You were born great
e grande hai da restà	And great you shall stay

Roma Roma Roma	Roma Roma Roma
core de sta città	Heart of this city
unico grande amore	The one great love,
de tanta e tanta gente	of many, many people,
c'hai fatto innammorà	That you have made fall in love.

Venditti's lyrics cast the A.S. Roma football team, called *Roma* in the song, as the 'heart' of the city that brings so many people together. The song calls on this community of Roma fans, who have fallen in love with the team, to sing together in a unified chorus in the second verse. The third verse creates an image of painting the city of Rome with the Roma colours, 'yellow like the sun and red like my heart'. The sun is invoked as the universal symbol of warmth and light and the heart represents warmth and determination. For the Romans, the sun represents the temperate climate of Rome, differentiating them from northerners, whom, Romans claim, are emotionally colder much like the climate in gloomy, Northern Italy. Roman dialect is sprinkled throughout the song. For example, in the phrase, *er sole* (the sun), *er* is Roman dialect that replaces the standard Italia, *il* (the). As discussed in the previous chapter, the use of dialect emphasizes the distinctly Roman nature of the event. The fourth verse reminds the fans of the grandeur of Rome and how it shall remain great. The fifth verse is a reprise of the first; however, the beginning of the fifth verse is sung as the culmination of a crescendo, as the Roma fans are becoming energized for the imminent match and sing as loudly and passionately as possible. As the Roma fans finish singing, the players and fans are ready. The match begins.

Venditti's warm melody and sentimental (melodramatic) lyrics contrast sharply with Lazio fans' scarf-twirling, rock'n'roll-oriented opening song, 'Non mollare mai' (Never back down). This rousing song cues Lazio fans at the beginning of every home game, to stand up, twirl their scarves overhead and shout, as much as sing, the chorus, 'Non mollare mai'. This song invokes a physically agitated and rowdy mode of fandom. It is as if the fans are getting themselves, and the team, ready for a fight.

Non Mollare Mai

Bianco e azzurro è il tuo colore,	White and blue are your colours
bianco e azzurro Lazio nel cuore	White and Blue, Lazio in my heart
Lazio da sola noi gente laziale	Lazio only, for us Lazio fans
non ti lasceremo mai! oh no, oh No..	We will never leave you, oh no, oh no
E quando qualcuno poi ti ferisce,	And if anyone ever hurts you
hai a fianco la Nord che non tradisce	At your side, you have the North which will never betray you
In alto i cuori, noi in campo con le voci e	We hold up our hearts, us, on the field, with our voices
Forza Lazio! Forza Lazio! Forza Lazio!	Let's Go Lazio! Let's Go Lazio!

Non mollare mai, non mollare mai,	Never back down, Never back down
non mollare mai, non mollare mai.	Never back down, Never back down
Forza Lazio alè, forza Lazio alè	Let's go Lazio, hurray, Let's go Lazio hurray!
Forza Lazio alè, forza Lazio alè!	Let's go Lazio, hurray, Let's go Lazio hurray!

The lyrics begin by asserting the blue and white colours of Lazio and how the blue and white is in the hearts of the fans. The lyrics shift into the first person plural, 'we' to sing about shared values of the fans. The song declares that if anyone or any team hurts Lazio, the fans (in the curva *nord*) will always be there faithfully to support the Lazio players. The fans pledge to 'hold up their hearts' and 'participate' on the field with their voices and the cheer of 'let's go Lazio'. The climax of the song is the chorus when the fans shout *Non Mollare Mai* (Never back down). The declaration of loyalty to the team is combined with the chorus, which might be considered an ultimatum to the team, to never back down. The lyrics of *Non Mollare Mai* affirm the loyalty of the fans and their commitment to the team, yet it contains a hard edge that reflects the core values of Lazio. The fans demand that the team play with toughness and a fighting spirit. This attitude contrasts with the attitude portrayed in Roma's song, which is one of pure passion and loyalty.

Stadium choruses are powerful in creating a sense of unity among fans. While the lyrics foreground unity as a central theme, it is the medium of music that has particular power to not only convey *ideas* of unity, but to actually evoke *feelings* of unity. In his article, 'Music and Identity', Simon Frith writes, 'Music seems to be a key to identity because it offers, so intensely, a sense of both self and others, of the subjective in the collective'.[23] Frith elaborates on how fans might feel during this process by quoting Mark Slobin, who notes how performers are, 'Working out a shared vision that involves both the assertion of pride, even ambition, and the simultaneous disappearance of the ego'.[24] Slobin puts his finger on exactly what these football songs aim to do: invoke the pride and ambition of the fans and to facilitate the process by which fans lose themselves in the collective. Part of the attraction of the football stadium is clearly the validation of identity that can only be found in a crowd that comes together as one – the feeling described by Victor Turner as *communitas*.[25]

The following song, also written by pop star, Venditti, is sung by Roma fans after every home victory. Like many such songs, the lyrics aim to unite the fans, but the reflexivity of the lyrics is uncommon as the song actually ponders the process by which fans are 'brought together'.

Grazie Roma by A.Venditti.

Dimmi cos'è	Tell me what it is
che ci fa sentire amici	That makes us feel like friends
anche se non ci conosciamo.	Even if we don't know each other
Dimmi cos'è	Tell me what it is
che ci fa sentire uniti	That makes us feel united
anche se siamo lontani.	Even if we are far apart?

Dimmi cos'è, cos'è	Tell me what it is, what it is
che batte forte, forte, forte	That beats strongly, strongly strongly
in fondo al cuore,	At the bottom of my heart
che ci toglie il respiro	That takes my breath away
e ci parla d'amore.	And speaks of love?
Grazie Roma,	Thank you Roma
che ci fai piangere	That makes us cry
e abbracciarci ancora.	And embrace each other again
Grazie Roma, grazie Roma, che ci fai vivere	Thank you Roma, that makes us live
e sentire ancora una persona nuova.	And feel again as a new person
Dimmi cos'è quella stella	Tell me what great, great
grande grande in fondo al cielo	Star in back of the sky
che brilla dentro di te	that shines inside of me
e grida forte forte in alto al cuore,	and screams loudly loudly from the top of my heart
Grazie Roma,	Thank you Roma
che ci fai piangere	That makes us cry
e abbracciarci ancora.	And embrace each other again
Grazie Roma, grazie Roma, che ci fai vivere	Thank you Roma, that makes us live
e sentire ancora una persona nuova.	And feel again as a new person
Dimmi chi è chi è	Tell me who it is, who it is
che mi fa sentì importante	that makes me feel important
anche se non conto niente,	even if I don't count for anything
che mi fa re quando sento le campane	that makes me king when I hear the bells
la domenica mattina.	On Sunday morning
Dimmi chi è chi è	Tell me who it is, who it is
che mi fa campà sta vita	That helps me endure this life
così piena di problemi	That's so full of problems
e mi dà coraggio	And gives me courage
se tu non mi vuoi bene.	If you don't love me
Grazie Roma,	Thank you Roma
che ci fai piangere	That makes us cry
e abbracciarci ancora.	And embrace each other again
Grazie Roma, grazie Roma, che ci fai vivere	Thank you Roma, that makes us live
e sentire ancora una persona nuova.	And feel again as a new person

Venditti's lyrics characterize a love for Rome that 'takes our breath away'. Venditti praises the power of the team to renew the fans and to make them feel important. His lyrics ask the rhetorical question 'What unites us?' The answer is, of course, the football club Roma. The community of Roma fans that Venditti invokes is an imagined community. Anderson writes of the notion of a national community, 'It is imagined because the members of even the smallest nation will never know most of their fellow members, meet them, or even hear of them, yet in the minds of each lives the image of their communion'.[26] Like the 'smallest nation' that Anderson theorizes, the majority of football fans of a major football team will never know each member personally, but they can feel as though they are part of community of people that share a common passion. Anderson emphasizes the importance of the newspaper in creating imagined communities. Football fan 'nations' similarly rely on media to disseminate information and to create the feeling of community among strangers. At the football match, the act of singing Venditti's 'Roma, Roma' or 'Grazie Roma' instantaneously actualizes the community of Roma fans. The lyrics to 'Grazie Roma' evoke and confirm the importance of the A.S. Roma football team in creating this type of imagined community through shared devotion to the team. 'Grazie Roma' is sung at the end of each game that Roma wins, thereby acting to confirm the frame of the event or to 'seal' the meaning of the preceding events.

The following song is an example of one of the Lazio fans' most heartfelt anthems. It describes the sense of anticipation that the fans feel waiting in the stadium for the game to begin.

Inno della Lazio

Sò già du'ore che stamo qui a aspettà	It's already been two hours that we have waited here
me batte er core cominceno a giocà	my heart beats in anticipation for the game to begin
mille bandiere famo sventolà	We wave thousands of flags
entra la Lazio lo stadio sta a scoppià	Lazio enters and the stadium explodes
Lazio grande Lazio che ce ponno fa'	Lazio, great Lazio, what can they do?
undici fiati tutti quanti a respira'	eleven breaths all together sigh
Lazio grande Lazio nata pe' domina'	Lazio, great Lazio, born to dominate
tu sei la mejo e nun ce vonno sta'	You are the best and they don't get it. (because they are sore losers)
Semo un'impasto de forza e volonta'	We are a mix of power and will
con tanto core come nessuno c'ha	With more heart than any other
fermate monno sotto al cuppolone	stop under the great dome
rifatte l'occhi stamo a gioca' a pallone	focus your eyes, we're here to play football
Lazio grande Lazio che ce ponno fa'	Lazio, great Lazio, what can they do?
undici fiati tutti quanti a respira'	11 breaths all breathe together
Lazio grande Lazio nata pe' domin'	Lazio, great Lazio, born to dominate,
tu sei la mejo e nun ce vonno sta'	You are the best and they don't get it. (because they are sore losers)

Daje aquilotti nun se pò sbajà *su c'è er maestro che ce stà a guardà*	C'mon eagles, you can't go wrong With you is the maestro that watches over

Lazio grande Lazio che ce ponno fa' *undici fiati tutti quanti a respira'* *Lazio grande Lazio nata pe' domina'* *tu sei la mejo e nun ce vonno sta'*	Lazio, great Lazio eleven breaths all together sigh Lazio, great Lazio, born to dominate You are the best and they don't get it. (because they are sore losers)

Lazio grande Lazio *che ce ponno fà* *tu sei la mejo* *e nun ce vonno sta*	Lazio great Lazio what can you do? You are the best and the others just don't get it they just don't get it. (because they are sore losers)

This anthem is one of the most traditional Lazio songs. Its emotional pitch is much more sentimental than the raucous 'Non Mollare Mai'. The song gives a descriptive story from the perspective of fans that have arrived early to the stadium and wait in the stands with great anticipation for their team to enter onto the field and for the game to start. When the team does arrive on the field, there is a figurative explosion of emotions complete with waving flags. The chorus is a sentimental praise of Lazio and hints at the outsider status that Lazio fans adopt. The lyrics ponder the question why 'Lazio fans know that Lazio is the best, but why don't the others understand?' In the second verse, the song boasts of the power, will and heart that Lazio displays. Throughout the song are references to Roman landmarks and symbols. For instance, the *cuppolone* refers to the dome of St. Peter's, the landmark of Rome of which the Lazio fans are proud. In the next verse of the song, the term *aquilotti* is a reference to Lazio's symbol and unofficial nickname, the eagles. The term maestro refers to former coach, Tommaso Maestrelli, who led Lazio to their first Italian championship in the 1973/1974 season. Maestrelli died a few years after Lazio's first championship, but he is still revered by Lazio fans.

The song employs Roman dialect in the pronunciation (and spelling) of several words such as '*ponno*' which is the dialect version of '*possono*' the third person, plural of the verb '*potere*', meaning 'can or may'. The song also uses the Roman phrase, '*Daje*' (c'mon or let's go), a common phrase for both Roma and Lazio fans. The Roman dialect and the reference to St. Peter's dome mark the Lazio fans' connection to Rome. Lazio and Roma fans constantly compete and bicker over which set of fans is the most authentically Roman. This song is a good example of Lazio fans proudly showing their Roman roots.

In direct contrast to the heartfelt, emotional anthems, sung in support of their team, a large contingent of Lazio fans spent a lot of time during the 2005–2006 season singing songs of protest against the team's owner, Claudio Lotito. The following is an example of a protest chant, against owner Claudio Lotito.

Forza Lazio	Let's Go Lazio
Forza Lazio	Let's Go Lazio
Sempre insiem' a te.	We're always with you.

Forza Lazio	Let's Go Lazio
Forza Lazio	Let's Go Lazio
Lotito vattene!	Lotito, piss off!!!

The chant reaffirms the fans' commitment to the team, but calls for the owner, Lotito, to step down from his position and sell the team. These mixed sentiments – on one hand, allegiance to the team and, on the other, protest against various segments of the team's structure – highlight one of the major discontinuities of professional football. For the fans, the team is understood as a timeless, idealized entity replete with valour and glory that transcends any single player or any owner. This ideal is worthy of the fans' unwavering faith and allegiance. The team colours – blue and white of Lazio and the red and yellow of Roma – represent the ideal for the fans. The ideal comes into conflict with the reality of modern football (and perhaps throughout the history of football) as a high-stakes business involving major capital risk. Cold-headed business decisions often are not reconcilable from the perspective of the emotionally committed fan. This particular Lazio protest chant distinguishes between the team from the owner, the ideal from the current reality. Football songs range from the nostalgic and mournful to the bitter and angry to the confrontational to the farcical. Football songs draw on a wide range of human emotions in order to engage the fans, motivate the players, and, ultimately, create the football stadium experience. Football songs and chants range from the nostalgic to the angry to the farcical. They draw on a wide range of human emotion in order to engage fans, motivate the players and, ultimately, create the football stadium experience.

Globalizing fandom

While the work of Lazio and Roma fans at the stadium highlights local language, local culture and local pride, fan culture is simultaneously influenced by fan culture that crosses national borders. Scholars, Carlo Podaliri and Carlo Balestri, argue that Italian *ultràs* displays have always borrowed from English models of fan support, resulting in an international cross-fertilization of *ultràs* pageantry. This phenomenon is the result of international media coverage of football as well as through the proliferation of intra-European club tournaments. Each year, as many as eight Italian teams join the top teams throughout Europe in the intra-European tournaments, the Uefa Cup and the Uefa Champions League.[27] Furthermore, fierce competition in the European airline industry has resulted in low-priced airfare and in increase in the number of fans that attend their teams' away games in all corners of Europe. In the days leading up the Roma match against the northernmost team in the tournament located in Tromso, Norway, newspaper coverage detailed the length of the journey, the town's proximity to the North Pole and the average amount of sunlight in winter. These away matches provide a lesson in geography, as well as the opportunity to steal ideas from competing fans.

A prime example of this cross-fertilization of fan culture in the 2005–2006 season happened when Roma played at Bruges, Belgium in the Uefa cup. After Bruges scored the first goal of the match, the Belgian fans started singing (or shouting), 'Ohhhh, oh, oh, oh, oh, ohhhhhh, oh,' to the bass line melody of the song 'Seven Nation Army', written by the White Stripes, an American rock band that had released the song several years prior. After Roma scored the equalizing and the winning goals, the Roma fans adopted the same chant in order to upstage their rivals. These Roma fans brought the chant back home to Rome and it became the unofficial anthem of Roma's record-breaking 11-game Italian league winning streak. The original song (or at least the 7 note intro section) spread like a contagion as it was soon heard on radio stations and hummed by fans walking in the streets of Rome. This previously obscure song had a commercial and cultural revival in Rome. The Roma fans added the lyrics, '*bianc'azzurro bastardo*' (white and blue bastard in reference to the blue and white of Lazio) for the derby game. Francesco Totti sang this verse on a radio programme and later apologized after the subsequent criticism from Lazio fans. Totti hummed the tune at the San Remo festival, an Italian musical event and cultural institution that was co-hosted by his celebrity fashion-model wife, Ilary Blasi. As the Italian national team advanced through the World Cup tournament, Italian fans united in singing this catchy melody. Ultimately, the players themselves led the 100,000+ chorus of Italian fans who turned up in Rome's Circus Maximus to celebrate Italy's World Cup victory. The journey of this song from the USA to Brussels, to the stadium in Rome, and, ultimately, to the World Cup celebration at the Circus Maximus illustrates one aspect of globalization and its effect on football fan culture. This particular chant proved so popular that it made into the stadium during the 2014 FIFA World Cup Finals in Brazil. The song has become a global phenomenon that typifies the multi-cultural fusion of global capital.

Protest

Unlike in the USA, where fan discontent is generally confined to individualized protest or media campaigns, Italian fans organize in person to protest. In the 2005–2006 season, the largest Lazio fan group of the time, the Irriducibili (Indomitables), protested against the owner of the team, Claudio Lotito, for most of the year. The Irriducibili used all of the expressive means at their disposal to orchestrate this protest. On several occasions, 1000s of Lazio supporters marched outside of the stadium hours before the match. They displayed banners, attached posters to trees and gave speeches denouncing Lotito and called for a brighter future.

In one in-stadium demonstration, the Irriducibili evacuated the entire *Curva Nord*, the sacred ground of Lazio fans. The *Curva Nord* is normally the territory that MUST be occupied and defended against outsiders and opposing fans. In place of their bodies, a handful of fans held up the banner reading, '*Il tifoso tradito ora va risarcito*', (The fan betrayed now gets recompense). The betrayal referred to in the banner is the referee scandal that Lotito and leaders from other teams were allegedly involved in. The lack of people in the Curva Nord was a grand symbolic statement by the Lazio fans and a major organizational accomplishment. Though fans pride themselves on loyalty, the Lazio fans' sense of betrayal was strong enough for them to symbolically withdraw their support. Disgruntled fans of struggling teams are not at all uncommon. The ways in which Lazio fans were willing to use the stadium and their own bodies make this type of protest remarkable, even if the ultimate effect of this protest was not successful.[28]

Derby

'Il derby' is the name of the rivalry match between A.S. Roma and S.S. Lazio. These biannual contests are the most intense games of the year for both players and fans. These are occasions for which the fans spend weeks and months preparing. Fans create some of the largest and most extravagant displays of the year that can cover the entire *curva* section of the stadium. The usual fan songs are supplemented by special songs that hurl invective at the rival team and fans. The derby is the foremost outlet to express the passion and partisanship that continually builds between these historic rivals. Since this game is a city-wide spectacle, even the least desirable seats are sold well in advance. The two teams share the same stadium. For the derby, the nominal home team controls the distribution of tickets. Normally, the home team allots a larger than normal number of tickets to the 'visitors'. Season ticket holders of both teams generally have priority in obtaining tickets. During the week-long build-up to the match, ticket scalpers hang out around the stadium and informally conspire to set ticket prices.

At the stadium on derby day, the *curve* sections of the stadium are nearly full two hours before the game. The two sets of opposing fans start singing their repertoires of derogatory songs hours before the match begins. They unfurl banners with provocative messages and wave their flags in anticipation of the most eagerly waited match-up of the year. Fans use anything in the history of the rivalry that might embarrass the opposition as inspiration for the derby displays. The derby matches are the pinnacle of fan participation at the stadium in Rome.

Conclusion

This chapter has catalogued the modes of expression employed by football fans at the football stadium. At football matches, the stadium becomes the forum for the expression and exchange of messages between competing fans. Using modest or even primitive media resources such as an old sheet and a can of paint or just their own bodies, fans broadcast their messages to the 1000s of in-stadium fans, as well as larger media audiences. Football matches are cultural performances that make overt the ideas, values and creativity of the fans. The ideas expressed by fans at the stadium are not limited to simplistic sentiment or partisan support. Messages of protest, anger and sorrow are displayed along with innocuous jokes and cheers. The enormous mass media attention paid to these performances makes the stadium an important site for the representation of the society from which it emerges (in this case, Italian), for locals and foreign observers alike.

The real power of the stadium is when the individual joins with others to create magnificent displays, powerful songs, overwhelming sound or, at times, equally as powerful silence. The degree to which any of the fan performance substantially affects the outcome of the match is a question for others to answer.[29] From this volume's perspective, the fan performances in the stands are at the heart of the game. They are what that give the game its flavour. The significance of the football match derives from its social meaning – the match is worth caring about because so many people care about it. It is a stage to be with others who support and encourage the expression emotion and passion. In a global economy where data analysis and markets grow in influence and attempt to measure the value of everything, passion may become even more precious. The chance to interact with others – to be vulnerable and to be validated in and through others – cannot be easily replaced. The stadium is the antidote to forces of alienation.

In the chapters to follow, my analysis considers the social organization of fan clubs and highlights the ways in which these fans use media to coordinate their fan activities. In a sense, these chapters give a 'behind the scenes' account of the activities of fans as they prepare for the ritual performances at the stadium. More importantly, these fans and these fan clubs do far more than just prepare for the weekend football match. Fan groups become communities that support one another in the rewards and struggles of daily life. Fandom is lived in bars, restaurants and websites, and, in short, in the spaces and practices of daily life, even as fans yearn to be back at the stadium.

Disclosure statement

No potential conflict of interest was reported by the author.

Notes

1. Ginsborg, *Italy and its Discontents*, 116.
2. see Singer, *Traditional India*; Bauman, 'Performance'.
3. Singer, *Traditional India*, xiii.
4. Bauman, 'Performance', 46.
5. MacAloon, *Rite, Drama, Festival, Spectacle*, 4. MacAloon is quoting the organizers of the conference on cultural performances.
6. Burns, *Barca: A People's Passion*.
7. 'Roma, Roma' and other songs are discussed in depth below.
8. Bauman, *Verbal Art as Performance*, 16.
9. Serie A referees are invariably male.
10. The death of Vincenzo Spagnolo is documented, along with other Italian football-related deaths in the Mariottini, *Ultraviolenza*.
11. Kendon, *Gesture*, 352.
12. For more information about the C.U.C.S, see http://asromaultras.it/2000.html#history.
13. *Striscia la Notizia* is a parody news show that airs on Mediaset's Channel 5.
14. The story of the Brigata Roberto Rulli can be found at the website, http://www.asromaultràs.it/fedayn.html.
15. trans. *Sei partita sola per l'ultima trasferta ... ma al tuo arrivo tanti amici ritroverai ... e insieme a loro forza roma sempre canterai! Ciao Luisa!* Banners dedicated to Petrucci can be found online at http://www.lamiaroma.it/cartellasalvaguai/Luisa%20Petrucci.htm.
16. Arkan was the nickname of Željko Ražnatović, a Serbian paramilitary leader who was accused of crimes against humanity committed during the violent breakup of Yugoslavia. Arkan was murdered in January, 2000, before his court hearing.
17. 'Olimpico, svastiche in curva sud'.
18. For example, the group, Boys, displayed a banner reading, *Nel cervello soltanto la Roma* (In our mind, only la Roma.).
19. Original text: *Con fedeltà e amore ti aspettiamo.*
20. Original text: *Mejo N'anno de galera che Laziale pe'na sera.*
21. The photo appeared in the La Repubblica website. The hyperlink was no longer valid as of June 2006.
22. The tune was sung by Manchester United fans to praise their hero, David Beckham with the lyrics, 'One David Beckham, There's only one David Beckham ...'.
23. Frith, 'Music and Identity', 110.

24. Ibid., 111.
25. Turner's concept of communitas is outlined in several of his works including *From Ritual to Theater*.
26. Anderson, *Imagined Communities*, 6.
27. Uefa Cup and Champions League are intra-European club competitions.
28. More on the Lazio brand of protest later in the book.
29. For instance, Kuper and Szymanski's *Soccernomics* has used statistical analysis to measure the home field advantage.

References

Anderson, B. *Imagined Communities: Reflections on the Origins and Spread of Nationalism*. New York: Verso, 1991.
Bauman, R. *Verbal Art as Performance*. Prospect Heights, IL: Waveland, 1984 (1977).
Bauman, R. 'Performance'. In *Folklore, Cultural Performances, and Popular Entertainments*, ed. R. Bauman, 41–9. Oxford: Oxford University Press, 1992.
Bauman, R. *A World of Others' Words: Cross-cultural Perspectives on Intertextuality*. Malden, MA: Blackwell, 2004.
Burns, J. *Barca: A People's Passion*. London: Bloomsbury, 1999.
Frith, S. 'Music and Identity'. In *Questions of Cultural Identity*, ed. S. Hall and P. du Gay, 108–27. Thousand Oaks, CA: Sage, 1996.
Ginsborg, P. *Italy and Its Discontents: Family, Civil Society, State, 1980–2001*. New York: Palgrave MacMillan, 2003.
Kendon, A. *Gesture: Visible Action as Utterance*. New York: Cambridge University Press, 2004.
Kuper, S., and S. Szymanski. *Soccernomics: Why Transfers Fail, Why Spain Rule the World and Other Curious Football Phenomenon Explained*. 3rd ed. London: Harper Collins, 2012.
MacAloon, J. *Rite, Drama, Festival, Spectacle: Rehearsals toward a Theory of Cultural Performance*. Philadelphia, PA: Institute for the Study of Human Issues, 1984.
Mariottini, D. *Ultraviolenza: Storie di Sangue del Tifo Italiano [Ultraviolence: Stories of Blood in Italian Fandom]*. Turin: Bradipolibri, 2004.
'Olimpico, Svastiche in Curva Sud [Olympic [Stadium]: Swastikas in the South Curve]'. *La Repubblica.It* (accessed April 4, 2015). 2006. http://www.repubblica.it/2006/a/sezioni/sport/calcio/serie_a/svastiche/svastiche/svastiche.html
Singer, M. *Traditional India: Structure and Change*. Philadelphia, PA: American Folklore Society, 1959.
Turner, V. *From Ritual to Theatre: The Human Seriousness of Play*. New York: PAJ Publications, 1982

Print media: circulating fandom

> This essay catalogues the variety of printed material that circulates among fans. In addition to the traditional newspapers available at newsstands, free papers are given away at the stadium. The images of football players are an essential part of the fan experience as they are posted on the walls of fan clubs. Mass distributed print media is social media; it educates fans, it fuels conversations between strangers and it is used by fans to decorate their clubhouse walls. Smaller scale, fan-produced media is used to proclaim and solidify group identity and to recruit new members. Though print media may seem outdated, it is still an essential social media, as evidenced by the uses and reuses of print by football fans.

Print media in the form of newspapers and magazines have been at the heart of fandom for over a century. The sports section of the daily paper is one of the foundational elements that have made football a culturally relevant phenomenon. This chapter covers a variety of different printed materials ranging from glossy magazines to the free papers handed out at the stadium. Each different paper has a slightly different format and is aimed at a slightly different audience, but they all contribute to fandom in some way, and they all rely on fans to justify their existence. All media are meant to grab the attention of football fans, and sell them ideas if not products. Most of the print publications rely on the visual aspects of football to grab the attention of their readers. Beautiful photography can be found in even amateur productions.

Print materials are created by a variety of producers ranging from the most professional publications that adhere to high journalistic standards to the fan-produced flyers printed on the fly with everything in between. The intention of these publications differs as well as some are created solely to advertise products while others recruit members and create solidarity. Beyond the production of media, this chapter will consider how media are 'consumed' and circulated. The cost, distribution and quality of a publication influences the ways in which fans approach the media. Some printed materials are discarded immediately while glossy books are designed to sit on bookshelves for years. To continue a theme developed throughout this volume, fans use the print media for their own purposes – the creation of meaning does not stop with the physical production and distribution of a medium. Fans cut out images, discuss provocative articles and they might passively agree or actively dissent from what they see and learn. Media facilitates the hashing and rehashing of the events of the stadium beginning with the performance of players and ranging outward to coaching and management decisions, and the gossip of celebrities and politicians.

This chapter begins with a short discussion of the history and development of the newspaper as a contributor to the ascendancy of football. The daily sports section may now be taken for granted, but a brief look at the history reveals a logic of how football developed as the people's game. The proliferation of print media has peaked with the production a commercial daily newspaper devoted to the doings of a single team. In more recent years, fans have become increasingly active in their creation of print content. Fan groups have the ability to create their own fanzines and commemorative books. This allows them to counter mainstream ideas with their own forms of resistance.

Of course, much of this fan production has gone online. One might rightfully ask whether the internet and portable media devices will supercede or even wipe out print media. In cataloguing various print media, this chapter implicitly argues that print media serve various functions in specific contexts that online media would have trouble duplicating or rendering superfluous. For instance, the physicality of print media makes them immediately 'post-able' on the walls of fan clubhouses or on the walls of a young fan's bedroom. The format of print media gives control of the visual representation and the timing of distribution to the producer. This lends itself to an effective advertising medium. For these and other reasons to be articulated below, print media will have an importance place in the lives of football fans for years to come.

Brief history of print media and sport

In critical discussions of the influence of media and football, print media seem to be almost taken for granted. The enormous financial and cultural impact of TV, internet-digital and so-called social media seem to be the topics of the most widespread interest. Newspapers, however, have had such a profound impact on sport that they have set the foundation for understanding the rise of sport and mass-audience spectacles that we know today. In addition to providing the descriptions and results, newspapers gave sport a narrative and created a sense of 'cultural continuity' through performing the following functions:

> Keeping records, lionising outstanding performers, developing the mythologies of 'golden eras' and in general operating as publicists, literary chroniclers and philosophers for the new codified games.[1]

Newspapers and sport have been mutual benefactors for over a century. The late nineteenth and early twentieth century was a time of 'significant growth and expansion'[2] for the daily newspaper and the mass popular entertainment. The development of the telegraph had a significant impact on the ability of papers to report results in a timely manner and it created the necessity for a cadre of sports journalists to report back from around the sprawling new world, and throughout Europe. The emergence daily sport sections in the 1880s in the newspapers was a significant milestone as it gave particular sports 'cultural legitimacy'[3] and mainstream appeal that niche magazines could not provide. This timeline coincides with the development of football around the world. In the era of commercial newspapers that relied on advertising sponsorship, the coverage of sport became an easy way to attract both subscriptions and sales at the newsstands. With easy to read articles and photographs that made heroes and villains, sport sold papers to expanding classes of barely literate masses. Football, in particular, was used to attract young and middle-class readers as it has long been considered a game 'of the people' due in part to its simplicity and lack of costly equipment. Its visual appeal and showcasing of the athletic body probably helped as well.

McFarland notes the development of sports journalism in Spain in the 1910s[4] with several sport-based publications arriving and disappearing starting around this time. Football coverage was aimed at the working class, while other motor sports and fencing were pitched towards the upper classes, though even the 'respectable' papers covered football. Early in the twentieth century, football became a 'true mass entertainment industry' in Spain through stadium construction, print media and the effective marketing football as an embodiment of local identity. Throughout Europe, football coverage appealed especially to young readers and to lower class readers as literacy rates in Western Europe increased in the earlier part of the twentieth century.[5] Supplemented by photos, the sports section was probably easier to read than most sections of the paper.

The inception of association football roughly coincided with the development of the sports section and other sport media in the early twentieth century. Newspapers and magazines, newsletters and fanzines have relayed the stories of the players and matches in text and imagery since the beginning of organized football. Over time, print media would celebrate heroes and castigate villains and goats and the papers would create celebrities out of sporting figures. Sport became an essential part of the newspaper because sport was popular. It used to be said that sport was a diversion from the tough issues of the rest of the paper. In more recent times, we might look to the sport page to see which social issues are being represented in the sporting world and how sport might speak to such issues. Also, the financial stakes of professional sports are so high that they might actually have a significant impact on the local economy. Now, sports news is integrated in the fabric of newspapers beyond the confines of the sport section.

Football became popular among the working class by emphasizing the 'associative nature of football fandom'[6] and in large groups setting social aspects. Where the 'new middle classes' experience football 'in a more solitary way' in smaller groups, including women.[7] This change in fandom is reflected and perhaps spurred by the expansion of football media. The new fans, that Giulianotti calls 'post fans'[8], are typically white collar, middle class and have a reflexive, ironic relationship with their fandom. They are more likely to create their own media or at least to comment upon and criticize the mass media.

One of the major social impacts of newspapers is that they give readers a common base of knowledge from which to discuss and argue about. In larger, industrialized societies, the newspaper was one of the few things that kept large groups of people in touch with each other. Larger societies could no longer rely solely upon word of mouth in face-to-face settings in order to interact meaningfully. The newspaper created the imagined communities[9] in that people who never met could imagine that their neighbours read the same things and were preoccupied with the same issues, and therefore, they were all connected even if they disagreed on particular policies or values.

While we might think of the power of the national newspaper to unite, or in some ways, even *create* a nation and the sense of nationhood, print media can do similar work on the local scale to both exploit and further a sense of community, and also to grab the attention of the local reader with more parochial concerns. The free newspapers distributed at football matches reveal one of the ways in which fans can be targeted as a demographically rich set of consumers, and how a newspaper might reach potential consumers at just the right time and place.

The free newspaper

One of the curious aspects of going to the Olympic Stadium in Rome is that fans are inundated with free newspapers. While surely game programmes are available to buy somewhere (I confess, I never bought one), the free papers would always feature attractive photos of the home team players on the cover. The inside would have rudimentary facts and figures and schedules, and somewhat rough articles concerning the rise and fall of players and coaches. The primary purpose of these papers was undoubtedly to carry advertisements. In terms of demographics, the soccer stadium is concentrated mass of male consumers with a range of ages, but most of whom reside within in the greater Rome area, and who have the extra time and money to attend football matches. It is no wonder, then, that sometimes I would arrive home with three or more of these free papers. As far as I could tell, the great majority of these papers were almost immediately discarded – no one except for this odd American academic would bring them home, but I would see people browsing through the papers before the matches began. From a marketing perspective, the interval between when a fan arrives at his or her seat and the opening kickoff is an opportune time to reach potential customers. Most fans have little else to do before the match. If a fan is waiting for their friend to arrive, they might be sitting alone, idly glance through the paper. They might be persuaded by the allure of a comfortable new couch, a shiny kitchen upgrade or even a new car – these are some of the advertisements that surround the player profiles or match notes that the papers provide. While these free newspapers were often treated with disdain, the papers were in high demand, if it had recently rained, or threatened to. These papers become improvised seat dryers and covers. The discarding of these papers was one of the more shameful things I had witnessed as they quickly became garbage, rain or shine.

The stadium comprised a prime audience for another targeted marketing scheme: the Panini sticker booklets. These booklets are designed to affix a sticker for each individual player and manager on every team. Panini would give away the booklets in order to stoke sales of the packets of stickers. The booklets begged to be fully completed, and of course, one would invariably end up with duplicates and triplicates of stickers of player a and b, but not player c, so you would have to buy more stickers, or trade with your friends. Though marketed at children, I witnessed one adult fan grab a huge stack of these booklets only to rip out the complementary first packet of stickers. Much to his chagrin, the packets contained the stickers of the exact same set of players. As these publication attest, the stadium is a prime distribution point for fan-targeted print media.

Il Romanista

Il Romanista was a daily newspaper dedicated primarily to coverage of the A.S. Roma football club. The paper was available at newsstands throughout Rome for 1 Euro in 2004. The paper was supplemented by news of other happenings in Rome and in the world, but most of the coverage was on every aspect of the club from the youth teams and charity games to the health of the top players and the intrigues in the administration of the club. Like any Italian sports publication, there was plenty of speculation on player transfers and other issues. *Il Romanista* had to compete not only with the sports sections of local and national daily newspapers, but also with the three national daily sport papers[10] that devote most of their attention to football. As is common at Italian newsstands, *Il Romanista* and other newspapers would increase sales by including special posters or prizes, or packaging the paper with a free DVD and DVD holder – the first DVD in series of DVDs, so one is induced to buy the remainder of DVDs in the serial release, along with the paper. Surely, many of these posters were destined to be tacked to the bedroom walls of eight-year-old players dreaming of playing professional football, while the DVDs were collected and perhaps watched once. *Il Romanista* ceased operations in August, 2014. Surely the paper was a casualty of the online sources of information as sustaining a full-colour, daily newspaper proved unprofitable. Ironically, the paper also maintained a website, though that is also no longer updated.

Glossy magazines are another source of information about the team. The club itself produces an official magazine that has lots of nice photos and often a poster or some other sort of pull-out feature that helps to spur sales. Top football players are celebrities, and, as such, are the subjects of tabloid papers and magazines targeted at female consumers who are not left out completely by the football media marketing demographic research. For instance, Roma star, Francesco Totti and his wife Ilary were pictured in their bathing suits on the cover of a prominent tabloid. In this way, football becomes more than a pastime for men, and becomes a cultural point of reference for a nation of readers, or at least, *browsers*.

Media circulation and identity

Fan clubs are the repositories and nurseries of fan culture. Part of this fan culture is the endless amount of images of football heroes and idols playing the game, advertising products or even making appearances at social benefits and banquets. The Roma Club Testaccio has turned its walls into a veritable museum of visual imagery of A.S. Roma – the players, the symbols and the colours. This section shows that ways in which the circulation of print media gives meaning to the images and contributes to fandom. The re-contextualization of the images – the craft of posting them, and sometimes modifying them, allows the fans to take some ownership in the meaning of A.S. Roma.

The Roma Club Testaccio's clubhouse is the heart of the club, and it is the place where Roma, the football team, and Rome, the city, are conjoined. Every surface of the clubhouse is decorated with images or objects that represent Testaccio, Rome and A.S. Roma. The clubhouse functions as a museum devoted to the exposition and celebration of culturally significant artefacts. Dondrea Thompson wrote, 'Public displays of any cultural sort ... are inescapably based on a constructed ideology intended to promote a shared vision of history, identity, and heritage'.[11] Roma Club Testaccio's 'shared vision of history, identity and heritage' is literally taped, painted and tacked onto the walls of the clubhouse as a selection of highlights from Roman history. Carol Duncan argues that museums edit out messy details in preference for uncomplicated narratives. 'In the museum, art history displaces history, purges it of social and political conflict, and distills it down to a series of triumphs, mostly of individual genius'.[12] In this case, art history is replaced by football historiography that is spearheaded by the efforts of 'individual geniuses' who score goals and command squads of players.

At the clubhouse, images of star players and championship teams are flanked by Roman columns. Many of these images are taken from mass media newspapers and magazines, though they are flanked by photographs of fans young and old, plastic centurions occupy the corners. Yellow and red, the colours of both team and city, blanket interior and exterior walls. Several images depict players in the guise of gladiators. The clubhouse contains artefacts that recall imperial Rome and present-day Testaccio. A replica coccio [clay jar] that symbolizes Testaccio rests in a corner near the ceiling. On separate walls are two large, framed, black and white photos of the Campo Testaccio, one of which bears the words 'Testaccio the cradle of Roma'. On one of the main walls of the club is a billboard entitled, 'From Testaccio – The roots and the history of A.S. Roma'. Under these words hangs a series of black and white photographs with captions that describe the early history of the team and the old stadium that stood a few blocks away. Above this billboard, black and white pictures depict the team from early in its history. Through these images, the fan club retains the memory of past players and managers. The images also imply: Roma was born here in this very place, and there is a tradition that continues here. Though the team now plays on the other side of the city, the Roma Club Testaccio documents and sustains Roma's roots. These images create a sense of historical continuity among generations of A.S. Roma players and fans.

This display constructs what Bahktin calls a chronotope – a narrative construct where 'Time takes on flesh and becomes visible for human contemplation'. Chronotopes 'stand as monuments to the community itself, as symbols of it, as forces operating to shape its members' images of themselves'.[13] The walls of the Roma Club Testaccio are where the identity of the club and the identity of its members are laid bare – the images connect the fans to the timeless community of A.S. Roma.

Current team's captain Francesco Totti is the most celebrated player on the walls of the Roma Club Testaccio. Born and raised in Rome, he speaks with a thick Roman accent. Totti has spurned offers to leave his home team to play for more glamorous and powerful teams in Milan, Turin and abroad. He is Roma's bandiera [flag]: literally, the player who anchors the identity of a team. At the Roma Club Testaccio, images of Totti document his rise from 16-year-old prodigy to incomparable icon. He is framed as a soldier, fashion icon, gladiator and philanthropist, as well as a football player. For Roma fans, Totti is not only the quintessential Roma player, he is the quintessential Roman.[14]

Images of rivals, Lazio, serve as counterpoints to that of Totti. One derogatory poster reads: 'A clean Rome depends on you'. It features a cartoon image of a wolf attired in a Roma jersey and holding an eagle in Lazio colours over a garbage can. Another image shows the Roma wolf biting the championship emblem off the Lazio eagle's chest. This image commemorates the 2001 season when Roma won the championship, thus ending Lazio's one-year reign. These images reflect, in a comical way, the strong feelings of identity and difference felt by the respective fan bases. Club President Sergio Rosi insists that he is an A.S. Roma fan because he was born in Rome. In other words, his fan identity is inseparable from his civic identity. He claims that the real Romans are Roma fans and that Lazio fans are burrini [country bumpkins] who live outside of the Aurelian wall, the 800-year-old wall that marks the old border of Rome). Sergio jokes that Lazio fans come into the city only to sell cheese, and when he speaks about the rivalry with Lazio, he speaks faster, uses Romanesco, and has a mischievous look in his eye. While much of the banter between fans of the two teams is often done with a sense of playful exaggeration, it reveals tactics by which the fans position themselves as authentic Romans. Their sense of identity is created in contrast to those who most closely resemble them – the football fans who share the same city and to whom they sometimes refer to as *cugini* (cousins).

The voice of the north

While the Roma Club Testaccio is not passive consumer of media – they do things with the print media, and use the images to decorate, they are still primarily stuck at the consumption end of the spectrum. The Lazio ultras fan group, the Irriducibili, produced multiple types of media in order to communicate to existing members, recruit new ones, and eventually, create an Irriducibili brand. The *Irriducibili* sell a game-day newsletter, maintain a hi-quality website[15], have a radio presence and produced a book and DVD. These media are created in addition to the in-stadium banners and flags, songs and choruses of the kind described in the first chapter. The print and video media documents the in-stadium fans performances and provides a way to disseminate the group's interpretation of events both inside and outside the stadium. The Irriducibili's media seem intended for insiders as a reflection of history and identity, and for outsiders as a defense against attacks from what they see as a biased mainstream media. The *Irriducibili*'s impressive repertoire of media communicates to current members and recruits new members.

The *Irriducibili*'s media provide images to model themselves after in the form of Lazio players, fans and political ideas and they give counter examples of what to detest in the form of A.S. Roma fans and owner Claudio Lotito. The content of the *Irriducibili*'s media creates and reaffirms their identity based on four central themes: (1) Praise of Lazio and its fans, (2) Belittling A.S. Roma and their fans, (3) Right-Wing Politics and (4) Resistance against team owner, Claudio Lotito.

La Voce Della Nord

La Voce Della Nord (The Voice of the North) is the game-day newsletter/fanzine that the *Irriducibili* have sold outside the stadium on game days since 1995. During the 2005–2006 season, *La Voce Della Nord* cost two Euros. The 'North' in the title refers to the *Curva Nord* (North Curve) of the stadium, the historic home of the Lazio fans. In its current form, *La Voce Della Nord* is a 16-page, full colour newsletter that functions as a game programme containing objective game-day information, such as the rosters and league standings, as well as decidedly partisan right-wing commentary, and parodies of A.S. Roma and their fans. The newsletter often contains small stickers with short sayings such as 'No to modern soccer' or 'Any Given Sunday' that eventually get attached to stadium seats, or are used to mark territory outside of the stadium on public road signs, walls and lampposts. As a regularly published, roughly bi-weekly,[16] publication, *La Voce Della Nord* chronicles the aesthetic of the *Irriducibili* and connects the fans with ideas and songs that unite the *Irriducibili*.

La Voce Della Nord devotes a considerable amount of space and imagery to the fans and to their activities. *La Voce Della Nord* documents Lazio's best banners and most inventive in-stadium choreographies, and praises the dedication of fans who travel great distances and in great numbers to away matches. These pictures model the *Irriducibili*'s standards of fan participation. For example, these images highlight the unity of the fans as a single force with one message. On the centrefold of *La Voce Della Nord* where one might expect the picture of the team or an individual player, there is, instead, a large picture of the fan section that went to the match in Florence the previous week to support Lazio. The centrefold photo literally and symbolically places the fans at the centre of 'Lazio' rather than the players or owners of the team.[17] The number of bodies as well as their flags, banners and scarves are indicators of the pride and dedication that the *Irriducibili* have for their team.

The centring of the fans is essential to the identity of all the soccer fans. While historically, players may have been drawn from local neighbourhoods, and the fans might have reasonable expectations of actually knowing the players, the current roster of players on any major soccer teams contains players from all over the world that are, in essence, free agents, or in the words of some fans, 'mercenaries'. Players switch teams, managers quit or get fired, teams are bought and sold, jerseys and even team colours are liable to modification based on current trends. Only committed fans remain. As an act of pride, foolishness or false consciousness, dedicated fans discuss their team's results in the first person plural as a way to claim ownership. For groups like the *Irriducibili*, 'We' are Lazio, and everything else is subject to change. *La Voce Della Nord* visually depicts this construction of reality through the literal and figurative centring of fan imagery.

Of course, another element of fandom remains the adoration of players as representatives of the group. Like most fan publications, La Voce Della Nord contains numerous pictures of prominent players in action during games. For instance, in 2006, La Voce Della Nord features photos of Valon Behrami, the young, handsome Swiss player with blonde hair, and Tommaso Rochi, the stout, hard-working, Lazio forward. The publication includes pictures of the team as a whole, and of significant actions during the game such as goals or goalkeeper saves.

For the *Irriducibili*, none of the players compare in popularity to Paolo Di Canio who seems to appear on every other page. He is depicted playing soccer, celebrating goals and even standing still in moments of apparent contemplation. The *Irriducibili* look to Di Canio to be a leader on the field and to exemplify of the *Irriducibili*'s entire way of thinking. Quoting from an article about Di Canio in *La Voce Della Nord*, 'I have someone who says on TV what I would say, who bites, on the field, as I would bite, who exults as I would exult ... salutes ... as I would salute'.[18] Di Canio's salute refers to the occasions when he gave the fascist salute (a straight right arm with fingers extended and arm raised forward above shoulder level) to his fans in the Curva Nord. Di Canio represents the rebellious nature and the right-wing militancy that the *Irriducibili* embrace.

The 26 February 2006 edition of the *La Voce Della Nord*, sold on the night of the Lazio-Roma derby game, depicts Di Canio on the cover in uniform, with clenched fist, clenched teeth, shaved head, tattoos and an apparent cut on his right arm.[19] Underneath Di Canio appear the words, *Sangue e Sudore* (Blood and Sweat). Behind the image of Di Canio is a Lazio jersey superimposed over the image of a throng of Lazio fans in the Curva Nord. The Jersey symbolizes the Lazio fans' role as the imagined '12th' player for Lazio. It also hints at Di Canio's identification with the Lazio fans, as he describes himself as a lifelong Lazio fan. As 'one of them', Di Canio is expected to lead the team. As written in the article, 'A Derby for Lions', 'We point to him (DiCanio) to win another battle'.[20]

Differentiation from Roma and their fans is a primary element of *Irriducibili* identity. Articles and cartoons constantly refer to the fact that Lazio was established in 1900 while the 'upstart' A.S. Roma was founded only in 1927. Lazio fans claim that since their team has been in Rome longer, they are more authentic Romans than the so-called visitors, the A.S. Roma fans. *La Voce Della Nord* prints images of the in-stadium displays that insult Roma fans including an image of a red and yellow vermin intended to represent Roma. Another shows a stadium banner of the endangered Panda bear and a wolf (a primary symbol of A.S.Roma). The image is accompanied by the phrase, 'Save us ... we are on the way to extinction'.[21] *La Voce Della Nord* published an altered picture of the daily A.S. Roma fan newspaper, *Il Romanista*, replacing their tagline 'The daily paper of the most *fanatic* fans in the world' with 'The daily paper of the *trashiest* fans in the world'.

The *Irriducibili* reinforce their own dedication to Lazio by denigrating the lack of commitment by many so-called Roma fans that, according to the *Irriducibili*, are only superficially connected to team. Lazio fans admit that they may be outnumbered, but their fans are more loyal and more dignified. An article written under the pen-name, Curvarolo, insists that, 'Once again, destiny calls (us) to confront the vulgarity, arrogance and superficiality of a segment of this city'.[22] The article invokes the *duty* of the Lazio fans to take a stand in the name of civility that the Lazio fans embody. The attacks on the A.S. Roma fans' undignified nature refer to the historical class differences between the teams. Originally, the Lazio fan base was centred in the affluent neighbourhoods of Rome, though the present situation is far more complex as fans of both teams can be found in every Roman neighbourhood. The article '*Un derby da leoni*' (A Derby of Lions) offers an affirmation of Lazio's supremacy and historical legacy in anticipation of the coming derby game against their cross-town 'cousins'.[23] It states, '[We are] proud to reaffirm once again our supremacy ... to demonstrate that we are the first fans of the capital and that we know no terms of comparison. With this spirit we seize the contest against our cousins'.[24]

Di Canio vs. Totti

The essence of these rivals is embodied in the contrasting players, Lazio's Paolo Di Canio and Roma's Francesco Totti. *La Curva Della Nord* continually draws comparisons between the two that flatter Di Canio and deride Totti. For instance, *La Voce Della Nord* printed the photo of a stadium banner shown by the *Irriducibili* that refers to a clause in Totti's contract that stipulates that he can leave Roma if they should ever become too weak to compete at a high level. The banner read, 'Totti: "For Money and a strong Roma team or else I'll leave" Di Canio: "I'll pay to return to Lazio, the team that is crumbling"'.[25] This direct comparison praises Di Canio's loyalty to Lazio and his role as saviour after a financial crisis almost destroyed the team.

The article entitled '*Ti Odio Perche*' ...' (I Hate You Because ...) lists the reasons why Lazio fans hate Totti. The list starts, 'I hate you because you are a phenomenal player, but crap as a person!'[26] Accompanying the article is a picture of Totti being driven off the soccer field on a cart after sustaining a serious ankle injury a month prior. Another of Totti's alleged failings is that he has not celebrated a goal during the derby in Lazio territory, under the *Curva Nord*. The article claims that he is not man enough to do so, unlike Di Canio, who actually did celebrate a goal in the derby in front of the *Curva Sud*, the heart of the A.S. Roma fan section.

La Voce Della Nord mocks the abundance of media coverage surrounding Totti's entire life. They complain that even when he does charity work, he is too immodest. After Totti was injured in the weeks preceding the derby, an article in the 22 February 2006 edition of *Il Romanista* described how a Caravaggio painting was damaged while in transit. *Il Romanista* declared divine synchronicity as, at approximately the same time that Totti broke his ankle, the figure in the Caravaggio painting was damaged at the same anatomical spot. *La Voce Della Nord* re-ran the article[27] without comment under the assumption that the reader already knows to interpret this image as emblematic of the childish devotion to the idiotic Totti. The article laments Totti's injury because it will deprive Lazio of the chance to defeat Roma properly – at full strength. *La Voce Della Nord* used Totti's injury relentlessly to make an unfavourable comparison with Di Canio who, according to the author, would cry because he could not play in the derby against Roma, the only game that counts for him.

In addition to the visual and textual insults, *La Voce Della Nord* provides Lazio fans with songs intended to be sung at the stadium to glorify Lazio and bash A.S. Roma. A critical function of *La Voce Della Nord* is to disseminate these new chants and cheers.[28] The *Irriducibili* take the lead in promoting these songs, some of which will catch on, and be sung by all the Lazio fans in the stadium. The following lyrics are meant to be sung to the melody of a popular Roma fan song.[29]

Giallorosso sei un papazzo,	Yellow and red you are a puppet
Resta zitto c'hai rotto il cazzo	Shut up, your dick is broken
Sei invidioso e complessato ...	You are jealous and have a complex
Da pagliaccio sei mascherato	You are disguised as clowns
Tutta Italia grida in coro:	All of Italy shouts in chorus
Romanista fai meno il boro	Romanista stop showing off
Dici a tutti che sei Romano	You tell everyone that you are Roman
Ma sei solo un Napoletano!!!	But you are only a Neapolitan!!!
La la la lalla ...	La la la lalla ...

In this song, yellow and red refers to A.S. Roma's colours, and thereby stands in for both Roma and its fans. In addition to the crude insults that call the Roma fans immodest, the lyrics are tinged with the regional antagonism that Romans feels towards Naples. In Rome, Naples is considered the beginning of the south, and the seat of mafia corruption, poverty and incivility.[30] For both the Romanisti and Laziali, Naples is the anithesis of everything Roman, and simply calling someone *Napolitano* is an insult. The expression of territorial or regional discrimination at soccer matches occurs often enough that, at the beginning of every soccer match in Italy, there is a public announcement warning fans that racial and *regional* discrimination will not be tolerated.[31]

Lazio's media is also a vehicle for their far-rightwing political stance. The most unexpected piece in *La Voce Della Nord* is an article on recent political issues entitled, '*Conflitto di Civilta: Un Inganno Pericoloso*' (Conflict of civilizations: A Dangerous Deception). This article recaps the controversy surrounding the publication of anti-Islamic cartoons in Denmark and the ensuing scandal involving Italian

Senator, and Lega-Nord member, Roberto Calderoli, who proudly wore a T-shirt with one of the controversial cartoons on it.[32] Calderoli eventually resigned from the Senate after pressure from both inside and outside of his party. After criticizing Calderoli's foolishness, the article concludes that Italy's current stance on globalism is not working. The article concludes, 'The most ferocious intolerance today is connected to those who would "give" the multi-cultural society to everyone'.[33] The appearance of overtly political commentary in a soccer publication is unusual, but for the *Irriducibili*, Lazio and right-wing politics are fundamental elements of their identity. This combination of soccer and politics is also indicative of the multi-valent points of identification that soccer fan clubs represent.

Anti-Lotito

The *Irriducibili* targeted a new enemy in the 2005–2006 season. In addition to their habitual denigration of A.S. Roma and left-wing politics, the 2005–2006 season was dominated by acts of resistance against the owner of the team, Claudio Lotito. In July 2004, Lotito literally saved the team by purchasing Lazio and taking on the debts accrued by its bankrupt owners. Lotito sold or released several high priced players in an effort to raise cash and cut spending. By August 2005, the *Irriducibili*, along with other Lazio fans, started to question Lotito's personnel decisions. The *Irriducibili* started a campaign to convince Lazio fans that Lotito did not have the best interests of the club in mind. They argued that Lotito was interested in the club only in financial terms and lacked the deeply emotional commitment that the Laziali believe that the club deserves. Perhaps they were spoiled by the success of the late 1990s teams that featured an international, star-studded roster and unprecedented success on the field. This success was financed by enormous debts that eventually led to the team's financial collapse.

Every game of the 2005–2006 season became an opportunity for the *Irriducibili* to protest. They used signs, chants, cheers and 'fan strikes' to protest against Lotito. At times, the action of the game became secondary to vocalizing protest. Early in the year, Lotito responded to these protests by calling them these dissenting voices a '*sparuta minoranza*', (insignificant minority). Lotito argued that the radical *Irriducibili* that did not speak for the mainstream Lazio supporters. The *Irriducibili* co-opted this phrase by making and selling T-shirts and banners declaring themselves the *Sparuta Minoranza*. As the season went on, the majority of Lazio fans supported, or at least did not oppose, the protests against Lotito.

La Voce Della Nord became the unofficial tool to organize and document the protest. The article '*Evviva La Sparuta Minoranza*' glorifies the protesters by declaring, 'We who protested at Via Allegri, who contested Cragnotti and who asked for justice ... We who make up the curva because Lazio is our source of pride'.[34] The article lists the abuses that Lazio and its fans have suffered and recounts the fans' heroic resistance. When I asked some of the *Irriducibili* why they disliked Lotito so much, they gave me vague and unconvincing answers about how he simply did not care enough about Lazio, or, more commonly, they would simply call him an insulting name. While the sale of star players might be enough to cause the protest of many fans, the unending criticism of the *Irriducibili* seemed intemperate considering the financial difficulties of the team.

While *La Voce Della Nord* provided a timely update of the fans and editorials on their position as fans in relation to the team, they also published a book as a lasting assertion of their identity and what they stand for. When I tried to arrange an interview with members of the *Irriducibili*, they advised me to buy their DVD and book at the 'Original Fans' retail store. While *La Voce Della Nord* covers the day-to-day updates of the Irriducibili, their hundred-plus paged book, entitled, *Irriducibili: Noi Siamo gli ultràs della Lazio* [We are the Ultràs of Lazio][35] and prefaced by the directive of Toffolo, Diabolik and Yuri recounts their origins and history. The book is filled with pictures of the fans throughout the years highlighting magnificent in-stadium displays such as an eagle that covered the entire Curva Nord and one in which fans wearing white T-shirts spelled out, 'Roma Merda' [(A.S.) Roma is shit]. The book also documents their militancy featuring photos of protest marches and clashes with police. The book recalls the history of their symbol, Mr Enrich, who was based on an English comic book hero and who symbolized a 'new style'. The book closes with a hand-written letter written by Paolo Di Canio who writes, 'It is an honor to be hated'. The Irriducibili book is another artefact that declares and consolidates the Irriducibili's way of thinking.

Conclusion

This chapter relays the importance of print media to football fandom. The appealing imagery and straightforward drama of sport were useful in attracting a working class readership to newspapers in the late nineteenth and early twentieth century. The emergence of the sports section coincides closely with the emergence of football as a spectator business at the dawn of the twentieth century. Undoubtedly, the newspaper helped to promote the game by providing, in effect, free advertising every day. Before sports radio and television, the daily newspaper or monthly magazine were what connected fans to their team. Newspapers remain as an important part of the football business. The efficacy of newspapers as an advertising medium is evidenced by the surplus of free papers that are distributed outside the Roman football stadium. Enough fans leaf through the papers and are influenced by the advertisements that flank the images and stories about their team to justify the production of these papers. The existence of these papers highlights one enduring advantage of print media over digital media – its relative stability. The layout of a newspaper is the same in every paper and the reader of a newspaper has fewer options when reading the text. As a result, they are likely to actually view the advertisements, and they are less likely to be distracted by the endless allures of hyper-connected media.

Newspapers and magazines provide the words and images that ignite and sustain fan culture. They provide the depiction of heroes to young fans and they provide the points of discussion for Monday morning chat sessions at cafes throughout Italy and around the world. Papers are influential in setting the agenda of conversation by what they feature and what they ignore. Newspapers have well-developed distribution channels and institutional authority, particularly if they retain high standards of writing and reporting. Print media create communicative resources – commonalities of knowledge and ideas that make fandom possible and meaningful. The Roma Club Testaccio demonstrates the ability of fans to repurpose media for their own use. Their clubhouse is a museum of fan culture (and media culture) as they cover their walls with images from the sports section and from magazine centrefolds. Through the arrangement of images, the club presents their identity as Romans and Roma fans. The thirst for football news in Rome was not satisfied by three national *sport* newspapers, nor by the myriad free papers. For over a decade, the daily newspaper,

Il Romanista, found an audience for news focused primarily on the daily activities of the A.S. Roma football team. While the paper went out of business in 2014, its very existence was a testament to the demand for print media and the fervour of the community of Roma fans.

In contrast to commercial media, fan-produced publications can fill in the gaps that are not covered by the mainstream media, and they also offer the opportunity for counter-messaging by fan groups that choose to dissent. Lazio's Irriducibili ultrà group became prolific media producers. Their book and newsletters allowed them to define their goals and their identity in contrast to the mainstream press that the Irriducibili viewed as ill-informed and prejudiced. Their newsletter, *La Voce della Nord*, helped the group to articulate their dissatisfaction and to galvanize a season-long protest against the team's owner.

Fans illustrate, sometimes dramatically, the processes by which readers/audiences construct meaning from the media that they consume. Fans discuss media stories obsessively, fans talk back to media producers, fans redeploy mediated images and fans create their own counter-narratives in conjunction and in contrast to 'big media'. This chapter has illustrated the ways in which print media are part of the social construction of meaning. They are a starting point in the process of meaning-making instead of a definitive endpoint that merely needs to be deciphered. Print media help fans in their efforts to create strong identities and to express their ideas that converge and diverge, to various extents, with the mainstream media. Ultimately, this chapter illustrates the ways in which fans continue to use print media in the social project of fandom.

Disclosure statement

No potential conflict of interest was reported by the author.

Notes

1. Goldlust, 'Sport as Entertainment', 40.
2. Ibid., 31.
3. Ibid., 41.
4. McFarland, 'Building a Mass Activity', 51.
5. The relationship between media and football starts with the newspaper. The accounts of matches past were vital to the promotion and dissemination of football in England and then throughout Europe and the world. See Giulianotti, *Football*, 149.
6. Giulianotti, *Football: A Sociology of the Global Game*.
7. Ibid., 149–50.
8. Ibid., 148.
9. 'Imagined Communities' was coined by Benedict Anderson and has been quoted extensively since.
10. La Gazzetta dello Sport, Tuttosport and Corriere dello Sport.
11. Thompson, 'The Politics of Display or the Display of Politics?', 38.
12. Duncan, 'Art Museums and the Ritual of Citizenship', 92.
13. Bahktin, 'Forms of Time and the Chronotope in the Novel', 7.
14. Klugman and Ricatti, 'Roma non Dimentica I suoi Figli', discuss the civic adoration of Totti and his predecessor as Roma icon, Agostino Di Bartolomei.
15. As of December 2007, the site is no longer online.
16. *La Voce della Nord* (LVDN) is produced for home games which generally occur every other week during the soccer season.
17. see LVDN April 15, 2006, 16–7 or LVDN February 26, 2006, 16–7.

18. Translated '*Ho qualcuno che in TV dice quello che direi io, che in campo morde come morderei io, esulta come esulterei io ... saluta ... come saluterei io*'.
19. The image appears to have been altered to enhance the blood on the arm. I saw virtually the same image without the blood.
20. Trans. From article '*Un derby da leoni*' (LVDN February 26, 2006, 5), '*Puntiamo su di lui (Di Canio) per vincere un'altra battaglia*'.
21. Translated SALVIAMOLI ... SONO IN VIA D'ESTINZIONE (LVDN February 26, 2006, 6).
22. Translated *Ancora una volta il destino si chiama a fronteggiare la volgarita, l'arroganza e la superficialita, di una parte della citta*.
23. The article, '*Un derby da leoni*' (LVDN February 26, 2006, 6) refers to A.S. Roma as their 'cousins'. Despite the antagonism between the two sets of fans, it is common for both sides to refer to the other group as their cousins.
24. Trans. *L'orgoglio di voler affermare ancora una volta la nostra supremazia ... per dimostrare che siamo la prima tifoseria della Capitale e che non conosciamo termini di paragone La voce della nord* (LVDN February 26, 2006, 6).
25. Totti: '*Di Soldi e una grande Roma o me ne vado*'. Di Canio: '*Pago per tornare nella Lazio che sta fallendo*' Ecco la differenza fra noi e voi (LVDN February 26, 2006, 7).
26. Trans '*Ti odio perche sei un giocatore fenomenale, ma un uomo di merda!*' (LVDN February 26, 2006, 10).
27. LVDN February 26, 2006, 11.
28. These songs, as described in the first chapter, use well-known tunes while adding novel lyrics.
29. The Roma song is *Passa il tempo*.
30. The Neapolitan version of the mafia, the *Camorra*, is profiled in Saviano's *Gommorah*.
31. Regional discrimination typically occurs between northerners and southerners. Attitudes in the more industrialized north tend to be negative towards the more agricultural and poorer south. A famous example of this type of expression in the stadium occurred when the visiting Naples fans were greeted by the home Verona fans with a banner that read, 'Welcome to Italy', implying that anywhere south of Tuscany is part of the uncivilized territory, sometimes mockingly referred to as North Africa.
32. BBC News, 'Italy Cartoon'.
33. '*L'intolleranza piu feroce giunge oggi proprio da chi ci ha voluto "regalare" a tutti I costi la societa multiculturale*' (LVDN February 26, 2006, 28–9).
34. LVDN February 26, 2006, 8. *Eviva la sparuta minoranza*.
35. Noi Siamo Gli Ultras della Lazio, 2006.

References

Anderson, B. *Imagined Communities: Reflections on the Origins and Spread of Nationalism*. New York: Verso, 1991.
Bakhtin, M. 'Forms of Time and the Chronotope in the Novel: Notes Toward a Historical Poetics'. In *The Dialogic Imagination*, ed. M. Holquist, 84–258. Austin: University of Texas, 1981.
BBC News. 'Italy Cartoon Row Minister Quits'. *BBC News*, February 16, 2006. http://news.bbc.co.uk/2/hi/europe/4727606.stm (accessed March 22, 2015).
Duncan, C. 'Art Museums and the Ritual of Citizenship'. In *Exhibiting Cultures: The Poetics and Politics of Museum Display*, ed. I. Karp and S.D. Lavine, 88–103. Washington, DC: Smithsonian Institution Press, 1991.
Giulianotti, R. *Football: A Sociology of the Global Game*. Malden, MA: Blackwell, 1999.
Goldlust, J. 'Sport as Entertainment: The Role of Mass Communications'. In *Critical Readings: Sport, Culture and the Media*, ed. D. Rowe, 27–47. Berkshire: Open University, 2004.
Klugman, M., and F. Ricatti. '"Roma non dimentica i suoi figli": Love, Sacrifice and Emotional Attachment to Football Heroes'. *Modern Italy* 17, no. 2 (2012): 237–49.
La Voce Della Nord. Irriducibili: Noi siamo gli Ultras della Lazio [The Voice of the North] [Irriducibili: We Are the Lazio Ultras]. Rome: Fotolito Moggio, 2006.
La Voce Della Nord [newsletter] No. 13, February 26, 2006. Rome.
La Voce Della Nord [newsletter] No. 16, April 15, 2006. Rome.

La Voce Della Nord [newsletter] No. 18, May 14, 2006. Rome.
McFarland, A. 'Building a Mass Activity: Fandom, Class and Business in Early Spanish Football'. In *Football Fans around the World: From Supporters to Fanatics*, ed. S. Brown, 43–58. New York: Routledge, 2007.
Saviano, R. *Gomorrah*. Milan: Farrar, Straus and Giroux, 2007.
Thompson, D. 'The Politics of Display or the Display of Politics?: Cultural Policy and the Museo del Hombre Dominicano'. *Museum Anthropology* 25, no. 2 (2002): 38–49.

Broadcast media: live and in-person

> Radio broadcasts brought fans into the drama of the football match in real time for the first time. The indelible impact of radio shaped the development of football fandom in the early to middle 20th century. While television is now the biggest financial supporter of top-level football, owners used to worry that TV would diminish gate receipts. Mass media are often suspected of contributing to social alienation, this chapter shows how fans use television broadcasts to create social events. This essay discusses various viewing contexts such as pubs and fan clubhouses in order to illustrate how media is used by fans to create social bonds.

One of the central motivations of this inquiry into football fan culture is the question of how football fans reconcile the tension between football as local passion and football as a global, corporate business. For me and for fellow researchers, and for many fans, I suspect, it is difficult to blindly pledge one's allegiance to a football club that can be bought and sold, and moreover, whose central mission is to sell goods and services to me, and people like me. I am not satisfied with the clear, crisp Marxist-influenced response that football is the current opiate of the masses or that people are essentially cultural dupes,[1] if only because I do not believe that I, nor many of the fans with whom I am acquainted, fit the description. We continue to believe in the power of sport to show us glimpses of greatness, of humanity, of tenacity, of hope, of disappointment, and, in short, of life, with its mixture of merit and luck along with the eternal renewal of opportunity. There is always the next goal or the next match or the next season (until, of course, there isn't). Football and football fandom are not wholly rational, and this we must accept, but there are bits and pieces of rationality, and there are explanations, and logic to much of what constitutes football. At least, I hope there is, as I continue to write as a way to explain how football fandom works.

So how do fans combat the potentially alienating effects of football as big business? I see the fans creating strong bonds with other fans that ultimately surpass the strength of their bonds with the team that they support. I would bet that many passionate fans would disagree with this assessment. For them, their love of the team is what motivates the communal celebrations at the stadium, the vibrant fan clubs and all of the social structures that make fandom meaningful. For me, the sociality of fans is far more important (and interesting) than the game team itself, or its products. The elaborate decorations of the Roma Club Testaccio, the intricate songs at the stadium, the passion with which fans follow the game are only meaningful when shared – when they become the foundation of community and togetherness. The lone fan may sit at home drawing cartoons of his favourite player or agonizing over the match on the TV, but I do not believe these activities could or would be sustained without the knowledge that the team means something to others. In this sense, the team gives the fan a place to fit in, a context with which to learn fandom, in short, a sense of identity within a community.

Of course, I am biased. My primary frame of reference is the Italian, and mostly, the Roman, football stadium. As an Communication Anthropologist trained in ethnography, I spent my time in the field in Rome attending matches, hanging out with fan groups, asking questions of any fan that would respond, watching TV, reading the newspapers and trying to gauge the mood on the street. Sometimes this 'mood' was indicated by spray paint on city walls; at other times, it was overheard conversations on the bus. For me, it is about being there in time and space, even as I tried to sort out how the internet could help fans attempt to overcome these limitations. As I have stated, the Roma Club Testaccio is as close to an authentic, pure fandom as I could hope for, even while I argue that they too, use fandom as a type of excuse to found a clubhouse, gather together, play cards and experience community. Testaccio has an air of nostalgia to it as a traditional working class community, even as it is a living, evolving neighbourhood. Testaccio is a leftist neighbourhood under a democratic socialist government. Italians are known for their strong family ties. All of this is to say that Italians have a sense of community and social equality that differs from my own background as an American kid who grew up in the suburbs of Chicago where maintaining a green, weed-free, lawn and a well-kept wooden fence were the primary ways to show one's status as a good neighbour. From this perspective, I offer my own take on what makes football and football fandom so compelling. As an ethnographer, my aim is to provide data in the form of accounts and descriptions that could be used to found a completely different reading, even if, as a writer, my goal is to provide a compelling analysis and interpretation. For those who disagree with my interpretations, may we some day hash them out over a cappuccino or a plate of Bucatini all'Amatriciana.

Italians like to congregate, and they are often emotional when they do it. The stadium and football offer opportunities to argue and celebrate in hyperbolic excess. Sport provides a structuring mechanism for social life in virtually all human cultures. Perhaps it is because it offers a set of rules for engagement. It helps us to overcome our fear of engagement by offering defined limits. The matches have a start time and an end time. Football gives us a wide array of topics of conversation. The game helps us act out aggression and rivalries in a somewhat civilized and socially manner. Football symbolizes 'us versus them', which seems, for better or worse, embedded in human DNA. Differentiation gives us something on which to found our identities. At the stadium, we recognize our differences, and at times, our shared humanity. There are times when the entire crowd – even rival fans – seems moved to a particular emotion. One such example was the memorializing of a murdered child that is discussed below. Football offers a context for ritual, the stadium offers a site. Sport gives a timetable of events, and a reason for fans (often men) to gather together in confined spaces. The analysis of male homo-sociality is beyond my expertise to adequately explain, but surely sport taps into men's simultaneous desire and reticence to gather together and experience some form of shared emotion (intimacy). In short, sport, and football in particular, offers an appealing structure from which fans can gather for a shared experience.

FOOTBALL FANDOM IN ITALY AND BEYOND

While sport is widely popular in the United States, the performance of its fans takes on a different character. Mark Cuban, the outspoken owner of the NBA basketball team, the Dallas Mavericks, agrees with the principle that sport's value is that of offering shared experience. In a blog post,[2] he articulates his take philosophy on the value of live sports in the age of home theatre systems, and how he wants fans that come to see the Mavericks to enjoy a shared experience that goes beyond the game itself. The difference between Cuban's vision of fandom and the fandom that I witnessed and participated in the Roman football stadium is that Cuban believes it is the function of his organization of marketers and promotion specialists to furnish this experience with constant entertainment ranging from cheerleaders, to big-screen TV's, to loud music and orchestrated chants, to half-time vaudevillian shows. He wants to provide wall-to-wall entertainment that makes it possible not to speak to the person next to you as you share an experience. Football fans the world over understand that it is their responsibility to construct the fan experience as a loosely organized force. Football fans do not need or want their chants and songs to be prompted by the public address system. They do not come to the stadium for free T-shirts and beer service. They come to express their thoughts and in emotions through fan-generated rituals and traditions.

Cuban's vision represents a strongly American, Disney-esque, version of the sporting experience where the business provides exceptional service and guides the consumer through a tightly orchestrated experience. Cuban's formula of serial distraction seems to work for American consumers. Despite fears that high-definition television and digital recording would ruin attendance, American basketball, baseball and especially football leagues fill stadiums with ever more expensive 'experiences'. In contrast, you never know what you are going to get at the Italian stadium. There are ritualized expressions of sentimentalism, humour, violence, chaos, irony, dissent and politics. Most essentially, these emotions come primarily from the fans and not from a furry mascot or a T-shirt cannon.

Italy, and most footballing nations are, perhaps, more collectivist and less individualist in nature, or perhaps it is the history of football teams that grew out of neighbourhood clubs to become badges of social identity. Though American sport teams are mostly franchises of a top-down corporation that are plopped down to exploit local communities, American fans are proud to wear sporting logos and insignia and to eat and drink together in parking lots in the tradition of tailgating, but they seem less apt to establish fan clubs, or to gather away from the stadium and in the course of everyday life to plan and to organize.[3] We do see something akin to the football's expression of identity in collegiate athletics. Obvious examples include big time college American football and basketball as well as relatively obscure competitions such as Ivy League hockey, all of which display traditions, rituals and elaborate fan coordination that relies on the idle time of clever undergraduates in conjunction with proud alumni who return to campus to reconnect with their alma mater. In many small towns, high school athletics can also produce a rallying point for the community.

An interesting hybrid of the American professional model and the non-American models of fandom is the emerging fan cultures of the American football league, Major League Soccer (MLS). Though derided by some as a second-class league, attendances at MLS matches are established as sustainable levels and rising. One of the reasons for this is the growth of active fan clubs that have borrowed the rituals of song and collective display and movement that characterize world football. For instance, in Chicago, the 'Section 8' fan club organizes fans of the Chicago Fire with an aim to 'create a dominant in-stadium force unseen in American sports'.[4] They occupy an all-standing section of the stadium and sing and chant continuously. Similar supporters groups have formed for most MLS franchises. Seattle has been a model of fan support as they average over 40,000 fans at their home ground that they share with an American football team. They have four recognized fan clubs. More interestingly, season ticket holders can vote to remove the general manager and on other team decisions.[5] The Sounders are also unique in that they have their own marching band that leads a march through the city to the stadium before matches. Another aspect of the Seattle fan culture is the Cascadia Cup trophy between geographic rivals, Seattle, Portland and Vancouver. Seattle is known as a progressive city in general and is certainly a leader of football fan culture. Their form of fan support for the Sounders could transform the American sporting experience.

Broadcast media and fandom

The chapter at hand considers how broadcast media fits into the fan experience. The traditional broadcast media of radio and television made football more accessible to the masses. They literally brought football into the home and into local bars where fans could see and hear their team compete even across continents. This boon to fandom has a dark side. Television companies have been known to exert pressure on leagues to air matches at times of the day that do not necessarily suit local audiences or foster optimal athletic competition. For instance, the English Premier League schedules some matches to suit Asian audiences.[6] The huge influx of money from television has changed the game from a local pastime into a global business. From a fans' perspective, the players often get paid in one week what a fan might get in a year. The influx of money means that fans might not be able to identify with the players and their celebrity lifestyles, though for now, it seems there is no shortage of interest in either football or celebrity gossip. But certainly, the character of the game has changed. Television has upped the stakes of football as business. The entire business model of sport leads to more and more matches, regardless of the fitness and durability of players. These decisions seem to place little weight on the health of players. The players themselves are under enormous pressure to perform, and some are quick to jump to greener pastures. While it may not be completely accurate to blame all of the changes on Television, it is clear that the huge influx of capital and the import of global audiences due to television have shifted power away from the local fan.

Fans have displayed a variety of responses. Some simply complain that players are now mercenaries who respond to the incentives of the free market rather than maintaining the irrational loyalty that binds fans to a local team. Others stage protests and demonstrations against their team. In Italy, the *No a Calcio Moderno* (No to modern football) movement organized protests and banners at stadiums throughout Italy. In England, organizations such as supporters' trusts have organized fans to create a powerful voice in order to influence the management of the club that they support. These are democratic, not for profit organizations of fans that have been organized with some government support.[7]

It would be a purist's stance to argue that attendance at the stadium is the essential act of fandom – that media simply builds off of the in-stadium experience. This narrow definition would exclude many fans that are passionate about their team, but are not from the team's home, or have never spent a season in the stands. This would exclude many of my compatriots who love to wear their Barcelona and Manchester United jerseys around town – people who huddle religiously to the bars and basements where fans gather at odd hours to watch the televised broadcast of their team of choice. This phenomenon of fandom would be an interesting subject of extended ethnographic study.[8]

Though mass media is often critiqued for its potentially alienating effects and its alignment with hyper-consumerism, any fan who has gathered at a friend's house or a local bar to watch a World Cup final or, for any American that has been to a Super Bowl party, we know that the consumption of mass media can be a prompt for sociality instead of a barrier to it. The Super Bowl is an occasion for parties that draws all types of viewers – some watch for the most expensive ads of the year, some wait for the over the top halftime show, while some gather for the sake of sociality, and/or guacamole dip and beer. In addition to in-person social interaction, online chat rooms host virtual communities that celebrate and critique sport. A central role of mass media is that they create common ground; they provide the material for the 'water-cooler' conversations that bring us from an imagined to a real community.

Another aim of this book has been to consider the tensions between the freedom and choice of the fan to express their support and the economic and social conditions under which those choices are made – in sociological terminology, it is the tension between structure and agency. The political economy of broadcasting structures the fan experience. Major broadcasters, in conjunction with government policies, determine when, where, how and how much of broadcasting, and ultimately, the conditions under which fans consume the mediated products. Therefore, it is worth considering the development and practices of broadcasting in order to understand the situation of the fan. The following section provides a brief overview of broadcasting, starting with radio and moving to television.

Brief history of radio

> *La frase piu bella del mondo non e 'ti amo', ma, 'La Roma in vantaggio!'* (The most beautiful phrase in the word is not, 'I love you', but, 'Roma takes the lead!') – Traditional Roman saying.

Beginning in the 1920s, sport played an important role in the developing radio broadcast schedule. Radio sport broadcasts offered the 'immediacy and authenticity of experience'[9] that newsreels and cinema failed to deliver. Though radio was exciting for fans, this is not to say that radio was immediately and universally embraced by the football industry. Owners worried about the effect that radio would have on gate receipts[10] despite early evidence to the contrary. North American sports led the revolution in sports broadcasting. Already in the 1930s, commercial broadcasters were paying for the rights to broadcast sporting events. This marked a tipping point wherein the broadcasters were begging for the rights to cover big events rather than sporting marketers begging journalists and broadcasters for coverage. There has been no looking back as TV rights deals seem to break every supposed ceiling to rights fees.

In Italy, broadcasting began in 1924 with the establishment of the Unione Radiofonica Italiana (URI), the national radio company that was founded during the fascist regime. URI would become EIAR in 1928 and then in 1944, it would adopt its current name, RAI. The first football transmission was an international match on 25 March 1928 in which Italy defeated Hungary 4–3.[11] Radio would be the primary real-time media of football until 1954, and even then, televisions were fairly rare in Italian homes until the 1970s. Football in the 1960s was a radio sport. The radio show 'Tutto il calcio Minuto per Minuto' (All the football minute by minute) would update the scores from around Italy in real time. The opening quote of this section is drawn from this programme. Roma fans would listen intently when the programme would be interrupted by a live update from the stadium. The words, '*La Roma in vantaggio*', were desperately hoped for.

Television

Television appeared in Italy in the 1950s. From 1954 to 1976, RAI was the only television broadcaster in Italy. Initially, public viewing in bars and cinemas and only the wealthiest private homes had their own TV set. RAI's second channel launched in 1961 and it was not until 1977 that colour television was decreed by law[12] to be legal in Italy. Italy may have lagged behind Western Europe in terms of the adoption of technology, but though TV was growing in stature, radio was still the medium of the masses in the 1950s throughout Europe. Merkel describes the momentous radio broadcast of the 1954 World Cup Final that saw the Germans defeat the favoured Hungarians of Puskas et al., 3–2. Merkel notes how the commentary of the announcer, Herbert Zimmerman, negotiated the terrain between the nationalist pride in the football team, and the all too vivid national shame of the German public. Merkel argues that the victory, 'contributed significantly to the promotion of a national identity.'[13] This victory brought international football to prominence in Germany and the audio broadcast was turned into a best-selling vinyl record.

The development of instantaneous mass communications in the form of radio and then TV contributed to and perhaps changed the character of fandom. Early broadcasts turned sporting events into serial dramas. Broadcasters were quick to realize that drama and emotion in the voice of the announcer drew more interest than encyclopedic knowledge of the sport or tactical expertise. The success of radio broadcasts energized and expanded the imagined community of fans that had theretofore been bonded together through the day old newspaper accounts. Radio telecasts reached the illiterate and literate alike and could set the emotional tone of a nation simultaneously. Radio continues to be an important source of fan news, especially for those who are travelling on game days. The radio broadcasts allow for fans to monitor several matches at once. It is not uncommon for fans to bring small radios equipped with an earpiece to the stadium so that the fans can tune into the matches involving their rivals. At Lazio matches, fans would start buzzing if their archrivals, Roma, had conceded a goal. The fans would start to cry out, 'oooooooohohoooohoohh' until the score was displayed on the screen at the stadium.

Contemporary Rome has a surfeit of local radio stations, many of which feature call-in shows devoted to their football teams. These shows allow the fans to voice their opinions and they also create celebrities out of fan leaders who host these shows. For instance, Fabrizio Toffolo, the leader of the Lazio ultras, the *Irriducibili*, often hosted a show. The Irriducibili's self-produced DVD, *L'amor per te mi fa teppista* (My Love for you has made me into a Hooligan)[14] features Toffolo making an appearance on *La Voce Della Nord*,[15] (The Voice of the North) a radio programme named after the North End of the Olympic Stadium, the home of Lazio Ultras. The clip in the DVD is unsensational as Toffolo puts on headphones and responds to various callers, but it exemplifies the ways in which the Irriducibili and Toffolo use radio as another tool used to disseminate opinions, recruit members, solidify opinion and demonstrate legitimacy. This is another example of fans using media for their own purposes, and to an extent, in contrast to the mainstream.

Impact of television

> Ignoring Media Sport today would be like ignoring the role of the church in the Middle Ages or ignoring the role of art in the Renaissance: large parts of society are immersed in media sports today and virtually no aspect of life is untouched by it. (MediaSport)

The fundamental goal of commercial television is to make money through advertising, or in essence, by delivering audiences to advertisers. In the words of David Andrews, 'Audiences effectively become commodities sold by media outlets to advertisers'.[16] As anyone with a television can tell you, sports media is intimately wound up with this system. It comprises a significant percentage of the content of both free and pay-television, yet its vital role in the political economy of television is not necessarily readily apparent. In this section, I will briefly outline the logic of televised sport programming in an attempt to clarify its value within the larger system of global broadcasting. As Andrews explains, sports programming offers distinct advantages in comparison with other types of programming: It is relatively inexpensive to produce, it has uncertain outcomes and it has historically and culturally entrenched popular appeal. Perhaps most importantly, sports programming 'delivers' the 18- to 34-year-old male demographic that is highly coveted by advertisers. In addition to the attributes that Andrews cites, I would add the relatively long and renewable virtually guaranteed shelf-life of sports. Sports teams rely on relatively interchangeable 'cast members' and seem to have infinitely regenerative fan bases. This makes sports broadcasting less of a gamble than other genres such as sitcoms or dramas that often rely on unique stars that are subject to the vagaries of life.[3]

Despite the challenges facing the television industry, television rights for the most popular sporting events continue to rise. In our age of media proliferation, online alternatives and audience fragmentation, the consistent audiences that sport offers makes them very appealing to television networks. For US broadcasting rights, NBC paid 3.5 billion dollars for Olympic Rights from 2000 to 2008 while the National Football League charged 17.6 billion for 8 seasons of football. The recent bidding on the English Premier League for the 2016–2019 seasons netted 5.1 billion pounds (or 7.8 billion US dollars) for domestic television rights, while the international broadcast rights are expected to bring in another $3 billion US.[17] Rupert Murdoch's Sky won the majority of rights, while BT retained rights to some matches.

The value of sports programming goes beyond its ability to temporarily attract eyeballs to the glitter of advertisements. Sports programming becomes a key element in global corporate strategy, as Rupert Murdoch's News Corporation demonstrates. David Andrews illustrates how, throughout the 1990s, News Corporation used sports programming as a '"Battering ram" for entry into new markets'[18] throughout the world. The purchase of NFL broadcast rights in the mid-1990s helped transform the upstart Fox network into a legitimate fourth network in the US. In England, the rights to league soccer turned Murdoch's BSkyB (now Sky) satellite television network into a national presence. Murdoch has expanded his interest in sports from broadcasting to majority ownership in teams such as the LA Dodgers of Major League Baseball. Murdoch's move towards vertical integration would seem to ensure long-term programming rights. For the time being, his initiatives have met resistance due to the potential conflicts of interest in the NFL and in the English Premier League, so he has pursued a strategy of gaining a minority stake in several clubs in order to retain influence. In Andrews' estimation, Rupert Murdoch is 'A masterly entrepreneur who recognizes the importance of sport's cultural significance to the process of capital accumulation within the media and communications industries'.[19] Sports provide instant and predictable audiences that are so precious in the televisual marketplace. Sports programming seem to hold the key for broadcasters to gain a foothold in virtually any broadcasting market.

Berlusconi and Italian football media politics

In Italy, the state broadcaster, RAI, had a legally enshrined monopoly on national broadcasting for decades. This meant that football was broadcast exclusively by RAI, and there was no competition for media rights, and thus, the football league and the clubs did not make the huge sums of money that are the norm today. The RAI monopoly continued until Silvio Berlusconi arrived on the scene to become synonymous with the nexus of Italian media, politics and football. Though Berlusconi is justly critiqued for his ineffective economic policies and for his alleged ties to organized crime, he can be given some credit for momentarily advancing Italian broadcasting – that is, until he used his power to stifle competition.

The market logic of broadcasting that makes sports programming valuable is as true in Italy as it is elsewhere, and in Italy, sports means football. Historian Paul Ginsborg wrote, in 2003, that 'Football has always been an abiding passion of the Italians, but in the last twenty years, this passion has reached new levels of intensity …to become a secular religion'.[20] Italy's football tradition spans the twentieth century and is marked by four world cup triumphs. Italian soccer is a performance of national identity, and as well as a part of daily life. It functions as a communicate resource that enables strangers to engage in conversation and argument in the ways that only Italians do. Football is by far the most dominant sporting form in contemporary Italy. Italy has a world-class volleyball league, and a high-level professional basketball, along with a historical devotion to cycling and motor sports, but all of these combined do not add up to the obsession with '*calcio italiana*' (Italian football) as represented on the Italian sports pages and television sets.[21] If you go to the web page of the national broadcaster, RAI, on any Sunday from September through May, the first thing you are likely to see is football results.

Televised soccer in Italy

Silvio Berlusconi capitalized on the power of football to sway Italian viewers and voters. As the owner of the TV conglomerate, Mediaset, and of the historically successful AC Milan football team, Berlusconi engaged in 'politics as spectacle'.[22]

The BBC has described the way Berlusconi has fused soccer into his political rhetoric in this way.

> Using the language and slogans of the football field, Berlusconi created a new simplistic political language which immediately won over many Italians used to the deliberately obscurantist terminology of the fusty old political parties. He talked incessantly about 'coming out onto the field', 'players' and 'winning the game'. He seemed to have a magic touch. (BBC Online, Reign of Two Halves)[23]

After his first election as Prime Minister in 1994, his team AC Milan won the domestic championship prompting him to declare that he 'Would do for Italy what he had done for his team'.[24] Berlusconi has tried to involve himself directly in the management of the national soccer team as well. His boisterous criticism led to the firing of Italian national coach, Dino Zoff after the team's heartbreaking loss in final of the European Cup in 2000. When Berlusconi was elected Prime Minister, he left the day-to-day management of AC Milan to his right-hand man, Adriano Galliani. Galliani subsequently became the president of the Serie A, Italy's top football competition. Berlusconi introduced legislation in 2003 that would have given public funding to indebted professional soccer clubs. Though this legislation was defeated, it was another one of Berlusconi's populist appeal to the football-crazed public.

Berlusconi's consolidation of media, political and cultural power is unprecedented in Italy's democratic era. Nevertheless, he could not control the advent of satellite television that emerged as the dominant economic model for soccer in the 1990s. With the development of licensing packages, fans could buy season 'tickets' for their favourite team or head to the local bar to watch the games with their neighbours. This new system inevitably disrupted the entire soccer market as individual professional clubs in Italy could sell the broadcast rights for their home games to one of two satellite providers, Stream or Telepiu. This system led to bidding wars which eventually bankrupted both satellite providers while also increasing the economic disparity between large and small clubs. Though an enormous amount of money has been injected into the soccer economy, the player market has grown exponentially causing many teams to spend foolishly. The implications of disparities are being negotiated and renegotiated every year.

In 2003, Rupert Murdoch's News Corporation aka News Corp (now twenty-first Century Fox) swooped on to capture the television rights to several *Serie A* (premier league) teams. The launch of News Corp's SkyItalia was an overt attempt to repeat the success that BskyB achieved through buying football rights in England. One Guardian newspaper headline read, 'Murdoch takes Sky to Italy: Tycoon extends his reach into Berlusconi's back yard'.Hooper, 'Murdoch Takes Sky to Italy'.[25] In a $1 billion deal, News Corporation purchased the Vivendi-owned Telepiu with their pre-existing stake in satellite provider, Stream, to consolidate satellite television in, 'one of the world's most locked-up markets'.[26] SkyItalia offered 120 channels including, significantly, Italy's first around the clock news channel. Football was expected to (and in fact, did) sell subscriptions as SkyItalia had signed most of Italy's top clubs, including Berlusconi's own, A.C. Milan. Berlusconi was not completely shut out of the football bidding wars. His free-to-air Mediaset network split the rights to Champions League matches between the best clubs in Europe. SkyItalia has been a success for Newscorp, though Berlusconi's Mediaset has not been completely defeated. In the latest deal, Mediaset has the retained rights to many games/teams. Gladwell, Serie A Clubs.[27]

As late as the mid-1980s, those in football management were weary about the potential negative effects of television on gate receipts and profits,[28] a fear that repeated the argument about radio decades before. Silvio Berlusconi updated this line of thinking when he publicly wondered whether the TV networks would have to pay fans to attend the matches in order to provide the atmosphere at the stadium in order to improve the experience of the television viewers watching at home.[29] As of writing, this fear has not exactly materialized, though there are plenty of concerns over match attendances, and a general unease about the state of fandom and of *calcio* in general. Outside of Italy, and particularly in England and Germany, match attendances are at historically high levels. Television and football are no longer considered enemies.

Media economics and fandom

The Italian case and the competition between Berlusconi and Murdoch dramatically illustrate the value of sports rights and their power to win audiences and ultimately to help build and sustain media companies. The ways in which football media rights are procured can be abstract for the average fan, but ultimately the logics of media influence the ways in which fans come to understand football and understands one's role as a fan. The following section broadcasting details the ways in which fans 'consume' televised football in various spaces. It shows the communal aspect of media spectatorship – aspects that can go overlooked if we think of media as inherently isolating or alienating. Instead, through a few examples, we can see the ways in which media broadcasts become social events. This section considers a few auto-ethnographic reflections along with a consideration of 'pub football' as described by Michael Weed. As this section will show, the game is globally intelligible while practices of viewership are adapted to local contingencies.

I return to the Roma Club Testaccio as it is a destination of *real* fandom in order to describe how these fans experience the televised match. This section illustrates how fans adapt to the institutional and structural realities of media, and ultimately how they use media for their own purposes. This is where the potentially abstract logic of corporate media meets the live experience of fans. The following examples explore the ways in which fans use media for their own purposes – how they create social occasions from the broadcasts.

Social viewing

> In all ritual sites, some kind of performance takes place. Ritual is often regarded as transformative: it confers identity or purifies or restores order to the world through sacrifice, ordeal, or enlightenment.[30]

On gamedays, the Roma Club Testaccio packs men, women and children into the clubhouse to watch the Roma games projected onto their big screen. Membership fees pay for the rent and the upkeep of the club, but it is not enough to cover all of the expenses of the satellite television subscription. To watch a televised game at the club, members as well as non-members must pay a fee of six Euros per game. The admission charge is a significant part of their operating budget for the club.

The Roma Club Testaccio is the site where fans gather to perform the ritual of watching A.S. Roma compete. This ritual happens on a weekly basis, and most often on Sunday, the Roman Catholic day of worship. The clubhouse itself acts in no small way to create the atmosphere and prepare the audience for the ordeal of urging Roma to victory. Screening A.S. Roma games has become one of the most important functions of the club. The club attempts to replicate the atmosphere at the stadium by gathering fans into tight quarters to watch Roma play on the projection television. These game screenings are popular enough to require advance reservations. The club was described to me by a club member as a miniature *curva sud* (the most vociferous section of the Roma fans at the stadium) with the crowd of people, the noise and the spirit. The Roma Club Testaccio sets up over 65 chairs organized into rows that cover the entire floor and are oriented towards the pull-down screen in the back of the club. The LCD projector mounted from the ceiling projects the game onto the screen.

My own experience watching a game at the club occurred on Sunday, 2 April 2006 at 3 pm. When I entered the club, each chair had a reservation tag on it. My chair was reserved with the tag reading 'Americano' accompanied by a small rendering of the American flag. Apparently, club President, Sergio, had remembered my reservation and my nationality, but had forgotten my name. I was seated next to Maurizio, a man in his 40s who was there with his two elementary or middle school aged nephews. Most of the people at the club were dressed not in the yellow and red team colours but in more formal attire, such as collared shirts, jackets and brown leather shoes, suitable for going to church. Among the crowd were several older men and women, a few families with children and one teenage couple. Before the match, people were chatting, children were running around and there was little in the way of organization or a shared focus.

Once the broadcast started, almost all motion stopped. Even the children who had been running around the room were settled in their seats. As people at the clubhouse settled in to watch the game, the TV broadcast showed a banner at the stadium in Florence that read, 'Goodbye Tommy, victim of an unjust world'.[31] The crowd in Florence and the spectators in Testaccio cheered when this banner dedicated to Tommaso Onofri, an epilectic, eighteen-month-old boy who was kidnapped for ransom and subsequently killed in a suburb of Parma, a north-central Italian city. Though Parma has no immediate connection to Florence or Rome, the story touched the entire nation. Storefronts in Rome, and presumably throughout the nation, posted images of the boy in hopes of rescuing him. Sadly, the story ended tragically. The posting of a message by the Florence fans and the reaction both in the stadium and at the Roma Club Testaccio show the ways in which football can reflect the mood of a nation and create spaces of communal grieving.

As the game started, conversation among club members ended. The lights were turned off and the room became dark as most of the windows in the room are painted red and yellow or covered with Roma paraphernalia. All heads turned to the screen, all ears tuned to the TV broadcaster. As I looked around the room, most people were seated, but one man was standing nervously at the back of the clubhouse with his hand resting on his chin. This particular game was an evenly contested match between A.S. Roma and Florence's team, Fiorentina. As the marathon season was nearing the May finish line, these two teams were fighting for the fourth spot in the standings which would provide a spot in the lucrative Champions League tournament the following season.[32] During the match, the only audible voices were the grunts, groans and short cheers that any decent football match elicits. The gentleman two seats away from me was with a young boy, but that did not stop him from repeating the offensive phrase, '*Mortacce tua!*' ('curse your ancestors', in rough translation). Communication was structured by the events on the screen that are more or less interpreted the same way by this partisan crowd – anything that goes in Roma's favour is greeted with enthusiasm – anything that goes in Fiorentina's favour is booed. As the first half proceeded, there more groans than cheers as Fiorentina had outplayed Roma.

At half-time, everyone in the room moved towards the 'bar' located under the TV screen and next to the merchandise table. The price of admission includes a complimentary beverage such as a soft drink, beer or juice. After getting a beverage, many people file out of the club and onto the sidewalk to smoke cigarettes as there is no smoking inside the club. I joined a circle of men who were puffing on their cigarettes and discussing formations, tactics and players. The mood was subdued, in part because Roma was losing 1–0. I broke off to speak a bit with Maurizio and his 10-year-old nephew. The precocious nephew, having already adopted a Romanesque pessimism, conceded that Roma would not win, but accurately predicted that they would score a goal, and the game would finish in a 1–1 tie. Less serious children were running around and playing during the 15-min halftime break. Undoubtedly, the 45-min halves that demand near silence and little movement had made the children restless.

Once the second half started, Maurizio and I shared a few comments, but then we both became too involved in the game to continue any conversation. Like the people around us, we spend most of the time watching silently. Only when the ball goes out of bounds, or the referee halts the game is conversation allowable within the etiquette of this occasion. At these times, people share comments, let out sighs or shout at the referee. This particular game ended in a draw so there was little celebration and only muffled frustration at the conclusion. The crowd exchanged their goodbyes and dispersed quickly, but I hung around to help put chairs away.

After the game, I spoke to Giancarlo, an older, bigger man with white hair. After explaining to him that I was an American, he informed me that Juventus always wins because the team bribes people, but that it is better to be a Roma fan. They do not win often, but when they won in 2001, it was a party for an entire year. He continued to say that Roma is winning without many key but injured players including Francesco Totti, Vincenzo Montella and Shabani Nonda. Giancarlo concluded by saying that Juventus, Inter and Milan have power, but Roma is better, or *piu bella*. This attitude towards Roma's northern rivals is a cornerstone of the Roman attitude. Traditionally, the northern teams have had the financial backing of rich, industrialist families, while Roma has had more modest ownership. Roma fans take pride in the passionate support that they themselves provide to the team, even if the teams have not been as strong as the Milan- and Turin-based teams. For Roma fans, supporting the team gives one a sense of honour that cannot be bought, but must be earned through supporting the team through its struggles.

Community business

Every other week, fans fill the Roma Club Testaccio to watch the Roma away games on satellite TV. Everybody, including club members, pays six Euros per game. This fee helps to cover the cost of the subscription to Sky satellite television and includes a half-time beverage. In comparison, in 2006, 12 Euro equalled roughly 15 US dollars while an espresso in a Rome bar cost about .65–.70 Euro and estimated GDP per capita in Italy was $28,100.[33] The Sky TV subscription cost the Roma Club Testaccio 210 Euro ($250) per month for the 2005–2006 season. The cost of satellite TV is second only to rent on the list of the club's expenses.

Satellite TV is a major cost for the club, but it also creates an opportunity for the club to raise funds by charging admission. Pay-per-view satellite television is an expense that many individuals cannot afford for their home television, so they are willing to pay money to the club in order to watch their beloved A.S. Roma. When Roma played a UEFA Cup[34] match that aired on free television, no one gathered at the club to watch because, as it was explained to me, they could watch at home for free. Though it may seem contradictory to some of the critiques about the alienating effects of mass media, the era of soccer on pay TV indirectly encourages socialization by forcing groups to band together just to afford the cost of watching televised games. In this sense, the practices of the Roma Club Testaccio, and countless groups of soccer fans throughout Europe, counter any easy argument that modern telecommunications are inherently alienating. The political economy of pay-television creates an opportunity for the Roma Club Testaccio and it provides the motivation for 'co-presence' or a communal experience as fans defray costs by gathering around a TV screen.

Though they subscribe to a satellite TV service, the Roma Club Testaccio is far from the cutting edge of technology. The rotary phone at the clubhouse has no answering machine, and the internet remains out of their sphere of interest. Club President, Sergio, does not carry a cell phone. Instead, the group favours in-person communication. They post information about upcoming games on a piece of paper at the entrance of the clubhouse, thereby encouraging people to visit the clubhouse to make seating reservations. The Roma Club Testaccio's preference for 'old' technology reflects their generation as well as their geography – they are so firmly entrenched in the local neighbourhood that they do not need new communication technology to organize or exchange information. Though the club welcomes younger members, the club is marked as a place for older men. The club members believe that the younger generation is more concerned with video games and television than they are in soccer and in playing cards.

The Roma Club Testaccio operates is a male space that centres around the soccer team, A.S. Roma. For these fans, soccer is an inexhaustible topic of conversation with its complexity and tactical ambiguities. Unlike some sports, the game resists statistical and objective analysis; thus, judgments are often supported with nothing more than one's interpretation of the quality of a player, coach or team. The fascination with soccer is fuelled by endless television coverage and the abundance of local and national daily sports journals that feed the flames of controversy. In addition to sophisticated analysis, these media sources recount endless details about the professional and private lives of the players and their associates. Gossip and rumours and the subsequent responses to the gossip and rumours are regularly printed in these papers and then circulated among these Roma Club members.

Though members of the club are old fashioned in terms of their relationship to information technology, the fan culture at the Roma Club Testaccio is still heavily influenced by mass media. Print media provides them with images to decorate the walls while satellite television allows them to watch their beloved team as well as to gather together and to collect money for the broadcast fees and for rent. Media provides the grist for the mill of everyday conversation and argument that forms the backbone of everyday life in Testaccio and the Roma Club.

Testaccio proclaims their attempt to recreate the curva sud of the stadium in their clubhouse, but I would argue that in their clubhouse, their style of fandom is every bit as worthy as that in the stadium. As I have argued throughout this volume, fandom is nurtured in everyday life in Testaccio, at fan clubs, and in the micro-social meetings among fans in the streets, cafes and living rooms wherever fans find themselves.

Pub football

Weed discusses the rise of 'pub football', the ritual practice of watching a football match in a public house (pub) with other like-minded fans. The fans in these pubs create a jovial atmosphere through song, shouting and wit as everyone stands facing the television while beer is readily available. Weed accounts for the apparently increasing popularity of pub football due to three factors. First, the decreasing cost of Big-screen TVs has made them affordable for most pubs. Second, the cost of satellite TV is prohibitive for some fans who might rather spend money at the bar instead of paying a monthly subscription fee. Third, reforms in English football starting in the 1990s have ruined the atmosphere at the stadium according to some fans. Now, fans are required to sit instead of stand, and with higher ticket prices, the mythologized 'working class fan'[35] has been purged from the stadium, and the stadium has been sanitized. English pubs had not been, though Weed did not rule out the repression of the pub as a possible trajectory. Weed makes a compelling argument that those who watch together enjoy a 'shared communal experience'[36] that can rival the experience of actually being there. Watching the match at the local pub has its advantages. Viewers benefit from multiple angles and replays that promise to improve with digital technology. Television screens add content in the form of graphics such as statistics and the game clock as well as audible and sometimes expert commentary that theoretically adds to the match. Pub football might have a purer fan base in the sense that it does not typically include the wealthy and blasé customers with connections to corporate tickets who seem to dominate the stadiums during World Cup final and other major matches. A fan can also avoid the hassles headaches of travel. The bar is a unique and shared experience, and a necessary one for many who do not have access to the home ground of their favourite team.

Fan Diaspora

While price might keep some fans away from the stadium, distance is another intervening factor in the behaviour of football fans. In our globalizing economy, people are often geographically displaced and cannot regularly return to their place of their fan origins. If the cases where there is a critical mass of similarly minded displaced fans, interesting diasporic groups can form. In the context of American Football, Jon Kraszewski writes about how fans of the Pittsburgh Steelers living in Forth Worth, Texas, congregate to watch their team. They try their best to recreate Pittsburgh by consuming Pittsburgh-centric food and drink, and moreover, they create a strong sense of belonging.[37] In a similar way, every major university in the Midwestern region of the US seems to have an established connection with a bar in Chicago where fans can go to congregate with fellow alumni and watch their football and basketball teams.

Large-scale public viewing is a growing trend in football. At the World Cup of 2006, there was the well-attended 'fan mile' in Berlin where fans watched matches on huge screen televisions. Now, public screening events are part of the organization of World Cup tournaments. During the World Cup of 2014, the US Soccer Federation organized public viewings, including several at Chicago's Grant Park where an estimated 20,000 fans showed up to cheer on the US Men's National Team in a match against Portugal. These big-screen viewing parties are a growing phenomenon that underscores how television can facilitate gathering for a communal experience away from the stadium.

Is the stadium experience necessary to be a good pub fan? Is the passion learned in the stadium and carried over into the pub or can it be developed in the pub? Is it second best, a substitute, a different thing or is it better in some sense? In particular, as many Americans become interested in European football clubs, most of them will never be able to attend matches regularly, if ever, yet there is a growing cognoscenti supporting various clubs, or in some cases, football altogether. Similarly, no World Cup will ever be able to accommodate every fan who would like to attend a match, so, large-scale viewing parties are able to offer views of the match along with a shared experience that is so vital in football.

My experience as a fan is firmly rooted in the stadium experience. I had played the game as a child in the suburbs, and I have vague memories of watching Socrates play for Brazil in the World Cup, and I even went to see Chicago Sting play in the US's defunct indoor soccer league.[38] Before attending my first Italian football match, I was not much of a fan. Watching the exuberant Lazio fans at the Stadio Olimpico as they celebrate the trophies won in the season past during an early round, Coppa Italia match, was transformative. I could not believe what I saw.

Perhaps like most readers of this text, I have watched football matches on a variety of screens in a variety of places ranging from a personal computer to an outdoor screen, and in the company of a group of close friends to watching alone among strangers. Likewise, the emotional tenor of these viewings has ranged from communal intensity to indifferent banality. I have watched VHS tapes with the previous day's game and I have had the internet shut off mid-match. I have watched matches in several different countries and time zones, in hotel rooms and in cafes. Perhaps the most remarkable experience was watching Italy play versus the United States at an outdoor screen in Salzburg, Austria, during the 2006 World Cup that was played just across the border in Germany. In the lead up to this match, I was conflicted since I am an American, but I knew far more about the Italian National team that featured two of my favourite players, Daniele De Rossi and Francesco Totti. These two are the stalwarts of the A.S. Roma team, the one that I had watched play, live, at least 25 times in the past year. As the game proceeded, and the Austrian beer took effect, I became an American fan. I could not go against my home country even if I could identify each member of the Italian team and the club that they played for while my knowledge of the US team was far more limited. I felt twinges of nationalist pride that I had not expected. I felt completely deflated when Daniele De Rossi elbowed the US player, Brian McBride, squarely, and with obvious intent, in the face. His inarguably deserved red card expulsion felt like a betrayal – why would he do that and hurt his team's chances against an inferior US team. Good for the US, I guess, but what a disgrace to football. In my position, I was hoping for a good showing for both teams, with the better team winning – I would have bet on Italy, the clear favourites. For neutrals, the fair play of Italy's footballers is always in question, and in supporting the US, I found their antics disappointing. In retrospect, I can at least say that I am glad it was an obvious referee decision instead of one that would have required a guess as to intent and would have made me try to balance my allegiances with a player, and the two nations of which I most closely align myself.

American fans – or, **Un Americano a Roma** *(an American in Rome)*

As an American fan of relatively obscure team (in the US, this means, more or less, NOT Manchester United), I have, more than once, been seated alone at the bar, begging the bartender to tune in the strange game from overseas on a seldom used satellite channel in the middle of the afternoon. The situation for Americans has been continually improving throughout my tenure as a fan. During the 2014 World Cup, it was easy enough to gather with fellow fans in bars in Eastern Washington state and in North Dakota. Any decent sports bar can tune in the biggest matches from England or the Champions League, but there is a critical mass of fans only for the biggest clubs of London, Madrid, Manchester, Munich, Milan or those that feature Mr Messi. The biggest American cities have pubs that specialize in showing football matches, even those starting at inconvenient hours. But there is one question I have. There is little dispute that the best club football is played in Western Europe and South America. Can an American that has never been to London be a true Arsenal fan? While Michael Weed Presents compelling evidence that the atmosphere of English pubs is lively and has some advantages over attending the live event in-person, his study implies that the fans that populate the pubs learn to be fans in the stadium and carry their knowledge and their passion to the pub. In the era of the internet, surely a fan can learn anything and everything about Arsenal, or any other major club. But is there something learned only in the stadium? Is the feeling of being in the stadium with thousands of others irreplaceable? Clearly, we could make distinctions and taxonomies of fans and place them in boxes. Surely, we can imagine an Arsenal fan in America, but would Nick Hornby or other self-identified lifelong loyalist fans accept this geographically misplaced fan as one of them?

Conclusion

Contemporary fandom comprises both in-person and mediated experiences. Media calls into question our assumptions about community as based strictly in geography. Fandom shows how identities are formed with often seamless transitions from mediated contexts to in-person spaces. We must shift our attention to the quality of social connection rather than the channel/s used. I cannot speak for Arsenal fans on the quality of their American fans. I will leave it to them consider whether they are worthy and to what extent their home stadium bestows authenticity. The subcultures of fans around the globe offer insight into the flexibility and ingenuity of fans to create meaningful experiences, regardless of what they think in north London.

This chapter has described a variety of ways in which fans watch televised football matches in distinctly social settings. At the Roma Club Testaccio, fans gather to watch matches in a place that is dedicated to celebrating Roma and Rome. The televised matches become a social event for regular club members as well as for other fans in the neighbourhood to congregate in a quasi-sacred space of Roma fandom. Throughout Europe, pubs become an ephemeral site of fan congregation. As

Michael Weed argues, the pub offers an alternative to the stadium for a meaningful social experience. Televised media offers a symbolic return home for those who are displaced. Pubs or living rooms become temporary space for the fan-diasporas to celebrate their home town team while gathered in a different city or even country. As Kraszewski notes, fandom becomes a ritual of home. These examples of group television watching demonstrate the ways in which fans use broadcasts to found social events and foster social connections.

International broadcasting exposes some of the tensions between the local and the global. The political economy of media broadcasting, and especially television, cultivates fandom around the world and is undoubtedly good for the economics of football. The developed international broadcasting system allows for the fan to watch their team play in real time from every continent and time zone. Television offers endless replays and slow-motion reverse angles that occasionally add to the comprehension of the match.

This chapter and this volume has focused mostly on fan empowerment, and how fans *use* media for the social project of fandom, but that does not mean that the global forces of media bend always to their collective will. There are clear drawbacks for local fans. Odd kickoff times to accommodate foreign audiences and the rise of lavishly compensated players that some fans perceive as spoiled turn off some fans. The fans that remain are expected to pay more and more for television subscriptions to fund the relentless financial expansion of the game. With a growing target audience, football teams can afford to lose some less affluent local fans. Yet, fans are creative and find ways to connect with fellow fans. One irony of higher media prices is that it might spur more socialization as fans band together to watch in pubs or in a friend's apartment. This is just one example of the ways that fans reclaim the game.

Disclosure statement

No potential conflict of interest was reported by the author.

Notes

1. See Adorno and Horkheimer, 'The Culture Industry'.
2. Cuban, 'The Fan Experience'.
3. Perhaps it would help American fans to organize to demand, for instance, cheaper tickets.
4. I must note that the team takes its name from the Great Chicago Fire of 1871. The team now plays its matches in Bridgeview, over 10 miles from the site of the conflagration.
5. Soundersfc.com, 'Alliance'.
6. Johnston, 'Juve Seek Bite out of Premier League's Asia Apple'.
7. See Supporters Direct.
8. Kraszewski provides a model for such work as he documents the ways that fans of the American football team evoke Pittsburgh, Pennsylvania, when they watch their team at a bar in Texas.
9. Goldlust, 'Sport as Entertainment', 43.
10. Ibid., 45.
11. See www.radiomarconi.com.
12. see Museum of Broadcast History, www.museum.tv.
13. Merkel, 'Milestones in the Development of Football Fandom in Germany', 66.
14. *Irriducibili Movie: L'amor per te mi fa teppista* [My love for you has made me a hooligan], DVD.

15. This is also the name of the Irriducibili's newsletter.
16. Andrews, 'Sport', 137.
17. Scott, 'English Premier League'.
18. Andrews, 'Sport', 140.
19. Ibid., 142.
20. Ginsborg, *Italy and Its Discontents*, 113.
21. Serie A TV rights sold for 943 Euros per season from 2015 to 2018. See Gladwell, 'Serie A'.
22. Ginsborg, *Italy and Its Discontents*, 132.
23. BBC Online, Reign of Two Halves.
24. Reign of Two Halves for Berlusconi. BBC Online. 14 May 2001. http://news.bbc.co.uk/2/hi/europe/1325122.stm (accessed April 4, 2014).
25. Hooper, J. 'Murdoch takes Sky to Italy'. The Guardian Online. http://www.theguardian.com/business/2003/jul/31/citynews.rupertmurdoch (accessed April 7, 2015).
26. Ibid.
27. Gladwell, B. Serie A Clubs Back New TV Deal'. 27 June 2014. http://www.espnfc.us/italian-serie-a/story/1916857/serie-a-clubs-agree-new-tv-rights-deal. See Giulianotti, Football: A Sociology of the Global Game.
28. Chandler, 'The TV and Sports Industries', 66.
29. See Giulianotti, *Football: A Sociology of the Global Game*.
30. Duncan, 90–91.
31. Trans. *Ciao Tommy, Vittima del mondo ingiusto.*
32. The Champions' League is an intra-European tournament among the top European club teams. Qualification is based on domestic league finish in the previous season. The lucrative tournament is organized by the European football association (UEFA). The tournament runs in parallel with most national competitions, starting in August and finishing in May. Ultimately, Fiorentina would finish fourth in the standings, but would subsequently lose their spot due to their involvement in the referee scandal of 2006.
33. According to the OECD, 2005, in comparison, US GDP/capita was $41,800.
34. The UEFA Cup (now called the Europa League) is the second-tier intra-European tournament that is organized similarly to the UEFA Champions' League, the top-tier European tournament.
35. Kuper and Szymanski, *Soccernomics*.
36. Weed, 'The Pub as a Virtual Football Fandom Venue', 246.
37. Kraszewski, 'Pittsburgh in Fort Worth', 155.
38. The indoor game featured lots of goals but could not, alas, sustain a niche in the US sporting scene.

References

Adorno, T., and M. Horkheimer. 'The Culture Industry: Enlightenment as Mass Deception'. In *Media and Cultural Studies: Key Works*, ed. M. Durham and D. Kellner, 71–101. Malden, MA: Blackwell, 2001.

Andrews, D.L. 'Sport'. In *Culture Works: The Political Economy of Culture*, ed. R. Maxwell, 131–62. Minneapolis: University of Minnesota Press, 2001.

Chandler, J. 'The TV and Sports Industries'. In *Critical Readings: Sport, Culture and the Media*, ed. D. Rowe, 48–69. Berkshire: Open University, 2004.

Duncan, C. 'Art Museums and the Ritual of Citizenship'. In Exhibiting Cultures: *The poetics and Politics of Museum Display*, ed. I. Karp and S. D. Lavine (Washington, DC: Smithsonian Institution Press, 1991), 88–103.

Ginsborg, P. *Italy and Its Discontents: Family, Civil Society, State, 1980–2001*. New York: Palgrave MacMillan, 2003.

Giulianotti, R. *Football: A Sociology of the Global Game*. Malden, MA: Blackwell, 1999.

Gladwell, B. 'Serie A Clubs Back New TV Deal'. *ESPN*, June 27, 2014. www.espnfc.us/italian-serie-a-story/1916857/serie-a-clubs-agree-new-tv-rights-deal (accessed March 14, 2015).

Goldlust, J. 'Sport as Entertainment: The Role of Mass Communications'. In *Critical Readings: Sport, Culture and the Media*, ed. D. Rowe, 27–47. Berkshire: Open University, 2004.

Irriducibili Movie: L'Amor per te mi Fa Teppista. DVD. Directed by A. Zappulla and R. Camolino. Italy: Lazio Irriducibili Video, 2005.

Johnston, P. 'Juve Seek Bite out of Premier League's Asia Apple'. *Reuters*, August 15, 2014. http://uk.reuters.com/article/2014/08/15/uk-soccer-asia-juventus (accessed April 2, 2015).

Kraszewski, J. 'Pittsburgh in Fort worth: Football Bars, Sports Television, Sports Fandom, and the Management of Home'. *Journal of Sport and Social Issues* 32 (2008): 139–57.

Kuper, S., and S. Szymanski. *Soccernomics: Why Transfers Fail, Why Spain Rule the World and Other Curious Football Phenomenon Explained*. 3rd ed. London: Harper Collins, 2012.

Merkel, U. 'Milestones in the Development of Football Fandom in Germany: Global Impacts on Local Contests'. In *Football Fans around the World: From Supporters to Fanatics*, ed. S. Brown, 59–77. New York: Routledge, 2007.

Scott, M. 'English Premier League Sells British TV Rights for $7.8 Billion'. February 10, 2015. Nytimes.com/2015/02/11/sports/soccer/english-premier-league.html (accessed April 7, 2015).

Weed, M. 'The Pub as a Virtual Football Fandom Venue: An Alternative to 'Being There'? In *Football Fans around the World: From Supporters to Fanatics*, ed. S. Brown, 237–52. New York: Routledge, 2007.

New media: online fandom

> Online media is a boon to fandom. It provides mountains of information for the devout follower, while it also provides the opportunity to create and share content. The internet allows fans to transcend geographical barriers to form communities that could not otherwise exist. One particular group of A.S. Roma fans show how fans can use the 'placeless' internet to invigorate a connection to place. They use their website in conjunction with meeting at the stadium and at other places in real life. The website provides the glue to their geographically dispersed set of Romans. The web is another tool that serves the social needs of fans.

A.S. Roma icon, Francesco Totti, celebrated his acrobatic goal in the Roma Lazio derby of 11 January 2015, by taking a 'selfie' in front of his adoring fans. One news article joked that the shocking aspect of all this was not the acrobatic goal that the 38 year old scored, but that he knew what a selfie was.[1] The facetious comment draws attention to the revolution in information technology that has occurred during the 'old man's' career that started during the early days of the internet. Digital media has had a profound impact on football fandom as football content is distributed in all varieties. Audio podcasts, video on Youtube and Vine, photographs of fans and of players and text-based commentary celebrate and critique every aspect of the beautiful game. The scope of this media cornucopia would have been unforeseeable when Totti made his first team debut in 1993. The internet and global telecommunications have dramatically increased the amount of available information on virtually every topic. For football fans, the effect has been that one must possess a greater amount of knowledge about their favourite team in order to be considered a *real fan*.[2] It is expected that a fan will know more than simply the score of the most recent match or who scored a goal. Fans might know who is dating a celebrity or which player is looking to leave the club in addition to the mundane facts that pertain to the football match.

This chapter begins with a discussion of some of the major issues surrounding the rise of internet-based, digital media, before continuing to a case study of an online football fan club. This chapter will focus on three areas of the so-called new media that have raised considerable concern. The first issue to be addressed is the rise of media consumers who become media producers. The second issue addressed will be the notion of virtual community along with its potential benefits and weaknesses. Third, the analysis returns to a discussion of globalization and how the internet might affect the sense of place. Various internet and information technology are often lumped together as 'new media'. The term 'new' signifies the threat of the internet to disrupt the 'old' or 'traditional' ways of doing things, and the term instantly casts air of nostalgia upon media such as analogue radio and the daily newspaper that might arrive at your doorstep. Newness promises a break from the past, though old arguments about the utopian or dystopian aspects of radio, telephony and television seem to find new life as they are applied to today's 'new' media. In media studies, these three issues have too often been cast in utopian and dystopian terms – the promise of liberation vs. the fear of disaster. While these discourses have inevitably led, over time, to more nuanced understandings of media, this brief introduction will introduce the hopes and fears of new media as a way to highlight the tensions in media, and not as a comprehensive analysis that these issues deserve. Finally, the chapter will highlight the fan group, Core de Roma, a fan group that hosts a vibrant website and global community while regularly meeting in person, at the stadium, and at banquets and other events. Core de Roma represents the ways in which the internet can be used to bolster social connections in the present day while trying to retain a sense of tradition and place.

Consumer–producer

New digital formats lower the barrier for the creation and distribution of content. Tired formulations that divided the world into neatly segmented producers and consumers have lost their explanatory power. Audiences are creative producers. The internet has lowered the barriers for fans to create and distribute their own texts and images. As a result, fans often co-create meaning with the formally recognized producers and they often contribute ideas, improvements and extensions to the professional producers of media content. 'Prosumers'[3] aid the creation of content, sometimes quickly as the speed of information travel has accelerated. As Henry Jenkins has documented, fans of all forms of popular culture have not only been consumers, but they are also producers of culture who modify, extend and expand the bounds of pop culture texts and narratives. As Giulianotti[4] points out, middle class and educated football fans (or post-fans, as he calls them) have spearheaded the production of football media to suit their own needs. In his telling, post-fans' media production diverges from the traditional working class roots of fandom that were based more in large group, face-to-face engagement. The ability of fans to express their ideas is, in many ways, liberating and utopian. On the other hand, many media platforms are controlled by corporations that attempt to monetize fan/audience production. Unlicensed creators of content can also be subject to copyright litigation if they attempt to use the symbols of the team that the hold dear.[5] These tensions are active and ongoing in fan cultures and in societies in general as they attempt to balance the rights of expression vs. the rights and power of business.

One of the promises of the internet is that it can bring together isolated, but likeminded people in order to find support and enact positive social change. Provided they speak a common language and have a reliable internet or mobile connections, people around the world can share knowledge, build relationships and connect with larger communities. Certainly, protest movements such as those associated with the Arab Spring used information technology to organize. On the other hand, technology is not a panacea, and there are fears that internet-based relationships can be detrimental to real community. Scholars have fretted about the potential of virtual (online, web-based) communities to save or destroy the face-to-face communities that we were accustomed to. Sherry Turkle's study of youth and technology documents how some of her young subjects replace deep relationships with shallow interactions, how the constant call for interaction produces anxiety and how young people can be cruel behind the distance of technology.[6] In terms of political actions, some fear that internet campaigns that do not demand real-life action might give the *impression* of action without the effects. Additionally, much of our communication online is subject to commercial monetization or government surveillance. Finally, the technologies available to those who seek to fight injustice are equally available to those who advocate intolerance and violence. For instance, Italian Sociologist, Antonio Roversi, has written about websites of radical right wing football fans that advocate hate and violence. While it is reductive to cast new media solely in utopian or dystopian terms, these issues need attention by citizens as governments create and enforce policies that attempt to balance personal rights of expression with societal safety.

The nature of today's digital information technology is a key part of the process of globalization. The multi-faceted, over-determined concept of globalization will not be sorted out here; however, I will point out a few key issues as they relate to football fandom. In the previous chapter, I discussed the importance of global audiences for televised football matches, and in particular, the English Premier League. The EPL has been able to cement itself as the richest league by garnering support around the world. The internet allows fans to learn more about their favourite teams and players, and to participate in online fan forums from virtually anywhere on the globe. Another advantage of the global internet is that, as a researcher, I am easily able to confirm the scoreline of matches played in another continent from a decade ago without putting on my coat and going out the door, let alone travelling to an archive abroad.

The rise of global media, and particularly television and internet, raises questions and potential challenges to the connection of football to place. Is there anything inherent in football that makes it a spectator sport or a powerful symbolic representation of neighbourhoods, cities, regions, countries or continents? Currently, top-flight football has incredible social meaning for all those who follow it, but the game itself is almost absurdly simple, and requires little more than a ball and some free time. Even an individual can gain satisfaction from juggling (aka keepie uppie) or kicking the ball at a net or wall. So how does this game attract such global attention? Sport's popularity is explainable, in part, because it takes on symbolic representational meanings. People pour their local and social identities into teams – a phenomenon that seems to be taken for granted at this point in history. It is so obvious for European or South American lovers of football that the game somehow *means so much more* than just a collection of players competing for arbitrary prizes.

While the influx of global capital would seem to erode local allegiances as owners, players and managers are sourced from distant lands, in some sense the opposite often occurs: local pride becomes emboldened as a response to the fear of global homogenization. Many fans of Manchester United protested the sale of the club to business savvy (but, presumed football-ignorant) Americans. The sale sparked a series of protests in the short term, but the club has only gotten larger with increases in global fandom and merchandizing that outweigh local grievances. We also know that teams attempt to monetize their 'authentic' connection to place,[7] even as they relentlessly promote their global brand to global consumers.[8] Every year, it becomes clearer that the game responds more to the demands of global capitalism than of local allegiances. If there is a breaking point, it has not yet been reached, in England, at least, are filled every week. I would like to predict that this cannot go on indefinitely – that fans will move on with their lives, and disregard a sport that seems to have little regard for them, but the game seems brilliant at regenerating itself, and generating more money at the expense of fans.

In stark contrast to the phenomenon of online, global fandom, the Roma Club Testaccio is a sort of ideal type of the 'old school' style of fandom. Neighbourhood locals support the local team, and over time, a tradition has developed that is revered and resilient against all threats. With the passing of time, the tradition becomes bigger and stronger and deeper, and the bonds between people who take part become stronger as the identity takes on a historical character that is just out of reach. Members of the club connect with something that is bigger than themselves and their limited lifespans. It is a glimpse of something that feels eternal. Testaccio maintains this aura through the photographic displays that document the history. The history is continually updated through the pasting of photographs and through the leadership of a core of people, such as Club President, Sergio Rosi.

The Roma Club Testaccio stands as an ideal and idealized neighbourhood club that offers a bit of nostalgia for those who do not live in the heart of Rome. For many of those living in the periphery of the city, they feel a loss of neighbourhood authenticity, and for working class values and ways of life. This sense of authentic leaving cannot be easily created, and perhaps cannot be achieved at all since it combines reality with idealized romanticism (pun intended). This tension – between the loss of authenticity and the desire to experience it and the impossibility of it fuels the Core de Roma website. The site has features of any website for fans – football fans – it has a chat room, news, photographs archives and editorials. What makes it stand out is the way that it embodies of a profound sense of place that draws upon and invigorates a pride in Rome, while residing in the placelessness of the internet.

Core de Roma – online and off

In Chapters 1 and 2, I described the clubhouse of the Roma Club Testaccio including the walls of images and their nightly card games. The clubhouse is a physical embodiment of Roma Fan culture set within a working class neighbourhood with geographical proximity to the quasi-sacred birthplace of the A.S. Roma football team. The Roma Club Testaccio embodies the traditional concept of community as its members live near each other, meet together often and have shared goals and interests. These men (and almost exclusively, men) have cultivated a pure fan culture built around loyal allegiance to A.S. Roma that is unsullied by commercial interests. Since the club is locally rooted, the members have little need for new information technologies such as the internet and mobile phones. Instead, members walk to the local club to play cards with other men of the same age and from the same neighbourhood. It is a traditional neighbourhood fan club tied to traditional Italian modes of sociability and community.

In the chapter at hand, I turn my attention to a fan club that strives to replicate the Roma Club Testaccio's traditional, neighbourhood-based fan culture in a virtual clubhouse that reaches across the city and to points around the world. Core de Roma is a fan group devoted to the A.S. Roma football team that is centred around their website, www.corederoma.it. In place of the decorated walls of the Roma Club

Testaccio clubhouse that are filled with collages of posters torn from magazines and personal photographs, the virtual clubhouse of Core de Roma has immense collections of digital images. Instead of the evening card games, they have a chat room where participants 'meet', share stories and make jokes, etc. Instead of serving as a place to watch games, the Core de Roma site catalogues previews and commentary and serves as an archive of visual and audio media from the matches. Through brash language and Roman imagery, the site is distinctly Roman. Above all, this fan club has adapted to the web and has cultivated a sense of 'Roman-ness' to fit a new set of social and technological realities.

The Roma Club Testaccio is threatened by changing economic and social forces as the neighbourhood gentrifies and the rents rise. The club stands as a relic at a time when many families are moving from central Rome to the periphery. Life in the urban periphery relies on the automobile for work and social lives. As the prevalence of local sociability declines, mass media and communication technologies become a more prominent element in some peoples' social lives. These Roman football fan clubs highlight the ways in which football fandom rooted in local support has incorporated the rise of mass mediation.

As this book has shown, football fandom embodies local pride to and global communities. Football fans can be described by Benedict Anderson's notion of the 'imagined community', in that the members of these communities may never know or meet each other face-to-face, yet they feel a sense of belonging that emanates from shared knowledge, often disseminated by TV broadcasts, newspapers and all other forms of mass media. Members of 'virtual communities'[9] might interact with other fans online, but never meet each other in actual life, or they might use internet to stay connected with friends *from the old neighbourhood*. Purely face-to-face social structures such as the Roma Club Testaccio appear to be less common than those who mix face-to-face with information technology. Core de Roma blurs any lines of distinction between in person and virtual communities as it encompasses imagined, virtual and local face-to-face communities. The site serves an information resource for the imagined community, a place to chat for the virtual community, and as a place to organize real-world meetings. In their own words,

> Core de Roma is not only a website. It is also a group of friends that frequently meet in real life. We are always present at the Olympic Stadium, in the *distinti* north, section, where we have been for years now, always located behind our banner. Our cheering and our colors can also be seen and heard at away games.[10]

This hybrid fan community mixes the local pride of the Roma Club Testaccio and brings it to a worldwide audience.

This analysis of Core de Roma is informed by scholars who see more coordination and cooperation between online and offline communities rather than distinction and separation between them. Online video game scholar, T.L. Taylor, critiques an earlier phase of the scholarship of web-based communities for inventing a false dichotomy between online and offline life. In her words,

> What seems more to be the case is that people have a much messier relationship with their off- and online personas and social contexts. That people can slip into and out of complex social networks that cross not only online and offline space, but genres within the online world is a fact often under-acknowledged.[11]

For the members of Core de Roma, their online social lives are always already intertwined with their actual world social lives. In response to critics who question whether online communities can be real communities, sociologists Barry Wellman and Milena Gulia respond, 'Pundits worry that virtual community may not truly be community. These worriers are confusing the pastoralist myth of community for the reality. Community ties are already geographically dispersed, sparsely knit, connected heavily by telecommunications ... and specialized in content',[12] Wellman uses the term, 'glocalized', to describe groups that are 'Heavily involved in both local and long-distance relationships'.[13] These scholars think about these groups as communities that incorporate telecommunications rather than as groups that are defined or limited by telecommunication technology. This line of thinking informs the analysis that follows.

This chapter describes the website and point out the ways in which fans interact with the site and with each other. While the website opens up new avenues of participation, my central concern here is not to find differences between the online and offline aspects of this community, but rather to think about how all of these levels of communities, from actual to imagined, contribute to the creation of a fan culture and a notion of *Romanità* (Roman-ness) that incorporates a wide community. My own relationship with this group might be described, in Taylor's terms, as 'messy' since I interacted with members both online and face-to-face, and in both local and long-distance contexts. My analysis is based on observation and participation of the site as well as time spent cheering with club members at the stadium, dining with them at banquets, watching games at members' homes and chatting with others in car rides in and around Rome in 2005 and 2006.

The Core de Roma site features a lively chat room where fans discuss every aspect of the A.S. Roma football team's history and future. Club members use the website to perform local identity through the display of Roman imagery and through the use of Roman dialect. The site promotes a vision of what it means to be not only a Roma fan, but what it means to be Roman. At the same time, the site embraces a worldwide audience. The site manages the global and the local by extending invitations to everyone to participate in their local events and by posting pictures of members throughout the world.

Fan club history

Core de Roma is a non-profit group that was founded by a small group of fans including Luca, Gigi, Maurizio and Stefano.[14] The original website was a simple chat room created without the help of professional web developers. The website was born just after archrival Lazio won the 2000 season championship. This was a difficult time for Roma fans, as Lazio were at the height of a successful period and had a powerful team filled with stars. Core de Roma was formed, in part, to defy the success of Lazio and to rally support for Roma. Since that time, the fortunes of the teams have been reversed with Roma now enjoying more success and a larger budget.

The founders of the site continue to be the leading members of the group, exerting organizational and editorial control of the site and managing the legal and financial responsibility for the club. Over the years, these responsibilities have grown as the traffic on the site has increased, and the number of contributing members has increased. The site was upgraded in December, 2007, in order to accommodate increased traffic and a growing archive of fan-produced material. In addition to the core members, there are various levels of affiliation. The entire site is publicly accessible, though in order to write in the chat room, one must complete a free registration. Regulars in the chat room include Roma fans from Denmark, France and Florida, among other locations dispersed all over the world. Official membership is open to anyone willing to pay yearly dues of 30 euros. Members receive an official membership card, an email account with the '@corederoma.it' suffix, a club scarf and a discount on any other merchandise purchases.[15]

Core de Roma is different from traditional fan clubs like the Roma Club Testaccio, in that, it does not have a physical clubhouse and its members are not bound by neighbourhood proximity, shared employment or childhood friendships. Members are distributed throughout disparate neighbourhoods in and around Rome, and, as mentioned, throughout the world. Core de Roma is exclusive in the sense that Italian is the primary language of the site and members must have consistent access to the internet to fully participate. This is a significant barrier since Italy lags behind much of Western Europe in internet connectivity.[16] My own struggle to keep online led me to sit on park benches in the rain, work at a thankless job, loiter by the columns of St. Peter's square, and meet and befriend Carabinieri[17] (military police) outside of a government building. The relative rarity of internet access in public spaces and private homes in Rome explains why the most active members of the group work in white-collar careers. Members include a travel agent, a retired Swiss patent office worker, an advertising consultant who relocated to Miami, Florida, a retired sports journalist, a contractor and an importer/exporter.

Though members tend to be family-oriented men over thirty, women are welcome to be part of the group as full participants. In addition to wives and girlfriends who are regular members, there are 'independent' members such as Paoletta. Paoletta is a young, devout fan who regularly posts articles to the website, writes in the chat room, attends the dinners and goes to all of the games. She is a relative of Roma star, Francesco Totti.[18] She could get tickets to sit in the VIP section of the stadium for free, but chooses to buy her own ticket in order to sit with the Core de Roma group. Her participation in the group is welcome and she is treated as a full member, unlike the Roma Club Testaccio, and many other fan groups that tend to be male-dominated. In terms of gender, Core de Roma is more progressive than many traditional fan groups. It serves as an arena for participation for underrepresented female fans, even if the communication style is normally masculine.

The openness of the group is exemplified by my own entry into the group. While surfing the web at my thankless job,[19] I happened upon the Core de Roma site. A pop-up window appeared advertising their upcoming banquet dinner. I sent an email message to the dinner organizer explaining that I was an American fan of Roma and that I would love to join them at the dinner. Despite the warning of a co-worker who thought that these fans might be 'crazy', which I understood to mean rowdy and dangerous, I accepted their invitation, and stepped into a car with a total stranger at the appointed time and place. In retrospect, this was a fortuitous decision as I gained entry into a group of fans that includes women, and non-native Italians such as Luca and myself.[20]

Another way that the Core de Roma group distinguishes themselves from other groups is through their charity initiatives. While European football fans often appear in American media as maddened, riotous lunatics in the mould of the mythic hooligan, Core de Roma and other groups use their social organization to support pro-social causes. For example, in 2006, the site had a banner ad with a link to *Aiutiamo Edoardo*, a campaign to cover medical and transportation costs for a boy afflicted with a disease that required treatment abroad.[21] In 2008, Core de Roma started an initiative to raise money for humanitarian aid for children in Malawi.[22] Core de Roma's charitable initiatives are indicative of their social values that extend beyond football.

Like many other Roma clubs, Core de Roma members gather at a regular spot at Roma home games wearing their fan club scarves and displaying their large Core de Roma banner. The group convenes in the often sparsely occupied north-east corner (named the *distinti nord-est*) of the stadium. They are situated opposite the *curva sud*, that is the historic home of the most intense Roma fans, the ultràs. Their position opposite the *curva sud* gives them an excellent view of the grand visual displays that the ultràs put on. In the more tranquil north-east corner of the stadium, they have more room to congregate and display their banner. Through their banner and their sheer numbers, the virtual fan club lays claim, however, ephemeral, to actual space in the stadium. Unlike most of the fans that surround them in the north-east corner section of the stadium, Core de Roma fans remain standing during the entire game. For them, standing is a show of support for the team and is a habit borrowed from the ultràs.

The most important signifier of support and allegiance for football fans is the football scarf. Like many fan clubs, Core de Roma produces a new scarf every year for their members. In the past, the club scarves bore the phrase, *C'e batte er core* (loosely translated – There is a beat in our hearts) and on the reverse, *C'e rode er culo* (and fire in our rears) meaning that they are fired up and ready to go. This vulgar phrase employs Roman slang to signify their brash attitude. In other years, they have produced scarves with phrases that refer in some way to A.S. Roma or to Rome, the city, such as 'Kin of the wolf' and 'Gens Romana' (Latin for Roman people). All of these scarves contain the red and yellow colours as an indication of their fidelity to A.S. Roma, while the unique design of the scarves distinguishes them as an organized fan club.

Aside from the habitual meetings at the stadium, organized banquets are a primary social activity for the Core de Roma group. I attended three of these dinners, all held at restaurants on the periphery of Rome. These dinners spanned several hours and included multiple courses of pasta and meat, plenty of wine and little regard for time. These dinners often marked a special occasion or had a particular theme. For instance, one dinner was organized to welcome the Roma Club Malta on their visit to Rome, while at another dinner, the group handed out football balls with the A.S. Roma symbol after we ate a specially made A.S. Roma cake and sang some of the Roma *cori* (songs). At other dinners, the club invites past players and coaches as special guests from Roma history. At these dinners, club members get to chat, take pictures with and honour the legends from Roma's past. These special guests are often pictured on the web site, thus giving the fan group a measure of publicity and legitimacy as a club that deeply respects the history of A.S. Roma.

While the website remains the hub of their community, a more traditional community of face-to-face contact has emerged. Members meet at the stadium, watch away games at each other's homes and gather at dinners. Some members have developed social and business relationships that have grown from their participation in the group. In 2006, Core de Roma started discussing possibilities to establish a physical headquarters and to found a youth football school. In this way, the group is moving against the current of technology, or against any argument that might find information technology to be alienating. Instead of becoming more virtual, the group is organizing on the web with aspirations of constructing a physical presence.

Evolution of the site

The original Core de Roma website was essentially a simple chat room. As time and technology has progressed, the site has evolved into a hub of activity and an archive of fan created material. The site houses a prodigious amount of material contributed by members including text and a plethora of multimedia content including photographs, audio and video. The original design and technical work for the site was done by volunteers. In December, 2007, the group unveiled a new, professionally designed site. The newer version is visually streamlined and better facilitates multimedia hosting. The new site also incorporates outside advertisements that generate money to offset the increased and increasing costs of storage and maintenance. Despite the new look of the site, the overall ethos of the site and the group has remained unchanged.

One of the primary features of the site remains its 'Muro' (literally, *wall*) or chat room. Members post messages as a way to discuss A.S. Roma, football in general, or most anything that might be of concern to the group and can be posted publicly. The chat room is monitored for offensive content, and users must register to post messages. Like many chat rooms, participants go by nicknames, which can cause confusion when meeting people in real life. At one of the group's banquets, I asked Luca for a person's real name, he could only tell me their chat room nickname, having momentarily forgotten their real name. The chat room is full of foul language, jokes, insults, as well as valuable information, biased opinions, rumours, curses, laments, provocations and good cheer. To choose but one playful example, on the day after the 2008 US election, Paoletta wrote, *Non si discute, si OBAMA*, (No discussion, yes Obama) a play on the typical Roma fan phrase, *Non si discute, si ama* (One does not discuss, one loves). In addition to text, the *muro* has animated miniature icons (emoticons) that users employ to accent their messages. For instance, after tough loss, the user named Vesenus posted a succession of crying faces that expressed his feelings more adequately than words.

The Core de Roma site exhibits a vast collection of fan-produced writings, drawings, poems and photographs. It is an example of the kind of participatory fan culture that Henry Jenkins describes: 'Fans construct their cultural and social identity through borrowing and inflecting mass culture images, articulating concerns which often go unnoticed within the dominant media'.[23] Core de Roma provides many opportunities for fans to express their ideas and beliefs that, as Jenkins predicts, are often not acknowledged by mass media. Besides Core de Roma members' unabashed bias towards Roma, they exhibit scepticism towards mainstream media and an absolute allegiance to a constructed sense of Roman-ness that I describe below.

The vast *editoria* (editorial) section of the Core de Roma website is filled with articles composed by members. Articles comprise a dozen different categories and range in length from a single page to a dozen, and vary in topic from reaction to the latest game to historical articles. Some articles contain basic information about the line-ups and statistics for matches. A section is devoted to drawings and poems that honour Roma. Another section contains a summary of the chat room for the week for those who might have missed a few days. The site pays homage to the

80 year history of the club by housing articles on past players and events. For example, club member and former journalist, Danilo Leo, contributed a series of articles profiling Roma players from the 1960s and earlier.

The 'front page' image of the homepage changes several times a week, but always comments on the day's news. For example, the image might be a message of congratulations when the team or a player does well, such as the image of Francesco Totti with text congratulating him on his 200th goal. On the occasion of defender Christian Chivu leaving Roma for another team, the front page expressed the fans' dissatisfaction with a cartoon of a foot booting another man out of the way with the words, *Ciao Chivu*. On A.S. Roma's eightieth anniversary, the front page displayed a black and white image of a Roma player holding a title cup, and the text read, '80 Years of Passion'.[24]

On the right side of the home page, there is a news 'ticker' that links to news articles relating to Roma. There are often interactive surveys that poll users for opinions on relevant and current topics related to the team. These surveys use humour to frame the current predicament that the team is experiencing. In response to a survey of opinion about the team's 80th birthday, 76% of the 993 respondents chose, 'Grand celebration. Grand emotion! Beautiful Roma I love you' while the more sober 24% chose, 'For now, let's think about the super-cup match'.[25] In addition to the frequently updated elements, there are several constant sections on the website such as links to other Roma websites, and links to newspaper articles that mention Core de Roma.[26] For instance, the link to the daily newspaper devoted to A.S. Roma and its fans, *Il Romanista*, highlighted the Core de Roma website, commenting that it is, 'Without a doubt one of the most up to date and complete sites dedicated to the giallorossa'.[27]

Multimedia

In addition to the massive textual archive, Core de Roma houses an extensive collection of photographs, video and audio files. Core de Roma has their own press-credentialed photographer, Luciano Rossi, who regularly contributes game photographs to the site. In addition, founding member Luca brings his professional quality camera to the games and updates the site regularly with pictures from the Core de Roma seats in the north-east corner of the stadium. The quality of photographs posted on the site has led Core de Roma to place a watermark and copyright notice on photographs since photographs have been copied from the site, and used without authorization on other fan sites.

The Core de Roma website exhibits many photographs of fans both in the stadium and around the world. Pictures of banners and fan displays from the stadium as well as photographs of members at the club's banquets are posted online. The section entitled, *Core de Roma nel mondo*, publishes pictures of members brandishing their scarves on beaches and cliffs and in front of monuments and landmarks all over the world. In addition to a host of European capitals, Roma fans have sent in pictures from San Francisco's Golden Gate Bridge, New York's Empire State Building, Machu Picchu, Tokyo's Zoo and Egypt's pyramids. I contributed a photograph of myself with my Core de Roma scarf outstretched in front of Chicago's skyline. These photographs of fans glorify the role of the fan contribution to the construction of Roma.

Core de Roma houses digitally recorded chants and songs from the stadium. An entire section is dedicated to the dozens of *cori* (choruses) sung at the stadium. One of the most famous *cori* is based on the bass line from an American punk-influenced, rock song, 'Seven Nation Army', by the White Stripes. Roma fans copied this chant from the fans in Brugges, Belgium, who performed this chant during a UEFA cup game between Roma and their local team. The song was adopted by not only Roma fans, but by Italy fans during the World cup. The song became a national sensation and spurred record sales for the White Stripes in Italy. The Core de Roma website posted (illegally) the original song and a remake of the song turned chant created by an Italian DJ.[28] The site houses several mp3 audio files from the radio broadcasts of legendary Roma announcer, Carlo Zampa. His deep voice, Roman accent and incredible enthusiasm make listeners fear for his health when he calls out, 'Go-go-go-go-go-go-go-go-go goooaaaaaalll!'

Video is becoming an increasingly important part of the website. The older version of the site housed downloadable videos including short segments of goals from the 2000–2001 championship season. The new version of the website is developing a video section that houses downloadable video as well as links to YouTube and other video hosting sites. One such video uses the 'Seven Nation Army' fan cheer to accompany video images of Roma players and fans.

Romanità

Apart from the immensity of the archive of Roma fan-produced material housed on this site, what I find most compelling about this site is the combination of historical consciousness combined with the performance and cultivation of a brash Roman identity, or *Romanità*. This site not only displays a distinctly Roman identity, but cultivates this identity through textual and visual representations. A visitor to the site is educated in what a Roman is, aspires to be, and what a Roman is not.

Based on my reading of this site, a Roman has the following attributes:

- Proud of Roma the team and Rome the city, and often conflates the two.
- Combative in daily life and in defence of both team and city.
- Loyal to the team in good times and bad, with the expectation that there will be more bad days than good.
- Uses Roman dialect.
- Considers A.S. Roma to be the team of Rome, and not SS Lazio, Roma's intracity rival.
- Roots against Juventus, the wealthy team bankrolled by automaker Fiat and the aristocratic Agnelli family.
- Despises Napoli, the nearest major city and football rival.
- Considers team captain Francesco Totti to be the ideal embodiment of a Roman.

Proud of Rome and conflating the two

At the outset of every A.S. Roma home game, fans sing, '*Roma, Roma, Roma*..heart of this city, the one great love that takes the breath away from so many people …'.[29] This official team anthem, written by Antonello Venditti, ritually reaffirms the team's and the fans' attachment to city. The members of Core de Roma embrace and embellish this civic identity. In an attempt to explain what Roma fandom means, Luca said to me that 'Sometimes Roma (referring to the city) and La Roma (the team) become the same thing'.[30] Roma fans exhibit an immense pride in their city as well as their team. Club member, Claudia, wrote in an article, 'To be Romans and Roma fans is a modus vivendi, an attachment to a team, to a city'.[31]

The A.S. Roma football team was founded in 1927, 27 years after rivals, Lazio was founded. Lazio adopted blue and white colours in reference to Hellenic ideals of mind and body. Lazio was originally the team of politically right leaning, upper-class fans. Roma was founded in 1927, as the 'people's team'. The team was formed when three teams, Roman, Alba-Audace and Fortitudo, banded together.[32] The newly formed A.S. Roma adopted the official city colours, red and yellow, and the city's insignia of Romulus and Remus and the she-wolf. From the start, the team closely aligned itself with civic pride. Roma now has a bigger fan base and is still considered, (at least by Roma fans) as the people's team and the city's team. Romanisti criticize Laziali and their founders for passing on the opportunity to name their team after the most glorious city of all, and choosing instead, the less resplendent name of the region.

Romans are proud of their city and their history. Before Roma's match at Manchester United, Paoletta posted an article entitled 'We will teach them how to be fans', which she begins with the historical titbit, 'Manchester was founded in 79 AD by the Roman governor Julius Agricola'.[33] This reference to antiquity is evidence of the historical consciousness and knowledge of the Roma fans, and, in this case, gives Romans a sense of superiority over the 'young' English city. This historical citation was especially well timed as the fans were preparing to see their team play as the underdog against the powerful Manchester United football team in Manchester.

Core de Roma consistently uses symbols of imperial Rome such as the coliseum and images that depict players such as Francesco Totti, Gabriel Batistuta and Marco Del Vecchio as a gladiator. The front page image that changes several times a week often contains an image of a Roman soldier, the Coliseum or Vittorio Emanuele monument in the background. One typical homepage showed 'S.P.Q.R.' the initials for the Latin phrase, *Senatus Populusque Romanus* meaning 'The Senate and the People of Rome', inscribed in marble overwritten with the phrase *Core de Roma Gens Romana* (*Core de Roma* Roman people). Roman governments from ancient times to the present day inscribe S.P.Q.R. on public works. After a tough defeat, the homepage featured the image of a Roman soldier, sword unsheathed, accompanied by the words, 'Enough with licking our wounds. Now is the time to fight. Wherever and for ever, Go Roma!!'[34] For the 2008–2009 membership campaign, Core de Roma adopted the theme, *L'Ultima Legione*,[35] a reference to the pseudo-historical film about the 'last legion' of Roman soldiers that, after having disbanded in Britain, reformed to defend the honour of Rome. Core de Roma pasted the motto onto the season's scarf.

In a special section of the site, a collection of photographs documents an Imperial re-enactment that took place on the *Via Foro Imperiali*, in the vicinity of the Roman Forum and the Coliseum. Though this re-enactment had nothing to do with football directly, it is a vivid example of the Roman spirit that pervades Core de Roma.

Imperial Roman images solidify the connection between the team and the city, but the pictures of gladiators and Roman soldiers also symbolize the qualities that the fans want to see in their players – bravery, tenacity and loyalty. The tattoo section of the site showcases the tattoos of loyal Roma fans who have inscribed Roman soldiers, she-wolves, S.P.Q.R. and various other Romans symbols onto their skin.

Romans are combative and loyal

Co-founder Gigi explained to me that a fundamental part of being Roman is the combative and defiant spirit. He said, 'You may not always win, but you must continue to fight'. This attitude is adopted fully by Core de Roma. In fact, Core de Roma was founded partly as an act of defiance during a difficult time for A.S. Roma when they were struggling to win and their rivals, Lazio, were very strong. Roma fans have had to learn how to accept defeat while still taking pride in their team. Co-founder Luca commented, 'You do not become a Roma fan because they win a lot'. After a successful run in the European Champions league (the most prestigious intra-European competition) in spring, 2007, Roma suffered a humiliating 7–1 defeat at Manchester United's home field. Some of the initial postings on the Core de Roma chat room were predictably negative and pessimistic, but other Core de Roma members fought off this attitude with comments of defiance in the face of defeat. Romaniaco wrote, 'Whoever is ashamed to be a fan of AS Roma is not a fan and can cordially go fuck themselves'.[36] Orco wrote, 'The day that I am ashamed to be a Romanista has yet to arrive'.[37] Sciamano wrote with pride about how the fans at the game continued to support the team despite the scoreline. He wrote, 'While [we were] losing so badly, the fans sung Roma's anthem at Manchester's stadium, Old Trafford, and for this, we are Roma, and the others aren't worth a damn'.[38]

During this difficult time, Romaniaco reiterated in the chat room what Luca had said to me, that 'Whoever wants to always win had better not become a fan of Roma'.[39] These comments portray the defiant spirit and their embrace of the underdog status and are an implicit dig against rivals such as Juventus who boast a large fanbase around Italy, and who have, according to Roma fans, won championships through dishonourable means.[40] These Roma fans are accustomed to fighting but not necessarily winning. These remarks also demonstrate the power of the group to validate what are considered to be worthy remarks, while attacking and regulating anything that might contradict this constructed understanding of Roman-ness.

Throughout Italy, Romans have a reputation for being boisterous, rude and vulgar. Core de Roma embraces this identity and performs it in the chat room. Being a fan of Roma is an endeavour filled with play and playfulness. Fans make threats in jest and make exaggerated rhetorical claims about their own team and against others. While the threats may be hollow and the language exaggerated, this kind of play is key to creating an identity. The Core de Roma chat room is a relatively safe place to hone an identity that might be more bombastic than the circumstances of one's daily life would allow. One section of the site in particular actively promotes vulgar statements. Romans use the term *coatto*, to describe the style or set of mannerisms that might be translated as unrefined and trashy. Core de Roma reserves a portion of its site, named *Pallone Koatto* (Trashy Football) for the most vulgar comments and provocations. The use of the *K* instead of *C* in the intentional misspelling of *Koatta* is another indicator of the unofficial nature of this section. The site is introduced by this disclaimer: 'This section was born from the necessity to gather the typical language of the fan, who, transformed by the passion for their team, becomes ... *coatto*'.⁴¹ Entries are structured by listing a victim, motive and the *Koatto* remark. For example, Club member, Tiziano, targeted Roma for the motive of 'their craziness'. He wrote,

> Hey, they gotta renew Panucci's contract cuz he plays better at 35 years than at 23 ... but if he goes, you put Cicinho in his place?? C'mon and end this and renew his contract ... if you want Aquilani, don't give him a lira because a real Roman would play for free.'⁴²

A less discreet writer, Iacopo, targeted Paolo Di Canio and his statement that he would never coach Roma. In his *koatto* comment, Iacopo wrote, 'Guys, did you hear what Di Cagno said ... "Never and then never to Roma" ... to Di Cagno ... you are an ass'. The misspelled Di Cagno is a play on the word, *cagna*, the word for a female dog. While this section encourages fans to express their rage, the site moderators do set limits. *Pallone Koatto* warns readers not to send in messages that are grave insults, threats or anything else that 'cannot be published'.⁴³

Romanesco

As discussed previously, regional linguistic dialects endure despite efforts to standardize the language. While cultural forces may work against the diffusion of Roman dialect in official circles, the Core de Roma website is a testament to the persistence of dialect, and moreover, how it has become a badge of honour and identity for some. Roman slang is alternately called *Romano* (Roman), *Romanesco* (which refers to a literary tradition of Roman poetry associated with G.G. Belli and Trilussa) or *Romanaccio* (meaning slang or vulgar language). I prefer the term Romanesco, as it implies more artistry than the other terms.

Romanesco is a vibrant enactment of Roman culture, or *Romanità*. Though Romanesco is not commonly written today, in the Core de Roma chat room, it is the norm. All of the excerpts from the chat room cited above were written using Roman slang. The chat room is a unique documentation of a marginalized spoken language. It is, for the users of the chat room, a way to punctuate ideas and to express authenticity with its implied brashness and pure Roman-ness. Though Romanesco is intelligible by most Italians, it is still a barrier to the participation of outsiders not familiar with its intricacies. Romanesco spelling condenses certain words by removing vowels, such as in the name of the group, *Core de Roma*, which uses *core* in place of the standard *cuore* (heart).

The legendary comedic actor, Alberto Sordi, was closely associated with Roman dialect. Sordi was allegedly kicked out of a Milan acting school because of his thick Roman accent. Eventually, this accent would become his trademark as he made his name in the Italian comedies of the 1950s and 1960s. Sordi was beloved by Roma fans for his support of the team and for his embodiment of Roman culture. At Roma games, at least one banner in the stands depicts Sordi, his mouth stuffed with pasta, in his classic role as Nando in, *Un Americano a Roma* (An American in Rome).

In the film, Sordi plays a young Italian who loves America and wants to do everything like Americans. In this scene, he starts eating what he considers American foods such as milk, yogurt and bread with mustard. He eventually succumbs to the temptation of the plate of pasta that his mother has left for him on the table. His famous line, delivered in quintessential Roman dialect, is 'Maccarone, you have provoked me, and now I will eat you'.[44] Upon his death in 2003, Core de Roma devoted a special section of the website to his life. His funeral in Rome was attended by an estimated 250,000 people, and in the days following his death, the site saw more online traffic than when Roma won the championship in 2001. Core de Roma memorialized Sordi by naming the chat room after him, and by maintaining clips from his movies, and providing links to articles about him.

Rivals

Roma fans are defined, in part, by their rivalries with other teams. Roma's primary rivals are Lazio, Juventus and Napoli. Lazio is their despised crosstown rival. Juventus is the most successful team in Italian history. Napoli is their nearest big-city rival. The rivalry with Lazio comes to a head twice a year in the 'derby' game between the two sides. Since both teams share the same stadium, it is never really a home or away game. At these derby games, fans of both teams show up hours before the start in order to shout insults, sing derisive songs and display messages that mock their crosstown 'cousins'.

On the Core de Roma website, Lazio players and their fans are regular targets of visual and textual ridicule. Roma fans consider themselves true Romans, and often refer to Lazio fans as *burrini*, or the country bumpkins who used to come into the city to sell butter (*burro*). The front page image on the website on the day of one derby showed a flock of sheep to represent Lazio fans, marked with the caption, 'They are coming'.[45] Former Lazio player, Alessandro Nesta, was once Lazio's counterpart to Roma's Francesco Totti. Like Totti, Nesta is from Rome. He became Lazio's and Italy's star defensive player. Nesta was a prime target for Roma fans. For example, after a derby game, frequent contributor Bobodrum posted a fictitious *locandina* (poster) for a mock film entitled, 'The Man Who Fell on the Ground',[46] with a picture of Nesta belly down on the turf. More recently, Roma fans have targeted Lazio player, Paolo Di Canio, as their most hated figure. Di Canio is famous for giving his fans the Fascist salute on multiple occasions. In the *Romanisti nel Mondo* section is a photograph of three Roma fans who dug a message in the sand. It reads, 'Di Canio Piece of Crap'.[47] The site proudly displayed an animated image of Di Canio sitting on the Lazio bench with a grim look of his frustration on his face as his team was losing to Roma in the 26 February 2006 derby. Core de Roma's archive of images reflects the depth of the rivalry with Lazio that is sustained throughout the year.

Roma's rival Juventus is Italy's most popular team, though the team is generally despised by fans of every other team. Funded by the Agnelli family, owners of carmaker, Fiat, Juventus, are the opposite of Roma. Based in the northern city of Torino, Juventus is the team that *does* win all the time. Juventus is immensely popular throughout Italy and abroad, but lack a strong local following in Torino as many locals prefer the city's other team, FC Torino. Roma, on the other hand, are passionately followed by millions of Romans, yet, their national appeal and their record of success are much more modest. Fans throughout Italy have believed for decades that Juventus use their immense financial power to corrupt the league and its referees and to win through any means necessary. Fans' suspicions were partly substantiated by the recent scandals in which the Juventus team doctor was found guilty of doping Juventus players.[48] The more recent scandal involved the general manager of Juventus, Luciano Moggi, who was found guilty of unfairly influencing the assignment of referees and threatening to ruin the careers of referees that did not follow his instructions. Members of Core de Roma seized the opportunity to chronicle Moggi's demise by posting actual news accounts as well as comically altered images. For example, one image mimicked a credit card advertisement showing fake Juventus credit cards with the names of allegedly corrupt referees on them accompanied by the words, 'A real Juventus fan always has victory in his pocket'.[49] Another fake advertisement pictures Moggi speaking on his cell phone accompanied by the text, 'With the new Moggy plan, talk for free with all the referees at all times!'[50]

Romans have a natural geographical rivalry with the city of Naples. Naples is the nearest major city, reachable by train in less than two hours. To Romans, Naples is a chaotic and uncivilized city run by the Camorra, the Naples mafia. Naples has its own dialect that is even further removed from standard Italian than is Romanesco. For Romans, it is an insult to call someone *Napolitano* (Neapolitan) because of the city's association with crime, poverty and general lack of civility. On the Core de Roma website, there is a picture of Lazio player, Paolo Di Canio, holding up a scarf of Naples' football team.

Di Canio is one of Roma's most despised rivals for, among other things, being an outspoken critic of Roma fans and insisting that Lazio, and thereby himself, are the true Romans. The implication that Di Canio supports Napoli in any way is an unambiguous insult. In the chat room, one Core de Roma contributor wrote the lyrics to a chant often heard in Roma's *curva sud*, even when playing a team other than Lazio, 'PAOLO DI CANIO NAPOLETANO ... PAOLO DI CANIO NAPOLETANO ... PAOLO DI CANIO NAPOLETANO ... CURSE YOUR ANCESTORS ALWAYS AND FOREVER'.[51] The writer adds the Roman curse that, unfortunately, does not translate very well into English. The rivalry with the team, S.S.C. Napoli, was on hiatus in the 2005–2006 season, because Napoli was playing in a lower division due to a financial meltdown, and therefore, was not the target of much derision. More recently, the rivalry between Naples and Rome has been fierce on and off the pitch. The rivalry between fans is such that both sets of fans have been banned from travelling to support their team in this match up. The matches have also been scheduled during the day to minimize potential violence.

Totti

Roma fans regard Francesco Totti as the living embodiment of what it means to be Roman. He was born and raised in a working class neighbourhood of Rome and speaks with a thick Roman accent. He is combative on the field, and he is loyal to Roma. Totti, who turned 38 during the 2014–2015 season, made his professional debut with the team when he was just 16 years old. He was given the Romanesco nickname, *er bimbo de oro* (the golden boy) or *er pupone* (the big kid). In the time since, he has become the indisputable leader and captain of Roma. He was also a stalwart of the Italian national team and is recognized as one of the most talented players of his generation, worldwide. Aside from his football talents, Totti is known for his thick Roman accent and for his alleged lack of intelligence. In an infamous interview, a journalist asked Totti, in Italian, if his philosophy could be summarized by the Latin saying, *Carpe Diem*. Totti responded that he could not answer because did not speak English. Roma fans, however, view this aspect of Totti as part of his good-natured naiveté rather than as an intellectual shortcoming.

Roma fans idolize Totti because of his fighting spirit on the field and because of his loyalty to A.S. Roma. While most stars tend to migrate to one of a handful of Europe's biggest club teams, Totti has refused offers to play at the biggest clubs in Milan and Madrid, preferring to stay at Roma for his entire career to date. Totti's retirement from the national team after the triumphant 2006 World Cup was justified, at least for Roma fans, by his desire to save his energy for Roma. Totti also mentioned the overly critical treatment of his performances by the northern press as a reason for his premature international retirement. His criticism of the north also plays well with his Roman fans.

Throughout Italy, Totti is a celebrity off the field, much in the mould of David Beckham. Totti is a sex symbol. A search on Google reveals shirtless images of Totti's body and an unofficial history of his various hairdos. Totti married the celebrity/model, Ilary Blasi. Their courtship, marriage and the birth of their children were and are prime fodder for Italian tabloids. Totti is featured in advertisements for a variety of products including cars, and cell phones in addition to football shoes and athletic clothing. Recently, he and his wife have started their own clothing brand, Never Without You. Though mocked for his lack of intelligence, he has turned the jokes aimed at him into a best-selling joke book, entitled, *All the Jokes About Totti*, of which the profits go to the UNICEF charity.[52] To his supporters, this act of charity exemplifies Totti's essential good nature. Unlike David Beckham, Totti has not become an international icon. While there are surely many reasons for this, one of the primary reasons is that Totti does not speak English, and he has not left Rome for the brighter lights (at least in football terms) of Manchester or Milan, Barcelona or Madrid. Totti remains distinctly Roman.

Core de Roma pays homage to Totti by posting pictures, screensavers, video, interviews and news items about him. The older version of the website had a section dedicated entirely to photographs of him. On the site alone, the search engine tracks 380 hits for his name. One notable Totti item is a video compilation of Totti's goals in the 2007 season when he won the Golden Shoe as Europe's leading goal scorer. The website also features a picture of two baristas that crafted a replica golden shoe to display in their bar in honour of him. Several pictures of Core de Roma members posing for a picture with Totti are included. Another addition is a picture of Totti at the San Remo music festival with a Core de Roma scarf draped on his seat. One particularly striking photograph shows Totti holding a book assembled by Core de Roma entitled *1000 Good Wishes* that consisted of fans' messages of encouragement for their injured *Capitano*. One cartoon caricature posted on the site comments, 'I went to the Louvre to see if there was the goal by Totti at Sampdoria among the masterpieces'. For Totti's birthday, two fans made a banner exclaiming, 'Congratulations Captain. Thank you for being'.[53] The image of Totti is the image of Rome and Roma combined. In the same way that Roma fans fail to distinguish between Rome the city and Roma the team, they have an equally difficult time distinguishing Totti from Roma or Roma from Totti.

Rome vs. Italy?

The discourse on the Core de Roma website concerning Totti's retirement from the Italian national team is emblematic of Romans' hostile, or at best, ambiguous feelings towards the nation. In a survey hosted by the Core de Roma website, almost 80% of the 2500 respondents were happy about his retirement, while 20% thought

Totti should continue to play for the national team. This response is indicative of the common preference of the local over national concerns. On the Core de Roma chat room, members often display contempt for the nation. Italy was a finalist in its bid to host the 2012 European Cup, but Italy lost to a joint bid by Hungary and Ukraine. On this day, the response was to ridicule Italy. Romatto wrote, 'Ha! These jerks really thought that they would have assigned the Euro Cup after all that has happened between the scandal and the fights outside the stadium??? What idiots'.[54] Criticism of the nation goes beyond mere football concerns. Chat room user, *er Pasquino* wrote, 'We must not wait for a European cup or World Cup to improve things in Italy. Now we need to do this without these resources'. The comment reflects dissatisfaction with Italy's basic infrastructure and a call to improve things without the financial influx that an internationally funded and attended tournament would provide. In some contexts, football is a cultural institution that can sew together the strands of a nation, but it can also invigorate local affiliation and rivalry that are antithetical to national unity. In the case of Core de Roma, the themes of civic pride and localism are much stronger than the themes of nationalism.

Conclusion

Core de Roma represents a technological and generational split from the Roma Club Testaccio. Whereas the members of the Roma Club Testaccio carve a club identity out of the neighbourhood they live in, Core de Roma develops their identity in an online forum since club members tend to live on the periphery of Rome. For them, the internet and mobile phones are integrated into their social lives. Unlike Testaccio, they use the web as a resource for reinventing community. Core de Roma strives to replicate the authentic mode of fandom exemplified by the Roma Club Testaccio. Instead of being geographically alienated, Core de Roma expresses a profound attachment to the city of Rome, as explicitly stated through commentaries, or expressed through visual and linguistic signifiers. Members of Core de Roma have invented ways to foreground their performance of *Romanità* since they cannot simply live it like those in Testaccio. As professional football globalizes, expanding its commercial appeal around the globe, attracting multinational sponsors, foreign investors and mercenary players, Core de Roma demonstrates a persistent attachment to the local and the desire for place-based identity.

One of the arguments of this volume has been that all media are social. Newspaper, radio and television are social in that they can give people common knowledge with which to interact, at least in the case of radio and TV, can be consumed in social settings. Internet technologies have, perhaps, increased the speed and immediacy of media sociality, but they also demonstrate the continuity of socialization. Groups like Core de Roma do not use their website as a substitute for the face-to-face meetings, but rather as a facilitator of sociality. The group demonstrates some of the best qualities of media: the fans produce and consume – they have contributed to a beautiful online 'home' that displays their pride in place. They have real community – they use the site not only to organize meetings for themselves, but to mobilize their members to help in charity and other pro-social campaigns. Finally, the site is able to bridge the local and global. Contributors to the site are scattered throughout the world, but are able to participate in some form of Romanita online.

Their use of the internet reflects a modern and mobile lifestyle, but not a lifestyle that disregards the importance of place and history. Conversely, the website displays an immense pride in Roman culture and offers multiple avenues to participate in *la magica* of Rome. The site represents a flexible formation of community that is evolving everyday to meet the desires of its local and global membership. Club member, Big Bastard, wrote in the chat room, 'There are good days and bad days … but tomorrow, I will wake up in Rome, and I'll always have these colors (of A.S. Roma) in my heart … and that's enough for me'.[55] While I can only dream of waking up in Rome, I share his adoration of the colours. Sitting at a café, I can join with others to exercise my own passion for Roma and La Roma by logging into the Core de Roma website. Rather than a break from the past, the website offers continuity to the spirit of A.S. Roma that started in Testaccio and now extends even to Juneau, Alaska or Bloomington, Indiana.

Disclosure statement
No potential conflict of interest was reported by the author.

Notes
1. Haisley, 'Francesco Totti Scores with Flying Kung Fu Kick'.
2. The idealized version of a fan is a construct used sporadically in this volume to refer to the unattainable ideal of fandom that includes comprehensive knowledge and unbridled passion. Though unattainable, it offers a model for behaviour for fans.
3. Ritzer and Jurgenson reinvigorated the term, a portmanteau of production and consumption in 'Production, Consumption, Prosumption'.
4. Giulianotti, *Football: A Sociology of the Global Game*, 150.
5. See the next chapter on branding for an extended discussion of a fight for the brand.
6. Turkle, *Alone Together*.
7. See, for example Edensor and Millington, 'This is Our City'.
8. See any number of examples, including Manchester United's deal with the New York Yankees baseball team.
9. See Boellstorff, *Coming of Age in Second Life*, 17 for a discussion of the definition and ramifications of the term 'Virtual'.
10. Translated from Core de Roma site, *COREdeROMA non è soltanto un sito web. Dietro c'è un gruppo di amici che nella vita si incontrano abitualmente. Siamo sempre presenti all'Olimpico, nei distinti nord lato Tevere, dove campeggia ormai da anni il nostro striscione. L'incitamento e i colori, i nostri, si fanno sentire e vedere anche nelle trasferte.*
11. Taylor, *Play Between Worlds*, 18.
12. Wellman and Gulia, 'Virtual Communities as Communities', 187.
13. Wellman, 'Little Boxes'.
14. Founding members Luca, Gigi, Maurizio and Stefano are listed by their nicknames on the credits page, http://www.corederoma.it/online/?page_id=332.
15. At the club dinners, members exchange assorted A.S. Roma-related items that might include a photograph or a DVD of game highlights.
16. As of 2006, Internet access in Italy was not widely available, particularly in private homes. Public wireless 'hot spots' were also difficult to find.
17. After I explained to the carabinieri that I was connecting to a wireless internet 'hot spot', one of the officers complained that there was a problem with my computer. It turns out, he was a fan of the Juventus football team, and he did not like the A.S. Roma sticker on my laptop. In an encounter with a different Carabinieri officer, he asked me where he could get a stronger wi-fi signal.
18. One of Paoletta's relatives is married to one of Totti's relatives.
19. I edited and wrote a few short articles for an Italian website that published in English.
20. My key informant and friend, Luca, is of African descent.

21. The boy suffered from a form of Leukodystrophia. More information can be found at the site, http://www.aiutiamoedoardo.it.
22. The Malawi campaign website.
23. Jenkins, *Textual Poachers*, 23.
24. Original text: *80 anni di passione.*
25. Original text: *Grande Festa Grande Emozioni! ... Roma Bella Ti Amo.*
26. The section *Miscellanea – Parlano di Noi*, contains links to articles that mention Core de Roma. http://www.corederoma.net/motore/showcat.php?Category=51.
27. Andrea Pandolfini, '*Foto video e cori ...*' Il Romanista 2 July 2006 Original text: '*CoreDeRoma.it è senza dubbio uno dei siti più completi e aggiornati dedicati alla squadra giallorossa'.*
28. The .mp3 file for Seven Nation Army is not available for download on the current version of the site.
29. Original text: *Roma, Roma, Roma, core de 'sta citta, unico grande amore che tanta e tanta gente, che fai sospira.*
30. Original text: *Roma e La Roma diventa la stessa cosa. Roma* is the Italian word for Rome, while *la Roma* refers to the football team.
31. Original text: *Essere romani e romanisti è un* modus vivendi, *è appartenenza ad una squadra, ad una città.* from the article, *Come Reagire allo Sfacelo*.
32. For history of A.S. Roma, see http://www.asromaultras.it/storia.html.
33. Original text: *Manchester fu fondata nel 79 d.C. dal governatore romano Giulio Agricola, che stabilì un forte chiamato Mamucium.*
34. Original text: *Basta leccarsi le ferite..e ora di combattere. Ovunque e per sempre Forza Roma!!*
35. Released in the US as The Last Legion (2007).
36. Original text:*Chi si vergogna di essere tifoso della Roma non e un tifoso e puo cordialment annassene affanculo.*
37. Original text: *Er giorno che me vergognero de esse ROMANISTA ANCORE DEVE DA ARIVA.*
38. Original text: *Sotto in quell modo e I ragazzi che cantavano l'inno della Roma all'old Trafford. E' PER QUESTO CHE NOI SEMO ROMA E L'ARTRI NUN SONO UN CAZZO* (04 October 07 22.47.22 message# 243885).
39. Original text: *Chi vuole vince sempre non deve diventare tifoso della Roma.*
40. For example, I purchase a T-shirt from a different fan group that reads, 'Juve ti odio' (Juventus I hate you) on the front, and 'C'hai fatto l'EPOca' (You are EPOchal). EPO is a doping drug that Juventus' doctors were alleged to have given to players.
41. Pallone Koatto, http://www.corederoma.it/pallonekoatto/index.php.
42. Translated loosely from Pallone Coatto post on 8 January 2008, by username Tiziano. Original text: *La vittima è: a roma Motivo: sta npazzita Koattata: ao a panucci o dovete rinnova sto contratto gioca mejo lui a 35 anni che certi a 23 ... ma poi se se ne va che ci mettete cicinho?? ma fatela finita e rinnovate sto contratto ... se volete ad aquilani nn je date na lira xke un vero romano gioca pure a gratise.*
43. Original text: *non scrivete 'vediamo se mi pubblicate' 'se avete il coraggio' etc. che chiaramente non pubblichiamo.* http://www.corederoma.it/pallonekoatto/index.php.
44. Translated from original text in Roman dialect, *Maccarone, m'hai provocato e io me te magno.*
45. Original text: *Stanno Arrivando.*
46. Original text: *L'uoma che cadde su terra.*
47. Original text: *Di Canio Pezzo di Merda.*
48. BBC, 'Juve Doctor Guilty'.
49. Original text: *Un vero Juventino ha sempre la vittoria in tasca.*
50. Original text: *Con la tariffa Moggi Parla sempre gratis con tutti i arbitri.*
51. Roughly translated from the Roman curse: *Mortacce tua.*
52. Totti, *Tutte le Barzellette su Totti.*
53. Original text: *'Auguri Capitano Grazie di Esistere'.*
54. Original text: *Ma davvero sti cojoni se credevano che all'Italia avrebbero assegnato gli europeo dopo tutto quello che è successo tra calciopoli e scontri negli stadi??? Che subnormali!*

55. Original text: *'ce stanno I giorni belli e quelli brutti ... ma io domain me svejo a ROMA..e c'ho sempre quei colori dentro er core ... e tanto me basta'* CdR Muro, 4 October 2007 22.53.13 #243902.

References

BBC. 'Juve Doctor Guilty in Drugs Case'. *BBC Online*, November 26, 2004. http://news.bbc.co.uk/sport2/hi/football/europe/4045525.stm (accessed March 10, 2015).

Boellstorff, T. *Coming of Age in Second Life: An Anthropologist Explores the Virtually Human*. Princeton, NJ: Princeton University Press, 2008.

Edensor, T., and S. Millington. '"This is Our City": Branding Football and Local Embeddedness'. *Global Networks* 8, no. 2 (2008): 172–93.

Giulianotti, R. *Football: A Sociology of the Global Game*. Malden, MA: Blackwell, 1999.

Haisley, B. 'Francesco Totti Scores with Flying Kung Fu Kick'. http://www.screamer.deadspin.com (accessed January 11, 2015).

Jenkins, H. *Textual Poachers: Television Fans and Participatory Culture*. New York: Routledge, 1992.

Ritzer, G., and N. Jurgenson. 'Production, Consumption, Prosumption: The Nature of Capitalism in the Age of the Digital 'prosumer''. *Journal of Consumer Culture* 10, no. 1 (2010): 13–36.

Taylor, T.L. *Play between Worlds: Exploring Online Game Culture*. Boston, MA: MIT Press, 2006.

Totti, F. *Tutte le Barzellette su Totti: Raccolte da me*. Milan: Mondadori, 2003.

Turkle, S. *Alone Together: Why We Expect More from Technology and Less from Each Other*. New York: Basic Books, 2011.

Wellman, B. 'Little Boxes, Glocalization, and Networked Individualism.' In *Digital Cities II*, ed. M. Tanabe, P. Besselaar, and T. Ishida, 10–25. Berlin: Springer, 2002.

Wellman, B., and M. Gulia. 'Virtual Communities as Communities: Net Surfers Don't Ride Alone'. In *Communities in Cyberspace*, ed. M.A. Smith and P. Kollock, 167–94. London: Routledge, 1999.

The football brand dilemma

> Brands symbolize our market-dominated, globalizing world. Football brands are particularly well suited for an economy of attention where branded goods are worth more because of their connection to abstract ideas. Football is media friendly, and, in its current incantations, corporate friendly. While football teams are bound to particular places such as Manchester or Madrid, they garner massive global TV audiences that dwarf the in-stadium crowd. The ambivalent relationship between a football team and a place is a hallmark of our times. Football teams are community goods – they require people to give them value and meaning, but what people and where? What happens when fans attempt to go from symbolic to real owners of a team? The mutiny of a group of Lazio fans serves as an illustration of the tension between the performance of fandom and the market logics of branding.

This volume has catalogued the various media that fans use to connect with their object of affection and, as I have repeatedly asserted, with each other. Fans consume, create and circulate stadium banners, newspapers, radio broadcasts and websites all as a way to connect with their team, to perform their identities as fans and to cultivate fan communities. Fans are exposed to a mulitiplicity of media that contribute to and compete to convey the *meaning* of the team. Fans might think of their team's essence in familiar terms, such as *la magica*, or they might refer to *the colours* as a purified abstraction distinct from the current instantiations of management, marketing or players. For marketers, however, the team's bottom line economic value is determined by the brand – the symbol of value in the twenty-first century economy. The brand is the umbrella that encompasses the various mediated and non-mediated narratives of a business or other entity. If brand managers are successful, the brand becomes an overarching narrative that invokes the positive aspects of a set of products or services. Sports teams are provocative examples of brands. They attempt to tie together disparate products – game tickets, TV subscriptions and merchandise with the illusory concepts that gives the products meaning and economic value – nostalgic history and local pride combined with the performances and personalities of players, and, ideally, moments of triumph. The brand synthesizes the history of the club and the experiences of fans into a narrative; this is invoked and monetized by slogans and trademarked logos that differentiate each team.

This chapter approaches sport teams and their supporters first from the lens of marketing and branding. This perspective defines supporters as loyal customers and potential commodities who can contribute to the economic value of the brand. Next, the analysis shifts away from a top-down, business-orientation to the perspective of fan studies – an approach that emphasizes the 'grassroots' or 'ground up' work of fans as meaning-producers who use fandom for their own uses. Professional brand managers whose job it is to build 'brand equity' are constantly developing new ways to harness the power of fandom. They have a potentially fraught task: they seek to incorporate into the brand the economically desirable aspects of fan participation while working to limit the potential damage to the brand that fans can inflict if they feel disaffected. From the perspective of brand managers, it is best if fans *feel* connected to the team, while they observe the distance mandated by the legal and social regimes of private capital in the neoliberal world. The *ideal fan* passionately and loyally supports and even promotes the team, but never attempts to make substantive claims to ownership or participation in the management of the team. The ideal team organization, from a fans' perspective, might be one that is successful on the pitch, serves the fans, and, in general, functions for the good of the community rather than for private profit. Fans yearn to be a part of something bigger than themselves but they are also weary of being exploited by the indifferent mechanisms of capital. The case study of Lazio's ultras, the Irriducibili, illustrates a dispute between football fans and an owner of a football team. This example dramatizes the tensions and contradictions that are inherent in the construction of the modern brand that relies on fans/customers.

What is a brand?

Brands are comprised essentially of signifiers that, if successful, create value. In the most basic model of market economics, the value of a good or service is defined by what the consumer will pay (where supply meets demand) rather than by the cost of material or the labour involved in producing said good or service. An essential, if not primary, purpose of a brand is to increase the amount of money a consumer will pay for an item by bestowing cultural meaning upon the item. In the early stages of branding, logos and labelling were used to distinguish items from their competitors – e.g. the smiling and resassuring face of Quaker oats as opposed to just oats. The brand came to replace face-to-face interaction with a merchant at the store who might actually recommend an item. A successful brand might create a bond of trust between a 'smiling' oat producer and a consumer. Brands developed slogans and jingles and, eventually, well-orchestrated media campaigns in order to construct an aura of desirability around a product. Desirability can take many forms such as superior quality or value or exclusivity, etc. Some of the most effective branding campaigns of our times no longer make direct reference to products at all. Instead they conjure cultural or aspirational values and subtly connect them to detached logos. For example, Nike commercials often focus on running or sweating rather than on footwear. The 'It' in 'Just Do It' is never clearly defined. The consumer gets to fill in the 'It' with something exciting or triumphant or worthy. Certain brands become so well known that they become shorthand for features of a society. Douglas Holt dubs brands that enter into the lexicon of culture, *iconic brands* – that is, commodities that 'help [consumers] express who they want to be'.[1] In certain cultural contexts, wearing the right Nike shoes gives one instantly recognizable cultural capital. Much of the recent literature on branding focuses on the social aspects of brands. Word of mouth advertising, socially 'viral' media,[2] and brand communities are all buzz words that point to the increasing recognition on the part of brand managers to value the (virtual or real) friend-to-friend, neighbour-to-neighbour communication that can so effectively build awareness (buzz), persuade consumers and sell product.

Sport teams as brands

Sport teams are ideal candidates for the twenty-first century branding economy because they are media friendly, corporate friendly, globally friendly and require few, if any, material assets.[3] Sport is so amenable to media that media companies are now, in many respects, beholden to sport, as I will argue below. Sports are visible manifestations of human drama that are distilled into discrete packages. Sports can be packaged and repackaged into highlight reels and documentaries or they can be used to sell advertisements in long-form, live matches. Newspapers, radio stations and magazines can garner audiences by analysing or glorifying sporting contests past, present and future. Sport continually and reliably provides content in the form of gossip and drama to media outlets. Sport are ideally suited for the increasingly global dissemination of media and of global exchange in general. Sport (and its attendant brands) can transcend national and linguistic barriers. Many sports, including football, are regulated by international rules that make the games recognizable and meaningful to global audiences. Unlike movies or sit-coms, the football match needs no translation, though, each linguistic region can provide commentators to narrate the action on the field, just in case. These aspects of sport make it amenable to the global flow of media and money that are hallmarks of the twenty-first century. Finally, sport teams require few, if any, material assets. If you owned a football team, what would you own? You might own a stadium and a training ground, but perhaps not. You would not actually own players or managers and you might not even own an office. What you would likely possess is a series of contracts with a league, players, managers, jersey makers, sponsors, municipal stadium owners and perhaps the owners of a clubhouse and football fields where your team can train. Your most valuable asset would probably be the intellectual property of a logo or two that you could slap onto jerseys or lease out to widget makers. The advantages of not owning any material assets are that you can change the business with relative ease. Contracts for players expire, coaches can be fired, and at least in European football, your team can be relegated or promoted to a different level of competition. In the USA, you can even more your team across the continent and you may not even have to design new uniforms, as the name Dodgers seems to work the same for baseball teams in 1950s Brooklyn as it does in 2015 Los Angeles.[4] You might have to replace your spurned old customers with eager new ones if the government of city X will offer you better subsidies than your current city. As a phenomenon of neoliberal global capitalism, brands like Nike have essentially whittled their labour down to creative product designers and media makers as they outsource the production of their products to faraway places with cheaper labour. Sport team brands are well suited to this new way of business as they are worth so much, yet are so flexible because they possess so little in terms of physical assets.

What do sport teams actually sell? The primary consumer 'products' of a sport team are tickets for live performances (matches), television/media content, and licensed merchandise. The least expandable of these are live match tickets as stadiums can only accommodate a limited number of fans, but prices, at least in the premier league, keep going up.[5] In addition to the ubiquitous official, and pricy, jerseys, fans can buy licensed merchandise ranging from coffee mugs to credit cards that bear the colours and logo of their team. Sport team marketers keep pushing to find new products to sell to new markets. Sport fits nicely with the business plans of television networks that need to draw large audiences to pay subscription fees, watch advertisements or ideally, both.[6] The marriage between sport and television is an integral part of the 'sport-media complex'.[7] The sale price of exclusive television rights has risen dramatically in the last two decades[8] as TV networks have found sport to be relatively cheap to produce and to be the one form of content that draws reliable audiences in an age of media overload. Sport matches are more likely to be watched live, and they attract desirable young male consumers who are prone to buy beer, energy drinks and high calorie, low-quality food.

The magic of the sport brand is that each product promotes the others. Television broadcasts act as advertisements for tickets and jerseys. Stadiums become shopping malls as they sell products to the dedicated consumers that have already paid the price of admission. Though once considered childish, it has long become socially acceptable for middle-class adults to wear the distinctive jersey of their favourite team on the streets of London and other otherwise fashionable cities. The parade of colour and logos on the streets helps to build and maintain brand recognition, and contributes to the sales of subscription television packages and match tickets. The football jersey reminds us of the other major revenue stream for football teams – sponsorship deals. Football teams lease out the front of their jerseys to the highest (socially acceptable) bidder. The faithful fan/consumer then, in effect, purchases a billboard when they buy the official team jersey with the official sponsor as the centrepiece of the design. Let us not forget that the sportswear brands pay large sums of money for the right to provide the team with their uniforms as well as auxiliary sportswear. While fans might take pride in their fidelity to one team, Nike and Adidas are openly promiscuous as they sponsor dozens of professional teams across the football playing continents as they try to connect their brand to the idea of sport. Sport is rife with co-branding as the potential brand 'synergies' between a team, a jersey-making brand, and a jersey sponsor are, I am sure, calculated in an office somewhere. The jersey is just one advertising space available for lease from the team. In-stadium advertising on placards and stadium-sized screens are standard while out of the stadium, commercial endorsements are another. In my head, I hear the words, '(CATCHY NAME) is the official (PRODUCT) of the (CITY, TEAM)'. Sports are generally seen as corporate-friendly because they display values that corporations would like to promote such as teamwork, meritocracy and dedication not to mention hierarchy. Football is well positioned for corporate sponsorship because it is, at least in comparison to boxing or mixed martial arts, non-violent and generally socially acceptable.

The sport team brand relies, to an extent, on the individual player brand. David Beckham is the poster child for this argument. His footballing talent was superceded only by his marketability. As a good-looking, working-class boy turned celebrity husband and father, Beckham was a marketing dream.[9] Star players develop their own brand in conjunction and in confrontation with team brands. It has been suggested that Beckham was hired by Real Madrid less to bend free kicks than to sell jerseys in Asia. Michael Jordan became synonymous with Nike, yet, had to wear the gear of the US Olympic sponsor at the 1992 games. Jordan agreed to wear the gear if he could cover the logo. Over-reliance on individual players can be a team liability as the career of a player is inevitably limited by age if not injury. Other players may publicly embarrass themselves and hurt their corporate-friendly image (see Tiger Woods), or worse.[10]

Perhaps the most succinct representation of the brand economy of football is captured in David Beckham's Real Madrid, jersey ca. 2003. His number 23 is a symbolic nod to personal idol, Michael Jordan, a man who immortalized #23 and blazed a trail of global sport marketing. The Real Madrid crest is one of, if not, *the* most powerful sport brands in the world, and is one of the most well-known brand logos, in general, in the world. The classic white jersey with black lettering along with a logo of the crown over purple signifies the 'royal' aspect of Madrid Club de Fútbol as the club was 'anointed' by King Alfonso XIII in 1920. The team's later connection to the Franco dictatorship is now out of fashion.[11] The Siemens Mobile on the chest of the jersey points directly to the sponsorship of a German mobile phone maker. The logo also references the vagaries of global capitalism as Siemens Mobile was sold to a Taiwanese company in 2005, and went bankrupt in 2006. The three black stripes on the shoulder and the logo on the upper right of the jersey signify the German giant of sportswear branding, Adidas. While the German company's triangular logo is proudly displayed, the country of manufacture is hidden on the inside, as the jersey was made by contractors, most likely in a developing Asian country, and quite possibly in what could be described as a sweat shop. This, of course, represents the less glamorous side of the global economy. The logo of the LFP, the Spanish professional soccer league, is attached to the right sleeve as a reminder that the jersey is connected to an actual sporting competition. Last but certainly not least, the black-lettered Beckham on the back culminates the synergies of co-branding as Brand Beckham meets Brand Adidas-Real Madrid-Siemens-LFP (minus foreign contractor unknown). Beckham conjures images of many concepts including haircuts, style, a pop-star marriage, free-kicks and global Britishness, if such a thing exists. We should also mention Pepsi and Gillette and his other endorsements.[12] With all of this advertising, you think they could give these jerseys away, but alas, they sold for roughly 100USD around the globe.

While sport teams brands are well known to highlight their local ties, many of them yearn to sell products the world over. I have written in Chapters 1 and 3 about the ways in which a football club can catalyse a profound sense of local pride.[13] In a globalizing world, sport can provide a sense of locality and differentiation. For example, the English football team, Manchester City created an 'Our City' campaign employing slogans such as 'Pure Manchester' and '100% Manchester' to brand themselves as *more authentically Manchester* than 'city' rivals, and global brand par excellence, Manchester United, who play their home matches outside the bounds of the city, in the borough of Trafford.[14] Manchester City's claim to localness might seem bizarre considering that they are essentially funded by middle-eastern oil and their squad of players features an international collection of talent with remarkably few British citizens, never mind residents of Manchester. Claims to local authenticity are often relative.

In their efforts to create a sense of identity, sport team brands cultivate a sense of nostalgia and myth. Sport teams highlight their past triumphs as a hedge against the vagaries of the present. Teams are known to trot out old players, build statues and create media representations that commemorate the heroes of yore. In the USA, teams regularly hang banners that mark past victories, 'retire' the jersey numbers of past great players, and, in some circumstances, name the field after a past player or coach. American Baseball is a particularly backward looking enterprise as amateur (and more recently, professional) statisticians[15] argue over the numbers of the past as compared to the present. Players such as Babe Ruth have become mythological beings. One of the advantages of the early history of the game is that while there is plenty of statistical evidence to pore over, there is comparatively little video of the performance of past legends. Much of what is circulated about Ruth and his larger than life presence comes from the unreliable stories of adults who saw Ruth play when they were children and from hyperbolic newspaper reports. Ruth's aura as player lives in the imagination more than in the evidence. The New York Yankees brand is imbued with the legends of Ruth and Lou Gehrig, Joe Di Maggio and Mickey Mantle. The recently retired shortstop, Derek Jeter, was the anointed heir to this legacy during his 20 year playing career. Jeter was a key member of the team during a resurgence that included five championships. He was marketed as a cleancut, humble star as he was able to keep his personal life away tawdry headlines. As the Yankees have struggled (by their standards) in the past few years, Jeter's retirement became a 162 game, 'relentlessly marketed unquestionably lucrative retirement tour'[16] that included ceremonies at every venue along the way. Fans could buy Jeter's game-worn socks or plaques with dirt from the playing field along with any number of objects that Jeter touched, signed or breathed upon. As one marketing researcher remarked, Jeter's six-month-long retirement party represents a new branding opportunity: 'This is the "feel-good" type of story that brands really pay for'.[17]

While the success of marketing schemes like Jeter's make fans look like cultish fools who seek salvation in consumer products, scholar Henry Jenkins' work has gone to great lengths to defend and re-cast fandom.[18] Jenkins trumpets the ways in which fans take popular culture characters and contexts, and re-write them to suit their own needs. Fans become creative producers in their own right. Though Jenkins writes little about sports fans, this volume provides plenty of evidence that sport fans are actively involved in creating images, banners and other auxiliary texts that complement and extend the meaning of the football team. Aided by the advent of the internet, fans gather online to celebrate and critique Star Trek as well as Bayern Munich. These 'virtual communities' are where Jenkins' concept of 'participatory culture' is most evident. Participatory culture is Jenkins' term that describes the ways in which fans co-create the meaning of texts. This concept directly challenges the received notion of the passive consumer who simply absorbs spoon-fed content. Jenkins' critique embraces fans' agency and their ability to not only to re-interpret messages, but to actively and creatively resist and re-purpose messages. Online fan communities become a place of solidarity where fans can share ideas and ultimately, hone identities.

Jenkins' idealistic account of fandom (for fans, by fans) is fundamentally threatened by the logic of capitalism that provides incentive to monetize any potential source of value. Fans generate an incredible amount of content, most of it without the aim of financial compensation. Fans do it for themselves and to create status within fan communities. The potential value of fan contributions has not gone unnoticed by brand managers. The concept of 'brand communities'[19] took note of the ways in which fans of products such as Jeep off road vehicles would gather to exchange knowledge and celebrate their bonds enthusiasts. While 'Brand Communities' might have glorified a 'do-it-yourself' ethos that had a vague sense of resistance, these communities were also identified by brand managers as a source of free marketing labour. Doubtless, businesses have courted loyal consumers since the beginning of organized markets, but the art of 'leveraging'[20] (i.e. exploiting) the labour and passion of fans has gone into hyper-drive in the age of instantly social media. Elsewhere, I have adopted the concept of brandom to describe the kind of brand manager-engineered sociality that seeks to create a pseudo 'participatory culture/brand community' that can be controlled as to not threaten the value of the brand.

As Jenkins asks, 'Where does grassroots culture end and commercial culture begin?'[21] Where can we draw the line between a public good and a private good when it comes to public–private entities that rely on community support? In the realm of football, this question is asked every week in the stadiums as fans, and in particular, ultràs try to take part in 'the team'. A.S. Roma player, Seydou Keita, said that a football club consists of three things: the administration, the players and the fans.[22] While undoubtedly sincere in his request for fan support, Keita did not discuss the direction of the flow of money that goes from fans to the administration to the players. The Irriducibili ultras of Lazio were not content with this arrangement, and fought to take control of the team.

History of *ultràs*

In the late 1990s and into the 2000s, the north end of Rome's Olympic stadium was home to one of football's most exuberant and notorious group of supporters. Devotees of Rome's S.S. Lazio gathered in their end of the stadium to cheer, to socialize, to raise banners, to sing choruses, to insult opposing players, to orchestrate magnificent displays and to occasionally disrupt the football match.[23] They were active participants in the football spectacle. Lazio fans were led by the *Irriducibili* (Indomitables), an organized ultrà group composed primarily of ardent young men who supported the team, and who socialized inside and away from the stadium. In 2005, the Irriducibili initiated protests against the owner of the team, Claudio Lotito. They organized a campaign against him including protest marches and a fan 'strike'. They railed against Lotito in newsletters, videos and on the radio. The Irriducibili envisioned an identity for themselves as resistance fighters pitted against the powerful and corrupt, Lotito. Through their activity and organization, they threatened the power of Lazio's owner. The Irriducibili were, however, far from left-wing, anti-capitalist revolutionary Marxists. They implicated themselves within the lucrative business of top-level football. Their attempted revolt exposed fissures in the conduct of sports teams as businesses that rely on emotionally invested fans.

Ultràs[24] are organized football fan groups known for passionate, well-organized and occasionally militant support of their team. At the stadium, they defend their 'turf' against ultràs of the opposing team. They create much of the atmosphere at football games through their constant singing and shouting and through massive coordinated displays that may cover an entire end of the stadium. Ultràs travel to the most remote away matches as a sign of their devotion. For the ultrà, one of the goals of going on these trips has been to represent and defend the honour of their team. Many of these early ultràs groups received direct support from the team, but, as Bromberger notes, ultràs' relationship to the team is marked by both the ambivalent 'assertion of autonomy and the thirst for recognition'.[25] Away from the stadium, ultràs groups meet during the week to socialize, to raise money, to arrange travel to away games and to plan the aforementioned demonstrations and songs.[26] The term, ultràs, first used by football fans in Italy in the 1960s,[27] was borrowed from radical leftist political groups of late 1960s, though as Podaliri and Balestri state, ultràs groups have been recruiting grounds for the entire spectrum of political movements. Tensions between left-wing ultràs and right-wing ultràs and waves of politicization and de-politicization[28] have become recurring themes of ultrà culture. The twenty-first century has seen a marked rise in the activity of right-wing ultràs in Italy, perhaps as the result of a stagnant economy and conspicuously rising levels of immigration from Eastern Europe and Africa.

Ultràs have become infamous in Italy and abroad for episodes of violence. In the 1970s, violent clashes between opposing ultràs groups were quite common. In the 1980s and into the first decade of the 2000s, clashes between opposing groups in the immediate vicinity of the stadium became less frequent as specially aimed laws and police crackdowns secured a tenuous peace. Instead, ultràs would organize clashes away from the stadium or impromptu violent encounters would occur on the tollways leading to and from the stadium. In recent times, ultràs have united, to a degree, in opposition to their common enemies: the police and any other form official authority.[29] The police presence inside and outside Italian football stadiums is highly visible and intimidating. At some matches, hundreds of police in riot-gear helmets, shields and body armour wield batons and line the streets while dozens of armoured police vehicles surround the stadium. New laws require individuals to provide official identification when they purchase a ticket and 'fan' identification cards will be implemented in 2010.[30] Such measures are designed to help secure the stadium, but these measures also discourage people from attending the game, and according to ultràs groups, impinge upon their civil rights.

Irriducibili Inc.

Ultràs have responded to the modernization and militarization of Italian football in different ways. For example, one pan-ultràs movement has assembled under the name, *No al calcio moderno* [No to modern football] to protest higher ticket prices, the influence of television and other 'modern' commercial aspects of the game. In his analysis of English football fans, Anthony King[31] suggests that the behaviour of fans and other subcultural groups' tends to waiver between resistance and compliance. He describes how the 'lads' of Manchester United disavowed certain types of consumption, such as the official team jersey, while continuing to emotionally and financially support the team through the purchase of match tickets. The Irriducibili took a radical path in relation to resistance and compliance by transforming into a commercialized entity. Founded in 1987, the Irriducibili were composed primarily of young men between the ages of 16 and 30, though some of the original members stayed into their 40s including the founder and leader of the group, Fabrizio Toffolo.[32] The group had a clubhouse where younger members carried out mundane chores such as cleaning, painting banners for display at the stadium and registering fans for chartered bus trips to away games. Unlike Lazio's archrival, A.S. Roma, which is supported by several ultrà groups that clash over politics and style, the Irriducibili became the singular dominant Lazio ultràs group in the early 2000s. The Irriducibili's dominance gave them tremendous power to control the behaviour of fans in the stadium and to gain the attention of the team's management. The Irriducibili drew negative attention for xenophobic and far right political displays. They have sung anti-semitic lyrics and chanted *Il Duce* in homage to Benito Mussolini. During a game in 2000, they raised a banner in honour of the slain Serbian war criminal, Arkan.[33] In 2006, their cheers for Paolo Di Canio and his fascist salute gave both Di Canio and the Irriducibili widespread media attention.[34] The Irriducibili became prime targets of journalists and TV pundits who have criticized their 'mindless heckling of black players'[35] and neo-fascist displays.[36]

From ultrà to brand

Police crackdowns at the stadiums and public criticism in mainstream media put tremendous pressure on the ultràs in general and the Irriducibili in particular, to change. The Irriducibili's leader, Fabrizio Toffolo, conceded that the days of battles among ultràs were near an end, and that ultràs must adapt. He said, 'The ultrà must use his brain [and be] much more aware of communication, much more aware of the problems that ruin the image of football'.[37] The Irriducibili changed into a branded organization with impressive media capabilities and business interests. Through these means, and through strategic alliances, the Irriducibili accrued enough real power to constitute a real threat to the Lazio owners. In doing so, they became 'professional' fans and disrupted the typical relationship between consumer-fans and producer-owners.

In addition to the banners, flags, songs and choruses used inside the stadium, the Irriducibili sold a game-day newsletter, maintained a professionally designed website,[38] controlled a radio programme and produced various books and films. Through this entire media, they cultivated a strong identity, and ultimately, a brand. Their game day newsletter, *La Voce Della Nord* [The Voice of the North], in particular, was an evocative recruiting and branding tool.[39] *La Voce Della Nord* was sold outside the stadium for one or two Euros, on game days since 1995. The newsletter's title refers to the *Curva Nord* (North Curve) of the stadium, the section controlled by the Irriducibili. In 2005–2006, *La Voce Della Nord* was a 16-page, colour newsletter that combined relevant information about the team with full colour pictures and fan-authored articles. The graphic design and layout of the newsletter are impressive for a newsletter with such limited distribution. As one might expect of a football fan publication, *La Voce Della Nord* contains many pictures of prominent players in action during games and articles praising Lazio and ridiculing rivals, A.S. Roma.

Beyond the predictable content that hails the football team, *La Voce Della Nord* celebrates the fans themselves and it pushes the group's right-wing ideology. The newsletter foregrounds the groups' travels to away matches through centrefolds and other full colour photos that feature fans. The newsletter features right-wing commentary on general political principles such as multiculturalism as well as specific Italian politicians and issues. For the Irriducibili, Lazio and right-wing politics are fundamental elements of their identity, and this combination of football and political commentary is indicative of the multiple points of identification that the Irriducibili constitutes.[40] The Irriducibili's idol, Paolo Di Canio, embodies this convergence. As an outspoken admirer of Mussolini, Di Canio has used his platform as a gifted football player to represent his political views, and provoke his opposition.

La Voce Della Nord became an important tool in the Irriducibili's campaign to overthrow team owner, Claudio Lotito. Lotito bought the team from its bankrupt owners in 2004 and initially, he was welcomed as a saviour by the fans. After a short time, the Irriducibili turned against him. They accused him of not spending enough money on the team and using Lazio only to enrich himself. The Irriducibili used all of their resources to protest against Lotito. Inside the stadium La Voce Della Nord became a key tool to distribute anti-Lotito songs such as the following:

Forza Lazio	Let's go Lazio
Forza Lazio	Let's go Lazio
Sempre insiem' a te	Always with you
Forza Lazio	Let's go Lazio
Forza Lazio	Let's go Lazio
Lotito vattene!	Lotito go away!

La Voce Della Nord carried pictures of protest banners that read 'Lotito Vattene'.[41] The newsletter claims that the Irriducibili are the 'Only defenders of this more than century old tradition' and that Lotito, on the other hand, does not even celebrate Paolo Di Canio's goals.

The Irriducibili-branded documentary, DVD, *L'amor per te mi fa teppista* [My Love for You Makes me a Hooligan][42] depicts founder, Fabrizio Toffolo, making business visits with various Irriducibili directors and associates. Toffolo is briefly shown guiding the Irriducibili at the stadium but most of the film portrays Toffolo as a businessman. With his closely cropped hair, unshaved face and aviator glasses, Toffolo defines the gruff 'look' that defines the Irriducibili. The film, like all of the other Irriducibili media, defends the right-wing perspective of the Irriducibili, which, they feel, is misrepresented in biased, left-wing mainstream media. Toffolo states that although violence is unpleasant, 'We live in a society of violence', and that the Irriducibili do not look to start problems, but that, true to their name (Indomitables), they will not back down either. Irriducibili leader, Diabolik, deflects blame onto the authorities by citing an incident where the police did not have the keys to release a gate during a match, a mistake, he argues, that could have led to tragedy.

The video highlights the Irriducibili's impressive media presence as Toffolo makes an appearance on the radio programme *La Voce Della Nord,* a programme that shares the same name as the Irriducibili newsletter. In the video, Toffolo wears headphones and responds to various callers. For the Irriducibili and for Toffolo, radio is another tool used to disseminate opinions, recruit members, solidify opinion and demonstrate legitimacy. As scholar Albertro Testa notes, the Irriducibili also use their media presence to promote social causes. Testa quotes Irriducibili leader Giorgio, who says, 'Just to have one of us on the radio speaking about the initiative is helpful'.[43]

The extras section of the DVD documents parts of their protest campaign against team owner, Claudio Lotito. One of these extras is a five-minute documentary-montage of protests titled, 'Sit In.' Led by Toffolo, the Irriducibili are shown marching, waving flags and shouting slogans outside of the Italian parliament. None of this footage is narrated or otherwise explained. One scene depicts Toffolo exchanging heated words with Lotito himself, though the video offers no context for this exchange. The entire montage is introduced by the words, 'Our battles ... we fight them alone'.[44] In the DVD, the Irriducibili frame themselves as heroes fighting against the 'villainous' Lotito.

Original Fans

Beyond the Irriducibili's impressive repertoire of fan-created media, their most unique and controversial accomplishment is their establishment of a chain of retail stores named, *Original Fans.*[45] In 2005, there were a dozen Original Fans stores operating in Rome, selling Lazio tickets and officially licensed Lazio merchandise. More significantly, they sold Irriducibili-branded t-shirts, scarves, flags, DVDs and anything else that might appeal to their members or admirers. The Irriducibili merchandise uses the light blue and dark blue colour scheme of Lazio and featured designs such as Mr. Enrich, a cartoon character who wears a British-looking bowler hat. The Irriducibili use the La Voce Della Nord as a promotional tool for the Original Fans stores. Prominent Lazio players such as Di Canio, Tommaso Rocchi and Valon Behrami modelled Irriducibili shirts in full-page ads in their newsletter.

Original Fans signifies a decisive departure from the traditional role of ultràs by turning themselves into a medium-scale, for-profit enterprise. The Irriducibili have faced criticism from other football fans that view them as traitors to an implied code that demands ultràs to be loyal supporters free from commercial concerns. Rival fans mockingly call them, Irriducibili Inc.[46] The notion that fans should not seek anything more than participation in a symbolic sense is reinforced by powerful football figures such as former Italian national team coach, Roberto Donadoni. After commending 'good fans' he continued,

> There is another [element of fans] that is in it to profit from football to gain wealth and make it a business. I believe that it is one of the maladies of our football, to marginalize and combat: it is an insidious practice without the intention to really support their club.[47]

Donadoni did not cite the lavishly paid football coaches, administrators or owners of football clubs as potential threats to the game, or acknowledge that his paycheck is ultimately underwritten by fans whether through taxes or consumer purchasing. From the fans' perspective, why should they be excluded from the economic benefits of the game when they add so much to the ambience of the stadium, and to the ultimate value of the brand?

The Irriducibili turned their fan culture into a brand of its own. Since their founding in 1987, the Irriducibili have sculpted a subcultural identity consisting of dedication to Lazio, to right-wing politics, and to the aggressive support of their team. They developed a style including short-cropped hair, black t-shirts and aviator-style sunglasses. Their identity grew from, and in key aspects, apart from Lazio and other Lazio supporters. Their brand challenges the usual relationship between fans as consumers and owners as producers. The Irriducibili wanted to be considered partners in the enterprise, and to be treated as equals. Instead, they were treated as criminals.

While the Irriducibili were protesting against Lotito in organized marches, fan 'strikes' and media campaigns, they began supporting former Lazio star, Giorgio Chinaglia, in his bid to wrest control of the team from Lotito. Chinaglia claimed to have the financial backing of a Hungarian pharmaceutical consortium.[48] Meanwhile, according to police reports, Toffolo and other members of the Irriducibili made threatening phone calls to Lotito, urging him to sell the team. Toffolo and other Irriducibili leaders were arrested and charged with extortion, while the financial authorities began investigating Chinaglia's supposed financial backing.[49] Police investigators allege that Chinaglia's bid to buy Lazio was secretly backed by the mafia. Chinaglia he never returned to Italy to face charges. He died from a heart attack in 2012 while living in exile in the USA . Investigators theorize that Lotito had demanded a portion of the profits of Original Fans, while Chinaglia had made a pact with the Irriducibili, promising not to interfere with Original Fans if they would support him in his bid to take over Lazio. In 2007, Fabrizio Toffolo, while serving part of his sentence under house arrest, was shot in the leg at the threshold of his apartment.[50] Some speculate that this shooting was a message sent by the mafia urging him to remain quiet. These events precipitated the demise of the Irriducibili as rulers of the *Curva Nord* with their leaders in jail and several other members banned from the stadium. Four of their leaders, including Toffolo, were sentenced to two to four years in prison.[51] The Original Fans retail stores began to falter as well.

The Irriducibili's cultural and financial power posed a serious threat to the Lazio brand and to its owner, Claudio Lotito. The Irriducibili, and ultràs throughout Italy, add value to the team/brand that they support through consumption, but also through productive labour. They add to the football stadium experience through dedicated support in the form of cheering and elaborate displays. Through their subcultural identities, they add to the cultural cachet of the team that they support. While many fan groups believe they deserve more credit and respect from the team owners and from the media for their activities, the Irriducibili were unique their ability to organize thousands of followers – a substantial segment of ticket holders – into a powerful and sustained protest against the team ownership. They developed impressive media capabilities, and economic power through the Original Fans retail outlets. While the ultimate tactics of the Irridicibili were, at the very least, questionable, they put into action the desire of many fans to gain a real stake in the team that they dedicate their passion and identities to. They took participatory culture to one logical extreme.

Conclusion

This essay has juxtaposed the language of participatory fandom with the language of brand marketing; On the one hand, fan culture can be a vibrant form of leisure that forms the basis for deeply felt emotions, relationships and identities. On the other hand, fan culture is rooted in a consumer culture that quantifies and monetizes human impulses under legal regimes that do not adequately recognize the contribution of fans. While the law may not adequately recognize the value of human sentiment, brand managers most certainly do. Douglas Holt's work on brands is just one example of an enormous literature (not to mention the almost unfathomably large industry) devoted to cultivating positive consumer sentiment (or branding). Fans and marketers share the understanding that the vital identity-producing 'stuff' of fandom cannot be reduced to a set of consumer goods[52]; Both groups understand that consumer goods are raw materials upon which identities are built whether we call these identities brands or fandom.

In football, fans/consumers are actual constituents of the brand. They add an essential element to the experience of the product. My personal interest in football was spurred by the fan orchestrations at Rome's Olympic Stadium more than by the performance of the players on the field or television broadcasts. Beyond the direct stadium experience, the subcultural identity of fan groups like the Irriducibili adds cachet to the brand. The Irriducibili were aware of their powerful role in the Lazio brand, and in response, they tried to convert that power into a share in the team. A more mainstream reading of the Irriducibli rebellion might be that the Irriducibili wrecklessly exaggerated their role. Certainly, official authority was on Lotito's side as there is no legal mechanism in Italy for fans to assert claims of ownership in privately owned teams. The Irriducibili appear to have aligned themselves with the unauthorized power of organized crime as a desperate option. In other contexts, fans have reacted to the perceived deficiencies of their team's management in other ways. Some fans simply opt out. In England, after the owners of Wimbledon FC moved the club, the fans formed their own club, AFC Wimbledon. Some fans of Manchester United staged protests against the team's then-new American owners,[53] while others shifted their support to the newly formed, Football Club United of Manchester. England also has the government supported, Supporters Direct organization that helps fans (supporters) to organize and gain a voice in the direction of their team. Spain's biggest clubs, Real Madrid and Barcelona, are actually owned by the fans who vote for the team's executives. The German league follows a different model altogether as most teams are community owned 'clubs'. Uli Hoeness, President of Bayern Munich, stated, in response to a question about the relatively low ticket prices in Germany compared to England, 'We do not think the fans are like cows to be milked. Football has got to be for everybody'.[54] In Italy, with limited options, the Irriducibili tried to compete with, and then, overthrow the owner.

The Irriducibili's rebellion was enabled, in part, by modern communication technologies that enabled them to coordinate their fans, but also to establish a business that outsourced the production of scarves, flags, hats and other Irriducibili-branded products. The power to make a brand is in the hands of consumers. Simultaneously, the power of fandom is within reach of brand managers who seek to harness the labour of fans under their terms. This struggle between fans/consumers/producers and power-wielding institutional producers will continue under different names and in different places. While one could imagine harmonious, cooperative alliances between fans and ownership, in Rome, there was an ugly struggle for power. The decline and fall of the Irriducibili marks one notable uprising in the conflict between football as private enterprise and football as communal good, and between fans as customers and fans as participants.

This volume has focused primarily on the positive ways in which fans connect with each other to celebrate their team, and ultimately, create community. Conversely, the ultimate focus of the brand is to convert the loyalty and dedication of their fans/consumers into tangible assets. Clearly, fans contribute to the identity of the brand, and some teams even promote their 'good' fans as part of the brand identity. But there are fans who do not cooperate with the logics of capital – they have their own agendas, and seek to influence the object of their desire beyond their place in the capitalist system. The *Irriducibili*'s actions may constitute an extreme response to a common situation – that fans are extremely loyal to something that may just be another business.

Disclosure statement

No potential conflict of interest was reported by the author.

Notes

1. Holt, *How Brands Become Icons*, 4.
2. I'm tempted here to write 'word of mouth to mouth viral transmission', but that would be mixing metaphors.
3. Guschwan, 'Fandom, Brandom and the Limits of Participatory Culture'.
4. The superficial (if not disingenuous or surreal) *connection* to place in American sport is exemplified by the Los Angeles Lakers who brought the name from Minneapolis (a city near many lakes) and the Utah Jazz who took their name from New Orleans, perhaps the most musically oriented city in the USA. I have yet to meet anyone who has gone to Salt Lake City, Utah for its jazz scene or anyone who has spurned the Pacific Ocean beaches in order to enjoy L.A.'s lakes. Perhaps, the Surfers and the Skiers would be better names, or better yet, both teams should be renamed the Valley Dwellers.
5. Sports Business Daily, 'EPL's New U.K. TV Rights Deal'.
6. Deloitte, *Football Money League*, see also note 8.
7. Rowe, *Sport, Culture and the Media*.

8. Sports Business Daily, 'EPL's New U.K. TV Rights Deal'.
9. Cashmore, *Beckham*.
10. The list of players making bad decisions is long, but the 2014 NFL football season was notable for domestic violence cases involving players and the murder trial of Aaron Hernandez.
11. See, for instance, Soccer Politics Blog, 'Franco Gets His Man'.
12. I was not compensated by any of the above brands for this essay.
13. Guschwan, 'Fans, Romans, Countrymen'.
14. Edensor and Millington, 'This is Our City'.
15. The very existence of www.BaseballReference.com, a trove of statistics, is testament enough to the obsession of baseball fans.
16. Barrabi, 'Derek Jeter Memorabilia'.
17. Ibid.
18. Jenkins, *Participatory Culture*.
19. Muniz and O'Guinn, 'Brand Communities'.
20. Heding et al., *Brand Management*.
21. Jenkins, *Participatory Culture*, 364.
22. Interview with Seydou Keita published on Roma News, 'Keita, "La societa, I giocatori e I tifosi"', http://www.romanews.eu/it,a140219.
23. Guschwan, 'Riot in the Curve'.
24. In Italy, ultràs is not necessarily the plural form of ultrà, though for the sake of this essay, I will use *ultràs* to denote the plural. Some Italian members call themselves ultrà while others prefer ultras (no accent). According to the Progetto Ultrà, ultras is more common among northern and newer groups, though this is not definitive. Testa and Armstrong, 2010, 2, use *UltraS*.
25. Bromberger, *La Partitia di Calcio*.
26. Testa and Armstrong, *Football, Fascism and Fandom*.
27. Podaliri and Balestri, 'The Ultràs, Racism and Football Culture in Italy'.
28. Podaliri and Balestri, 'The Ultràs, Racism and Football Culture in Italy', 95; Roversi, *Hate on the Net*.
29. Testa and Armstrong, *Football, Fascism and Fandom*; Guschwan, 'Riot in the Curve'.
30. Guschwan, 'La Tessera della Rivolta'.
31. King, *The End of the Terraces*.
32. Toffolo led the Irriducibili, but, as will become clear, the status of the Irriducibili, and Toffolo himself, has changed.
33. Arkan was the nickname of Željko Ražnatović, a Serbian paramilitary leader who was accused of crimes against humanity committed during the violent breakup of Yugoslavia. Arkan was murdered in January, 2000, before his court hearing.
34. The story of Di Canio's fascist salute can be found at Fenton, 'I'm a Fascist'.
35. See Speck, 'The Ugly Face of Italian Football'.
36. See Testa and Armstrong, *Football, Fascism and Fandom* for an analysis of neo-fascist displays by the Irriducibili.
37. Translated, *Uso molto il cervello ... [essere] Molto piu attento alla communicazione. Molto piu attento ai problemi che rovinano l'immagine di calcio.*' (from Irriducibili DVD, *L'Amor per te mi fa teppista*).
38. As of December 2007, the site is no longer online.
39. Discussed in further detail in Chapter 3, Print Media.
40. The social significance of the Irridicubili's right wing politics and their connection to contemporary Italian politics deserves more attention than I can write in this essay, though I intend to pick up the subject in subsequent essays. For more information on the relationship between radical politics and Italian football fans, see Testa and Armstrong, *Football, Fascism and Fandom*, 2010. My concern in this essay is how right-wing politics informs the self-described identity and the Irriducibili as a branded identity.
41. La Voce Della Nord, May 14, 2006.
42. Also known simply as Lazio Irriducibili DVD, however, the outside of the DVD case has the name '*L'amor per te mi fa teppista*' on the side.
43. Testa and Armstrong, *Football, Fascism and Fandom*, 17.

44. Original text: *Nostre battaglie ... combattiamo da sola.*
45. Original Fans is *not* a translation.
46. The nickname, *Irridicubili, S.p.A.,* is the equivalent of Irridicubili Inc. or Incorporated. This insult appears, for example, on a fan site of rival Fiorentina fans in an article entitled, Irriducibili *S.p.A. la vergogna dei gruppi ultra* [Irriducibili Inc., the shame of *ultràs* groups], http://magnifico.tifonet.it/2000_1/irriducibili.htm.
47. Translated from: *Un altro è approfittarsi del calcio per lucrarci e farne un business. Credo sia uno dei mali del nostro calcio, da arginare e combattare: è un'usanza subdola senza l'intenzione di supportare realmente il proprio club. original.*
48. BBC, 'Police Move in Over Lazio Shares'.
49. Hawkey, 'Wanted. Giorgio Chinaglia'.
50. La Repubblica, 'Capo Ultrà della Lazio Gambizzato'.
51. Corriere dello Sport, 'Cronaca, Scalata Lazio'.
52. Horne, *Sport in Consumer Cutlture*; King, *The End of the Terraces*.
53. See Scott, 'Anti-glazer Protest Leads to Slump'.
54. Evans, 'German Football Model is a League Apart'.

References

Barrabi, T. 'Derek Jeter Memorabilia'. *IB Times*, September 25, 2014. http://www.ibtimes.com/derek-jeter-memorabilia-1694607 (accessed March 3, 2015).
BBC. 'Police Move in over Lazio Shares'. *BBC*, October 13, 2006. http://news.bbc.co.uk/2/hi/europe/6047864.stm (accessed January 7, 2011).
Bromberger, C. *La Partita di Calcio: Etnologia di una Passione* [The football match: ethnology of a passion]. Translated from French by L. Casalino. Rome: Editori Riuniti, 1999.
Cashmore, E. *Beckham*. Cambridge: Polity Press, 2004.
Corriere dello Sport. 'Cronaca, Scalata Lazio'. *Corriere dello Sport*, January 29, 2015. http://www.corrieredellosport.it/calcio/serie_a/lazio/2015/01/29-394117/Cronaca,+scalata+Lazio%3A+7+condanne,+anche+4+capi+ultras.
Deloitte. *Football Money League*. Manchester: Deloitte, 2014.
'Di Canio Banned for Fascist Salute Once Again'. *ESPN*, January 23, 2006. http://footballnet.espn.go.com/news/story?id=356189&&cc=5901 (accessed March 29, 2015).
Edensor, T., and S. Millington. '"This is Our City": Branding Football and Local Embeddedness'. Global Networks 8, no. 2 (2008): 172–93.
Evans, S. 'German Football Model is a League Apart'. *BBC.com*, May 24, 2013. www.bbc.com/news/business-22625160 (accessed April 1, 2015).
Fenton, B. 'I'm a Fascist, Not a Racist Says Paolo Di Canio'. *The Telegraph*, December 24, 2005. http://www.telegraph.co.uk/news/1506262/Im-a-fascist-not-a-racist-says-Paolo-di-Canio.html (accessed June 10, 2015).
Goal.com. 'Donadoni contro i tifosi di professione che lucrano sul calcio'. Goal.com, January 4, 2008. http://www.corederoma.it/online/?p=1244 (accessed January 7, 2011).
Guschwan, M. 'Riot in the Curve: Football Fans in Twenty-first Century Italy'. *Soccer & Society* 8, no. 2–3 (2007): 250–66.
Guschwan, M. 'Fans, Romans, Countrymen: Football Fandom and Civic Identity in Contemporary Rome'. *International Journal of Communication* 5 (2011): 1990–2013.
Guschwan, M. 'Fandom, Brandom and the Limits of Participatory Culture'. *Journal of Consumer Culture* 12, no. 1 (2012): 19–40. Abstract: http://joc.sagepub.com/content/12/1/19.abstract.
Guschwan, M. 'La Tessera della Rivolta: Italy's Failed Fan Identity Card'. *Soccer & Society* 14, no. 2 (2013): 215–29.
Hawkey, I. 'Wanted. Giorgio Chinaglia: Italian Police would Like a Word'. *The Times* [London], October 22, 2006. http://www.timesonline.co.uk/tol/sport/football/article608920.ece (accessed January 7, 2011).
Heding, T., C.F. Knudtzen, and M. Bjerre. *Brand Management*. New York: Routledge, 2009.
Holt, D.B. *How Brands Become Icons: The Principles of Cultural Branding*. Boston, MA: Harvard Business School Press, 2004.
Horne, J. *Sport in Consumer Culture*. New York: Palgrave Macmillan, 2006.

Irriducibili Movie: L'Amor per te mi Fa Teppista. DVD. Directed by A. Zappulla and R. Camolino. Italy: Lazio Irriducibili Video, 2005.

Jenkins, H. *Textual Poachers: Television Fans and Participatory Culture*. New York: Routledge, 1992.

Jenkins, H. 'Afterword: The Future of Fandom'. In *Identities and Communities in a Mediated World*, ed. J. Gray, C. Sandvoss, and C.L. Harrington, 357–64. New York: NYU Press, 2007.

'Keita: "I Campioni Nei Momenti Difficili Alzano la Testa"'. *Roma News*, March 18, 2015. http://www.romanews.eu/it,a140219.

King, A. *The End of the Terraces: The Transformation of English Football in the 1990s*. London: Leicester University Press, 1998.

La Repubblica. 'Capo Ultrà della Lazio Gambizzato'. *La Repubblica*, August 6, 2007. http://www.repubblica.it/2007/08/sezioni/cronaca/capoultras-lazio/capoultras-lazio/capoultras-lazio.html (accessed January 7, 2011).

La Voce Della Nord, ed. *Irriducibili: Noi siamo gli Ultras della Lazio*. Rome: Fotolito Moggio, 2006.

La Voce Della Nord. [newsletter] No. 13, February 26, 2006. Rome.

La Voce Della Nord. [newsletter] No. 16, April 15, 2006. Rome.

La Voce Della Nord. [newsletter] No. 18, May 14, 2006. Rome.

Muniz, A.M., and T.C. O'Guinn. 'Brand Community'. *Journal of Consumer Research* 27, no. 4 (2001): 412–32.

No al Calcio Moderno. http://www.noalcalciomoderno.it (accessed March 8, 2008, inactive as of April 2015).

Podaliri, C., and C. Balestri. 'The Ultràs, Racism and Football Culture in Italy'. In *Fanatics!: Power, Identity and Fandom in Football*, ed. A. Brown, 88–100. London: Routledge, 1998.

Roversi, A. *Hate on the Net: Extremist Sites, Neo-fascism On-line, Electronic Jihad*. Burlington, VT: Ashgate, 2008.

Rowe, D. *Sport, Culture and the Media: The Unruly Trinity*. 2nd ed. Maidenhead: Open University Press, 2003.

Scott, M. 'Anti-glazer Protest Leads to Slump in Manchester United Shirt Sales'. *The Guardian*, February 21, 2011. www.theguardian.com/football/2011/feb/21/manchester-united-glazer-shirts (accessed February 23, 2015).

Soccer Politics Blog. www.sites.duke/wcwp/.

Speck, I. 'The Ugly Face of Italian Football'. *ESPN*, October 19, 2000. http://footballnet.espn.go.com/archive/columns/2000/1019/20001019featspeck.html (accessed March 7, 2015).

Sports Business Daily. 'EPL's New U.K. TV Rights Deal Worth Record $7.8B'. *Sports Business Daily*, February 11, 2015. Sportsbusinessdaily.com/Daily/Issues/2015/02/11/Media/EPL-TV.aspx (accessed March 3, 2015).

Testa, A., and G. Armstrong. *Football, Fascism and Fandom: The UltraS of Italian Football*. London: Black Publishers, 2010.

Fan politics: dissent and control at the stadium

This essay delves into the theoretical and practical dimensions of political expression at the stadium. While previous chapters are organized around the form of media, this essay considers the breadth of media put to use to convey political sentiments. While the notion of sport as apolitical has surface appeal, the stadium has always been political, and provided that sport continues to aggregate tens of thousands of fans in an enclosed space, there is little hope of eliminating politics. The stadium offers the chance for average citizens to gain a voice and, I argue, the stadium is an important part of the public sphere. The chapter considers how the stadium is used for dissent in several contexts. In Italy, the stadium has long been a site of political expression while more recently, in Cairo and Istanbul, football fandom has provided the tools to directly confront the state.

The goal of this volume has been to consider the ways in which football fans communicate through particular media in order to create individual and group identities as fans. Unlike previous chapters that focus on a particular medium or particular context of communication, this chapter delves into the ways in which fans communicate political messages. Previous chapters have included examples of politically motivated fan groups, and the display of political messages inside and outside of the stadium, but this chapter will consider the theoretical and practical implications of fans as citizens. In particular, it thinks through the ways in which fans create solidarity, express dissent, and in some cases, lead political protests.

This chapter considers the connection between politics and football fandom in a variety of ways. My definition of political is broad to include anything that affects the lives lived in common rather than a focus on electoral politics. The first section theorizes the football stadium as a political space – as part of the public sphere. Most essentially, the stadium can become a site for the expression of political dissent. Fans are active in their local, national and international communities, and through their organizational structure, support and protest a wide variety of issues. The next part of the chapter focuses on the history and development of the Italian ultras. Politics have been a part of Italian ultras since their start in the 1960s. Some take on the commercialization of the sport, some fight against the state while others are concerned with political ideology. The actions and image of Italian ultras have led to a variety of restrictions on fans, including the *tessera del tifoso*, the much maligned fan identity card that threatens to change the character of the stadium in Italy. Through formal and informal networks, Italian ultras have created an ideal of fan culture that other groups have mimicked and built upon. The last section of this chapter considers how fans have used their organizational and oppositional savvy to get involved in direct political action.

As this volume has shown, football fans are communicatively competent and media savvy. Through trial and error, they have learned how to get the attention of other fans, their team's players and management, local media, and at time, global media. As yet another entertaining example of fans attracting global media attention, the disgruntled fans of the first division Polish team, Zawisza Bydogoszcz, broke into their home stadium and left individualized coffins on the pitch for members of the team and the owner after the team had gone on a ten game winless streak.[1] The story made international news as a clever ruse by dedicated fans. While it might seem that only established groups of fans can garner media attention, I offer my own experience of displaying a banner, and successfully getting the attention of a photojournalist who placed the photo into the online section of an important daily newspaper. I made the banner after A.S. Roma had been suffering a poor run of form leading up to the Christmas break. The gifted but impetuous Antonio Cassano had not been playing well and was often left on the bench. He was rumoured to have been disrupting team harmony. Over the January transfer window, he was moved to Real Madrid. After his exit, Roma won a then-record tying, ten matches in a row. The 11th match was the derby against archrival, Lazio, which they won to set off a great celebration. At the local hardware store, I procured the plastic poles and black spraypaint I needed to construct a banner on an old bed sheet. Before the match, I found a conspicuous area of the Curva Sud to raise the banner as the photographers were milling about after the players had finished warming up and had disappeared back into the locker room. My banner read, 'Thank you Real Madrid, for taking out the trash'. In the stadium, I had a received a few smiles and head nods for my work, but I went home unsure of the impact of my statement. In the morning, I received a phone message and an email from friends who had seen the 'crazy American' with the banner raised overhead, in the online section of the newspaper. This was a moment that turned me into a *real fan*, in a way. My more upstanding friends could not believe I did this, while the members of Core de Roma asked me to bring the banner to the next banquet. I had succeeded in becoming a Roman fan – they accepted me as a contributor to the Roman culture of wit and pugnaciousness. At my job teaching English, one of my clients suggested that I had used incorrect grammar. Fortunately, the grammarians at the stadium are lenient. The members of Core de Roma suggested that the only thing that could have improved my sign is if I had used a more Roman word for trash.[2] This is a grammar lesson that I will never forget.

Another example of a fan display that made international news occurred in January, 2015, when fans of the Belgian first division club, Standard Li'ege, greeted former player, Steven Defour, who transferred to rival club Anderlecht, with a huge banner that read, 'Red or Dead', in reference to the home teams' red jerseys.[3] The words of the banner would have passed unremarkably if it were not for the caricature of Defour having been beheaded. The depiction stirred particular controversy because it comes at a time when western democracies are battling the self-proclaimed Islamic state, a group that has brazenly released video footage showing their brutal beheadings of western journalists and aid workers. Additionally, the massacre of the creators of Charli Hebdo in Paris, and the lingering resentment over the publication in Denmark of cartoons featuring the Islamic prophet Muhammad, conditions the ways in which the imagery was interpreted. It is unclear whether the creators of the banner fully understood or anticipated the reaction that the banner would generate, though it would seem clear that they intended to be provocative. Belgian authorities have threatened fines and stadium bans against the fans responsible for the banner that was in 'bad taste'. This event is just one example of how the greater political context of world affairs enters into the stadium and conditions the construction and reading of messages displayed there. It is likely that if this banner had been displayed five years ago, it might still have been in bad taste, but would not have caused nearly the international stir.

Sometimes football matches are more directly political. The international match between Albania and Serbia, hosted in Sarajevo, in October of 2014, was interrupted by a drone holding aloft an Albanian nationalist flag flying above the pitch.[4] As the drone flew too close to the pitch, the referee suspended the match. Events turned ugly when a Serbian player reached up and grabbed the flag. The Albanian players were offended by the Serbian player's handling of the flag, and they jostled with him and other Serbs in order to recover the flag. This incident escalated into a pushing match among players until a few fans invaded the pitch. The referees eventually decided to abandon the match as the overall situation in the stadium deteriorated and the Albanian players felt unable to continue.

This last example is the clearest example of politics entering into football. The tension between Albania and Serbia is part of the recent history of conflict between the nations and the match was known to be risky and tickets were not made available to Albanian fans. The stadium has long served as a space for the exhibition and promotion of political agendas. Hitler used the Berlin Olympics to promote his ideas about racial supremacy, while the more recent Beijing Olympics of 2008 were a not so subtle showcase of China as a rising world power. The African Cup of Nations football tournament was 'saved' by Equatorial Guinea and its dictator, Teodoro Obiang Nguema,[5] after Morocco declined to host the tournament as scheduled due to fears over the spread of the Ebola virus. Organizers and politicians recognize the power of the stadium and try to bend that power towards their will.

Leftist critiques of spectator sport commonly focus on their role in promoting commodity fetishism, division of labour, and ultimately, alienation through distraction.[6] The American sporting venue seems to be a case study of these critiques. In the United States, every major sporting event is preceded by the playing of the national anthem. Some baseball games play the song, God Bless America, during the seventh inning stretch, a ritualized break in the game that traditionally featured a song that encourages fans to consume 'peanuts and Crackerjack'. The invocation of God, in song, has been more prominent since 11 September 2001. Major US sporting events are often accompanied by military officers transporting the flag and military jets screeching over the tops of the stadiums in rituals that are, I surmise, intended to remind fans of the immense human and capital resources that go into preserving the freedom to choose to spend leisure time and expendable income on sport entertainment, though the meanings and significances of these rituals are always left somewhat open to interpretation. The orchestration of political meanings at the US stadium is commandeered by the organizers of these events who, through symbolic action, tie the sporting entertainments to larger sociopolitical ideas such as patriotism and support for militarism.[7] In the US, authorities are experts in controlling the messages inside of the stadia as proudly patriotic and blandly obeisant. These demonstrations add fuel to the remarks of Noam Chomsky, who has said that sports are 'a way of building up irrational attitudes of submission to authority, and group cohesion behind leadership elements – in fact, it's training in irrational jingoism'.[8]

In the rest of the world, fans, and football fans in particular, behave *badly*, at least by the standards established by the public–private American sport entertainment industry. Football fans are savvy in the ways of resisting authority and in attracting, manipulating and producing media. The first two examples above demonstrate fans' dedication and their abilities to provoke. The third example involving the Albanian flag displays the significance of football as a symbol of national rivalry and the vulnerability of the stadium as it attempts to simultaneously exploit and contain deeply felt political identities and tensions. Pierre De Coubertin, founder of the modern Olympics, along with innumerable other political and social leaders, have tried to promulgate a vision of sport as apolitical – as a space set apart from the divisions, inequalities and realities of life outside of the stadium. Many fans reject this artificial separation entirely. Ultras, in particular, are well known for their integration of football fandom and political ideology.[9] On a weekly basis, they organize themselves to resist rival ultras and state authority. Ultras are often responsible for the anti-social violence and disruptions that make newspaper headlines. Football stadiums are resistant to control, and are 'to the annoyance of football and non-football authorities alike, an ungovernable environment'.[10]

The events of Spring 2011 in Cairo's Tahrir Square highlighted the ability of organized fans – in this case, self-proclaimed ultras – to organize resistance against authority.[11] The fans of Cairo's rival football teams, Al Ahly and Al Zamalek, were instrumental in organizing protesters and training them to deal with riot police, tear gas and other practical matters. Likewise in Turkey, ultras were fundamental organizers to the resistance against Prime Minister Erdogan In Gezi Park, as will be discussed below.[12] Clearly, the stadium is a good training ground for resistance against authority in North African and Turkey. Elsewhere, I have argued,[13] in some depth, that the sporting stadium should be considered as part of the public sphere. Here, I will layout the basics of the argument for why we should consider the stadium to be a politically active and relevant space.

The public sphere
The public sphere is a critical concept in political theory generally attributed to Jurgen Habermas. He conceived of the public sphere as a place set aside from work and from home that would function as a space for political discourse. The ideal public sphere would be a place where logic and reason would mitigate conflicting viewpoints about issues of public concern. While the ideal of reasoned political discourse is a lasting aspect of political thought, the everyday functioning of democracy reveals the gap between the ideals and the practices of political decision-making. Even in the best examples of democracy, those in power are liable to trivialize or ignore the less powerful. Margaret Kohn offers a response to the politics of power that offers potential visibility and voice to the less powerful. She is concerned with physical space and the ways how it is controlled or manipulated to encourage or discourage social interaction and dissent. She makes a strong argument for the value of public space in which different people with different needs and agendas might be encouraged to interact with each other, and thus confront their differences. Her politics of confrontation work against the privatization of space in which the privileged can pass from private homes, to underground garages, to sociopolitically

homogenous workspaces and thereby avoid potentially uncomfortable interactions with those who have not benefited from the current economic and social order. For Kohn, out of sight is out of mind, while the beggar or picketer, 'draws attention to the irrationalities produced by our society'.[14] Her ideas count on a notion forwarded by Hannah Arendt, that public opinion should not merely be the sum total of private opinions, but rather, individuals must take into account the good of society in formulating their political opinions. This trajectory of thinking can also go against the most radical visions of individualism where the self-obsessed concerns of the powerful trump those of the weak or the poor.

The stadium is one site where tens of thousands of people from different backgrounds come together on a regular basis. As this volume attests, different ideas circulate around the stadium as expressed in the form of signs, banners, chants and fundamentally, the physical presence of others. At the very least, at the stadium, one is reminded that there are thousands of other people, and that we must find ways to occupy the same space together. The stadium can also confer a sense of solidarity when the mood of the stadium palpably shifts, or when a song unifies the crowd into a single voice, and what feels like a single body. In addition to the mass co-presence of spectators, the stadium is site of the intense gaze of media producers both professional and amateur. An artfully constructed banner can get the attention of a photographer, and be published for national and international audiences. Fans stage elaborate displays that can become 'image events',[15] the powerful, and often irrational, insertions into the public discourse in the form of evocative imagery. Images events are particularly useful for those who are ordinarily excluded from the public sphere by regulations of decorum or rationality.

The typical sport stadium is a space governed by both public and private interests. Many stadiums, particularly in Italy, are publicly owned. Most stadiums around the world are buoyed by public subsidies and/or services while most top football teams are privately owned and managed.[16] Through a series of contracts, the private team rents the stadium and governs the space for the duration of the event. Tickets are sold to control entry into the stadium, and the arrangement of fans within. Ticket holders implicitly agree to a range of controls over their behaviour with the threat of revocation or legal punishment if a ticket holder breaks the rules. In some circumstances, fans can be arrested and jailed if they break the 'contract' of the ticket. Most famously, fans who enter onto the field can be jailed even if the field is technically public owned. In Italy, there are special laws that increase the weight of punishment for actions in and around sporting events. These restrictions are reasonable if they are used to ensure public safety but they are a touchy subject for many fans who feel unfairly targeted by special laws that can be used to discriminate against fans. For example, in Italy, the distrust between average citizens and the state is exacerbated by laws that target ultras, as I will discuss further below. Regardless of the special circumstances of the stadium, it has a public aspect to it even if it is privately owned. This quasi-public space (Kohn calls them *social spaces*) offers the possibility of interaction and public confrontation that is vital to her vision of democracy. The governance of public stadiums restricts the rights of citizens. It is worth reiterating that free speech is restricted to in football stadiums, through explicit law and through implicit signals. Should we concede that stadiums are used to promulgate and solidify the ideas of those in power?

The stadium is not an ideal public sphere and it has aspects that limit its value as a place of public discourse. The poor are excluded by price, and those disinterested in football are excluded by choice. The stadium is not rational or reasoned. It is a place dedicated to the emotional force and spectacle of the football match and not to political discussion. But the problem is that if we look for an idealized space designed for rational discourse, what will we be left with? Elite social clubs and exclusive college campuses? Certainly any theorist who would argue that mass media or the internet are a space guided by ideals of objective, fact-based, rational discourse has not turned on a TV or an internet browser lately. Despite its shortcomings, the football stadium consistently draws large crowds and fanatical media interest. It is a political space where individuals and marginalized groups can have a voice regardless of any attempts to 'cleanse' sport of politics. The football stadium is just one political space, but, a highly visible space for the expression of political identity and public opinion.

Political sentiment in the stadium is often crude and sometimes vacuous, not unlike a great deal of political discourse. Sometimes displays in the stadium are irresponsible and incendiary, and should be opposed by civil society, but the problem is that many of the measures used to *stamp out or weed out the troublemakers* (variants of this refrain are used worldwide to justify increased security and oppression) violate the civil rights of citizens and compromise democratic ideals. How can one set restrictions, a priori, that can stop an abuse of the public space before it happens without *stamping out* the festive and convivial atmosphere that is a strong pull to the stadium in the first place? In Italy, this question might be framed as 'How to fight Fascism without resorting to fascism?' Italian ultras have long made the stadium not only a place to observe a football match, but also a place to express the sense of wit and irony makes the Italian stadium a place to watch.

Football and politics in Italy

The intriguing history of the Italian ultràs has been covered in depth elsewhere,[17] but I will give a brief sketch of relevant aspects. Organized fan support has been a part of Italian football culture since the early part of the twentieth century.[18] Initially, fan groups helped distribute tickets and organize trips to away matches. The early days seem innocent by today's standards. Professionalization did not fully take hold in sport until the post war period. *La Fossa dei Lioni* (The Den of Lions), a group that supported A.C. Milan, is often recognized as one of the first hardcore ultràs group in Italy. Ultràs borrowed ideas from the English supporter culture while subsequently influencing English, European and South American fan cultures. Ultràs post large banners proclaiming their identity. They continue to make enormous banners, organize spectacles with sparklers, paper and other materials, they orchestrate songs and chants, synchronize physical movements such as jumping up and down, beat drums, and in general, encourage their team, disparage the opponent, excite the stadium and each other. The ultràs took over *la curva* (the curve), the curved ends of oval stadiums, throughout Italy. The curva became the symbolic territory to be defended against rival ultràs who would try to steal their banners. In the early days, the rivalries were expressed primarily in the stadium and in the immediate confines of the stadium. The ultrà culture became quite well known in Italy and has been dramatized in films such as *Ultrà*[19] and parodied in films such as *Eccezzziunale ... Veramente*.[20]

Perhaps inevitably, organized fan groups became popular recruiting grounds for political movements as politicians exploited the social organization of these groups to rally supporters. Additionally, some fan leaders became powerful figures and launched political careers. Overall, however, the curva developed into a 'free zone' where mostly young, mostly male fans could beat drums, smoke marijuana and stage ever more outrageous displays. Some of these fans and fan groups became attracted to extremist politics – in some cases, these identities may have been adopted as a way to provoke mainstream culture and to articulate an outsider identity rather than to promote political ideology. However, certain fan supporters became synonymous with their political stances – for example, the Livorno fans are known as devout Communists, while the Lazio fans represent the right wing. Politically like-minded fan groups would form a symbolic *gemellagio* (twinship) that signified mutual support. What developed from these alliances was a convoluted web of friends and friends of friends, and enemies of enemies, etc. These alliances were often volatile and not necessarily driven by strong ideology. Writing in 1997, De Biasi and Lanfranchi wrote, 'political ideology is not the main issue in the ultrà gatherings, the cognitive framework of the *curves* is metaphorical and can assimilate young people of opposing ideologies'.[21] What may have been true in 1997 is clearly no longer an uncomplicated rule of the curva. Political affiliation can, and does, override team affiliation in certain contexts. Testa and Armstrong found that, in some contexts, the neo-fascist politics of Roma and Lazio ultràs groups trump even the football rivalry.[22]

The A.S. Livorno football club provides a particularly interesting case study of the confluence of politics and football.[23] The town of Livorno gave birth to the Italian Communist Part in 1921 as Antonio Gramsci, among others, split from the socialist party.[24] One of the Livorno's primary ultras groups, the *Brigate Autonome Livornesi* (Autonomous Brigade of Livorno), was known to wear Che Guevara shirts, or wave flags of the Soviet Union or Cuba. Livorno ultras were also known to ignite anti-Berlusconi chants in the stadium as Berlusconi represents a form of the new right wing. The group also expresses solidarity with those who have suffered such as the survivors of the earthquake in Haiti. Livorno fans are associated with the larger Antifa anti-fascist networks and they have formed alliances with other left-wing fan groups across Europe such as those of AEK Athens, Marseille, Beşiktaş (Istanbul), Celtic (Glasgow) and St. Pauli (Hamburg). In addition to the heated political rivalry with the right wing fans of Lazio, Hellas Verona is another fixture that brings out exaggerated political sentiment.

In the late 1990s and into the early 2000s, the display of right wing political sentiments became a worrying development for the organizers of Italian football. Of particular note were the exposition of Fascist, xenophobic, Nazi and anti-semitic displays. Lazio fans raised a banner in support of a Serbian war criminal and applauded Paolo Di Canio's fascist salute.[25] The Roma curva was marked by a display of Nazi flags in 2006,[26] and the increasingly common exposition of the celtic cross of Forza Nuova,[27] a right wing political group. Overt racism has been another troubling occurrence at the Italian stadium as black players face taunts all too often and fans of Verona were reported to have convinced the team owners not to acquire black players.[28] As mentioned in Chapter 5, the confluence of radical politics and football is evident online as groups use internet to further their agenda.[29]

Christian Bromberger, writing in 1999, found that racism was less important than team affiliation: a successful black player on *our* team would be lauded, while the black opponent would be subject to racialized taunts with little awareness by the fans. Race, in other words, was just another feature for opposing fans to disparage.

Bromberger's comments point to the peculiarities of the Italian peninsula where immigration and racial heterogeneity were, and are, a relatively new phenomenon. In the Italian context, racial abuse may reflect a profound ignorance rather than the effects of colonialism and/or long-standing racial tension. In recent years, right-wing Roman ultràs have been vociferous in their rejection of multi-culturalism. They see themselves as not racist – they believe in cultural essentialism where every race should stick to their own culture. Herzfeld examines and dismisses such views as disingenuous rationalizations.[30] Whatever the ideological underpinning, the racist behaviour of certain fans has earned public condemnation by politicians and has fuelled perceptions to outsiders who see Italy as lagging behind the rest of Europe in terms of race relations. Italy has failed in its bid to host major football tournaments, in part, because of its public problems with racial intolerance.

Before every match in Italy, a message is read aloud that prohibits, among other things, the exposition of provocative symbols or messages. Provocative is defined by the league as anything discriminatory in terms of race, religion *or* territory. The category of territory is necessary due to the long history of regional prejudice, and particularly of northerners against southerners. Verona fans were particularly notorious as they constructed banners that 'welcomed' Naples fans to Italy, and banners that wished volcanic eruptions on the Neapolitans. Though the stadium officially prohibits xenophobic or racist symbols, there are several well-known examples of fans breaking these restrictions. Monkey chants directed at black players have been too common. Mario Balotelli, the gifted Italian player of African heritage, has been a particular target of racism as some have questioned his Italian-ness.[31] Anti-semitic songs were a regular part of the Lazio fans' repetoire.[32] Verona fans were known to be particular intolerant, having been vocal in their opposition to black players.[33] When it was rumoured that Hellas Verona would acquire a black player, in the stadium, among their ultras, two fans dressed in Ku Klux Klan robes 'hung' a black mannequin in effigy. The black player transferred to a different team. Verona fans combined their skin-based racism with territorial discrimination when their dark-skinned Brazilian player, Dirceu, transferred to Napoli. The fans' farewell banner informed him that would no longer be a foreigner – he was returning to the dark continent.[34] More recently, ugly displays of racism have been targeted at one of the Italy's best players, Mario Balotelli.[35]

Distrust of state

Through the decades, the antagonism and violence that arose between rival fan groups was gradually redirected towards the common enemies of the police and the state itself. The mistrust between fans and the police has a long history and mirrors more general themes of endemic distrust in Italy. Perhaps the first tragedy in the Italian football stadium[36] occurred in Salerno in April of 1963. A controversial decision by the referee led the home fans to invade the pitch causing general chaos. The police rushed to the centre of the pitch, and one officer fired three shots into the air. One of these bullets apparently hit Giuseppe Plaitano in the head and killed him. The official investigation found that Plaitano died of a heart attack even though witnesses reported blood flowing from his temple. The official autopsy was mysteriously lost and the investigation was abandoned. Major newspapers in Italy now report, as fact, that Plaitano was killed by one of the officer's bullets, and that the investigation was a poor attempt at a cover-up.[37] The absurd tragedy and cover-up conjured a profound feeling of distrust between Italian citizens, and in particular, fans, and the state. In a country with a history of low levels of trust in authority, this event is one of the series of injustices that have caused ultras to feel marginalized as scape-goats.

Fan violence and disruptions have become something of a regular event in Italy. The Roma-Lazio derby of March, 2004, was interrupted when a rumour spread through the stadium that a child had been accidentally killed by police. Despite the official announcements over the public address system that there were no reported casualties, several fans, with the encouragement of thousands, entered onto the pitch and pleaded with the players to halt the match. Journalists later speculated that the incident was a pre-meditated show of power by the ultras. The theory was that the Roma ultras and Lazio ultras that are normally rivals overcame their differences in order to stop the match. The theory was plausible because of the well-known distrust of the police.

The 2007 tragedies involving the death of a police officer and the shooting of a Lazio fan demonstrate the violence and distrust between fans and police. In February, 2007, police officer Fillippo Raciti was killed amidst fan violence outside of the stadium in Catania. After initial reports of an explosive were found to be false, it was deemed that Raciti died of liver injuries caused by blunt force trauma, possibly by a dislodged sink. Raciti died in the hospital. After a lengthy judicial process, two young fans were convicted of the crime. Ultras believe that the fans were wrongfully convicted. The death of Raciti caused a halt to all football matches for a week and had caused league to actively enforce the so-called Pisanu Decrees that had mandated several safety requirements, but had ultimately made several temporary exemptions for stadiums that could not immediately comply, such as in Catania.

In November 2007, Gabriele Sandri was travelling with some fellow Lazio fans to Milan to see an away game when they stopped to get gasoline in Tuscany. Their group was involved in a scuffle with Juventus fans who happened to be at the same rest stop. A police officer on the other side of the highway attempted to respond. With his gun held aloft, officer Spaccarotella rushed across the highway. According to his account, he inadvertently pulled the trigger. One of the bullets went through the window of the car, hit the 26-year-old Sandri in the neck, and killed him. Roma and Lazio fans united in their reaction to the killing by throwing rocks and setting fires outside the Italian Olympic Committee headquarters and the Olympic stadium. Roma fans 'adopted' Sandri as one of their own. After an initial lenient sentence for manslaughter, the Italian courts found that the officer had intentionally fired at the vehicle in a reckless manner. The events incited fan protests and further eroded relations between fans and the police and in many people's belief in the justice system. Sandri became a martyr and a symbol of the struggle for justice among Italian ultras. His name is spray-painted on the walls of Rome as a memorial and a reminder of injustice. Another common slogan seen in the stadium and streets alike is the acronym 'ACAB' which stands for All Cops Are Bastards.

Militarization of the stadium

Through the years, the Italian stadium has become ever a more militarized zone. As part of the aforementioned Pisanu Decree, stadiums are required to cordon off the area 500 metres around the stadium to ensure that those without tickets cannot approach the stadium. Tickets required personalization so that one could not enter the stadium with a friend's ticket without prior authorization without incurring the risk of steep fines. Banners were severely limited at first, by special patrols that would check each banner at the gates, and later, through a system of prior authorization via fax. Needless to say, these controls on banners limited the improvisation and spontaneity of banner makers. For decades now, Italy's military police, the Carabinieri, have conducted security 'pat downs' in search of flares or other contraband on every young man that wished to enter one of the curvas. As I often carried a camera and an audio recorder into the stadium, often with extra batteries, I would speak in loud English in order to convince the authorities that I was not an ultra, but rather, a naive tourist. This security stop was a normal part of going to the stadium every week even as many outlawed flares and explosives were smuggled in and set off at every match that I attended.

Military vehicles and riot police line the routes leading up to the Olympic Stadium, especially before high-profile matches such as those between Roma and Lazio, or involving another big team, or even with smaller teams if there was a known political clash between supporters. As described previously in Chapter 1, it has become something of a Sunday ritual for the Carabinieri to escort fans to away matches in a military-style convoy. The Italian highway, the *Autostrada*, becomes a moving display of fan culture as fans traverse the country to support their team.[38] In addition to the overt military and police present outside the stadium and in transit, the Italian bureau of special investigation, the Digos,[39] has a team of officers dedicated to tracking ultras who are deemed a particular threat. The ultras are aware of these investigations and believe that they are being unfairly targeted. It is not uncommon to see the phrase, *Digos boia!* (Digos to the gallows) spray-painted on the walls of Rome or other cities.

In this atmosphere of distrust, the *Tessera del Tifoso* (Identity Card of the Fan) was introduced as another step to *weed out the troublemakers.* The Tessera del Tifoso (hereafter, Tessera) was promoted as a way for fans to exhibit their loyalty, and gain special privileges and discounts. It was supposed to make it easier to purchase tickets for home and away matches by linking the card to a bank account. Privacy advocates, and the already suspicious fans were quick to attack the Tessera as an illegal way for the police to track and harass fans. The database of fans was to be shared between football league officials, banks and the state. Any fan with any sense of twentieth century history and Italian Fascism had reason to be weary of such a scheme. The head of the European Football Association (UEFA), and former Juventus player, Michel Platini, thought the Tessera was a bad idea. Playing to his fans, Roma's Daniel De Rossi commented that he thought the police would do better to track themselves than to track innocent fans. Various fan protests and legal challenges ensued.

The league delayed the imposition of the Tessera, but has been trying to reinvent it. The political savvy of the fans in this case helped to modify and delay the potentially repressive fan identity card. A quick internet search of the term, *no alla tessera*, reveals a wide collection of images and articles that express fans' opinions of the original scheme. As of March, 2015, there is an active public discussion about the future of the Tessera along with other stadium initiatives in an attempt to make the stadium safer as well as to increase attendance at Italian stadiums. The Tessera had discouraged many fans from going to the stadium at all as even occasional fans and children needed a Tessera to attend. The newly branded Fidelity Card could function to actually help fans to acquire tickets and enjoy the stadium, while the league could enact other measures to isolate and identify those who 'sing racist choruses or display shameful banners'.[40]

Ultràs against commercialism

In the 1990s, ultràs began protesting the increasing commercialization and 'modernization' of football. For some ultràs, part of the *la mentalità* (proper mentality or attitude) consists of rejecting anything that interferes with allegiance to the team. This meant that financial matters and politics *should be* secondary to the team. Ultràs protested against rising ticket prices and the inflated salaries of players and coaches. They hated pay-per-view televised football. Another element of la mentalità is to attend matches wherever and whenever possible. Ultràs around the country organized to resist the increasing power of television companies that advocated midweek games in place of the traditional Sunday afternoon kick-off time, because it made travel to away games more difficult. The now defunct website, '*No al calcio moderno*'[41] (No to Modern Football) displayed photos of protest rallies staged throughout Italy. Ultràs also protested against the corruption scandals involving players, referees and team directors and they railed against various doping scandals. They verbally, and sometimes physically, attacked team owners who appeared to be more concerned with the bottom line than with winning. The politics of money sometimes conflict with loyalty to the team.

The increasing visibility of global capital in football has been met by resistance as well as more ambiguous reactions. As discussed in the previous chapter, the Lazio ultras, the Irriducibili, embraced commercial opportunities. Police crackdowns and increasing media scrutiny on ultràs groups led them to change their tactics. As Fabrizio Toffolo, the former leader of the Irriducibili, said 'The ultrà must use his brain [and be] much more aware of communication, much more aware of the problems that ruin the image of football'.[42] A.S. Roma fans were initially sceptical of their new American owners who bought the team in 2011. For example, fan group, Core de Roma, resisted a change to the traditional logo of the mythical She-Wolf and Romulus and Remus by posting an image of the new logo with an 'x' through it on their home page. The new logo was a slight modification of the old logo, but from the perspective of the fans, it seemed needless and, moreover, seemed to be indicative of the new management's desire to make Roma into a global brand.[43] Perhaps they thought the logo needed an update, or perhaps they believed the new logo would give them stronger trademark rights. Whatever the case, the fan unrest seemed to be quelled by success on the pitch. The 2013–2014 season saw Roma contend for the title and qualify for the Champions League. The new coach and a new stream of players combined with stalwarts, Francesco Totti and Daniele De Rossi, to become a formidable team with high expectations were high for the 2014–2015 season. The loyalty of fans seems to derive from some fragile balance of adherence to tradition balanced by progress that leads to victories. Waves of resistance and surrender to the demands of global corporate capital are a defining trait of the contemporary game.

Direct political action

In May 2013, a small protest against the demolition of trees in Gezi Park in the Taksim neighbourhood of Istanbul turned into a widespread protest against the regime after the initial sit-in was violently disrupted. As the protests grew, the regime responded with police commanded to subdue the crowds with water hoses and tear gas. The protests became a global media spectacle symbolized by the iconic image of the 'lady in red' being sprayed with tear gas. Local football fans came to play an important part in the protests as the police 'cracked down'.

> Later, many reported the important role of the Çarsi group, the Beşiktaş futbol team fans, in raising their spirits. Famous for their rhymed slogan '*Çarşi! Her şeye karşi!*' (Çarsi! Always in opposition!), these futbol fans had a tradition of getting organized, producing slogans and rallying the crowds. All of a sudden the performance of futbol fandom was transformed into a chant for Gezi protesters.[44]

The skills honed by football fans that continually struggle against opposition became quite useful in a protest that brought enthusiastic but inexperienced citizens to resist the authorities. The Taksim protests spread to other parts of Turkey and lasted through the summer before dying down. Their legacy is still being written, but it is clear that for those who were there, they tasted the power of collective action – a power that manifests itself weekly in football stadiums.

While this essay has focused considerable attention on the place of the Italian football stadium as a place of resistance, perhaps football takes on a larger role in societies that are less accustomed to protest and disagreement. As Turkish author, Saadet Özen remarked, 'the stadium is one of the rare places in Turkey where the masses can organize, brandish slogans, and learn to take common action and confront official authorities'.[45] This seems to be a common attitude in which the stadium as a political space is overlooked by authorities or is considered an innocuous 'safety valve' for the cathartic expression of political and emotional angst. But the record shows that the stadium is a political space and it has been the recruiting and training grounds for not only protesters, but for paramilitary troops. Take, for example, Serbian war criminal, Arkan and his so-called 'Tigers' that were recruited, in part, from the ranks of the Belgrade Red Star fans. Arkan was the leader of a fan group before the breakup of Yugoslavia opened an opportunity for him to lead his group into an actual war zone. The stadium brings together energetic young citizens (largely, but not exclusively men) who desire to be part of something larger than themselves. The stadium offers an enticing mixture of emotional commitment and communal expression that make it rife for collective action for any number of purposes.

Conclusion

This chapter has reviewed some of the theoretical and practical dimensions at the conjunction of politics and football fandom. If we consider the stadium as a part of the public sphere, we see a place that is rich with political opinions and a valuable place for dissent. The history of Italian football reveals the development of politically astute, hardcore fans that blur the lines between football and politics. The modern mediation of sport gives the football stadium an even higher stage with which to broadcast political messages. Italian ultras are castigated (and feared) by Italian officials, and these fans are subjected to an array of restrictions on their rights. For foreign fans, the Italian ultras represent a model of subcultural style and resistance against authority. Their influence can be seen even in the Arab Spring where football fans were instrumental in organizing resistance.

This chapter has, once again, focused attention on the Italian case. While it is a useful and conspicuous model of fan culture, the political implications of football fandom need to be better understood in a variety of other contexts.[46] I have a particular interest in the American context where, under our constitution, individual citizens have the rights of freedom of expression, though, rarely is this right exercised in any meaningful way in the stadium. We, as consumers and sports fans, seem willing to leave our political identities behind when we approach the publicly funded stadiums, and we expect our athletes to do the same.[47] Perhaps even more intriguingly is the place of football in more unstable political climates. James Dorsey's Middle East Football Blog[48] provides a fascinating look at the place of football in that region. The protests surrounding the Brazilian 2014 World Cup offer a glimpse of the ways in which the publicity surrounding football can be redirected in order to show more pressing social concerns such as the plight of the poor. Football has been a source of inclusive (as opposed to divisive) if ephemeral, nationalism in Iraq as their victory in the 2007 Asian Cup momentarily transcended religious divisions.[49] Can the stadium be an agent of positive social change in places like North Korea or in troubled African nations? Surely, there is no singular answer, but the stadium is vital public venue that might act as a barometer of public opinion, as a site of dissent, or as pep rally for authoritarianism – but not a site of meaningless diversions from real life. The old notion of bread and circuses must be updated in the era of Twitter and ultras.

Disclosure statement

No potential conflict of interest was reported by the author.

Notes

1. Chandler, 'Polish Soccer Fans'.
2. The original banner read, 'Real Madrid: *Grazie per portare* via *la spazzatura*'. Members of Core de Roma suggested using *immondizie* as a more Roman alternative to *spazzatura*.
3. The Guardian, 'Standard Liege Fans'.
4. Ames, 'Serbia v Albania'.
5. According to one exiled writer, Obiang uses sport to prop up the unequal social structure of the country. See Laurel, 'Why We shouldn't Support'.
6. Kennedy and Kennedy, 'Introduction: Reflections on the Context of "Left Wing"'.
7. See, for example, Butterworth, 'The Athlete as Citizen'.
8. Chomsky, *Manufacturing Consent*.
9. See, for instance, Testa and Armstrong, *Football, Fascism and Fandom*.
10. Kennedy and Kennedy, 'Introduction: Reflections on the Context of "Left Wing"', 119.
11. James Dorsey's blog, www.mideastsoccer.blogspot.com, has done outstanding work in covering the effects of soccer in broader culture throughout the Middle East. Egyptian Ultra Tactics Evident in the Battle for Cairo's Tahrir Square.
12. Öztürkmen, 'The Park, the Penguin, and the Gas'.
13. Guschwan, 'Stadium as Public Sphere'.
14. Kohn, *Brave New Neighborhood*, 59.
15. Delicath and Deluca, 'Image-events'.
16. Notable exceptions are Real Madrid and Barcelona that are owned by fan associations.
17. See Podaliri and Balestri, 'The Ultràs, Racism and Football Culture in Italy'; Foot, *Calcio*.
18. Podaliri and Balestri, 'The Ultràs, Racism and Football Culture in Italy'.
19. *Ultrà*, directed by R. Tognazzi.

20. *Eccezzzuniale ... Veramente*, directed by C. Vanzina.
21. De Biasi and Lanfranchi, 'The Importance of Difference', 96.
22. Testa and Armstrong, *Football, Fandom and Fascism*, 36.
23. Doidge, 'The Birthplace of Italian Communism'.
24. Ibid., 248.
25. Agnew, *Forza Italia*.
26. Ibid.
27. See their website, http://www.forzanuova.org/.
28. Parks, *A Season with Verona*.
29. Italian sociologist, Antonio Roversi, in *Odio in Rete*, found that the internet became a breeding ground for radicalism.
30. Herzfeld, 'Small Mindedness Writ Large', 269.
31. Balotelli was adopted by white Italian parents early in his life.
32. One self-identified Jewish Lazio fan that I interviewed remarked that the anti-semitic songs were the one imperfection of the Lazio fanbase. Though he sat in the Curva Nord, he sat higher up in the stadium from the more avid ultras.
33. See Parks, *A Season with Verona;* Sansonetti, 'Ultras Verona'.
34. Sansonetti, 'Ultras Verona'.
35. Doidge, 'If You Jump Up and Down, Balotelli Dies'.
36. This was the first death during a football match to be widely publicized in Italy.
37. Mariottini. *Ultraviolenza.*
38. See Parks, *A Season with Verona*, for a wonderful description of travelling on the road with the ultras.
39. Digos is an acronym for the Divisione Investigazione Generali e Operazioni Speciali (General Investigation Division and Special Operations).
40. Bianchi, 'Stadi, Ecco Cosa Cambia'.
41. *No Al Calcio Moderno*, website defunct as of writing. www.noalcalciomoderno.it.
42. From *Irriducibili Movie*. Translated, *Uso molto il cervello ... [essere] Molto piu attento alla communicazione. Molto piu attento ai problemi che rovinano l'immagine di calcio'*.
43. Straus, 'American Pallotta out to Turn AS Roma into a 21st-century Empire'.
44. Öztürkmen, 'The Park, the Penguin, and the Gas', 47.
45. Ibid., 53.
46. See the Soccer Politics Blog (http://sites.duke.edu/wcwp/) hosted by Duke University for an invaluable portal into the football around the world.
47. Butterworth, 'The Athlete as Citizen'.
48. Dorsey, *Turbulent World of Middle East Soccer.*
49. Hendawi, 'Iraqis Bask in Rare Joy'.

References

Agnew, P. *Forza Italia: A Journey in Search of Italy and its Football*. London: Ebury House, 2006.

Ames, N. 'Serbia v Albania: Drones, Flags and Violence in Abandoned Match'. *BBC.com*, October 15, 2014. www.bbc.com/sport/0/football/29624259 (accessed December 14, 2014).

Bianchi, F. 'Stadi, Ecco Cosa Cambia: Nasce la Fidelity Card'. *La Repubblica.it*, April 6, 2014. www.repubblica.it/rubriche/spycalcio/2014/04/06/news/club_senza/.

Butterworth, M. 'The Athlete as Citizen: Judgement and Rhetorical Invention in Sport'. *Sport in Society* 17, no. 7 (2014): 867–83.

Chandler, R. 'Polish Soccer Fans Break into Team's Stadium, Leave Coffins for Each Player'. *Sportsgrid*, January 28, 2015. www.sporstgrid.com/soccer/polish-soccer-fans-break-into-teams-stadium/ (accessed February 2, 2015).

De Biasi, R., and P. Lanfranchi. 'The Importance of Difference: Football Identities in Italy'. In *Entering the Field: New Perspectives on World Football*, ed. G. Armstrong and R. Giulianotti, 87–104. Oxford: Berg, 1997.

Delicath, J., and K. DeLuca. 'Image Events, the Public Sphere, and Argumentative Practice: The Case of Radical Environmental Groups'. *Argumentation* 17, no. 3 (2003): 315–33.

Doidge, M. '"The Birthplace of Italian Communism": Political Identity and Action Amongst Livorno Fans'. *Soccer & Society* 14 (2013): 246–61.

Doidge, M. 'If You Jump Up and Down, Balotelli Dies: Racism and Player Abuse in Italian Football'. *International Review for the Sociology of Sport* 50 (2015): 249–64. doi:1012690213480354.

Dorsey, J. *The Turbulent World of Middle East Soccer.* www.mideastsoccer.blogspot.com.

Eccezzzuniale ... Veramente. Directed by C. Vanzina. Cinemedia, 1982.

Foot, J. *Calcio: A History of Italian Football.* London: Harper Perennial, 2007.

The Guardian. 'Standard Liege Fans Face Five-year Stadium Bans for Steven Defour Banner'. *The Guardian.com*, January 26, 2015. www.theguardian.com/football/2015/jan/26/standard-liege-fans-stadium-ban-defour-banner (accessed January 30, 2015).

Guschwan, M. 'Stadium as Public Sphere'. *Sport in Society* 17, no. 7 (2014): 884–900.

Hendawi, H. 'Iraqis Bask in Rare Joy after Soccer Win'. *Washington Post*, July 30, 2007. washingtonpost.com/wp-dyn/content/article/2007/07/29/AR2007072901047.html (accessed January 20, 2015).

Herzfeld, M. 'Small-mindedness Writ Large: On the Migrations and Manners of Prejudice'. *Journal of Ethnic and Migration Studies* 33, no. 2 (2007): 255–74.

Irriducibili Movie: L'Amor per te mi Fa Teppista. DVD [Irriducibili Movie: My Love for you Makes me a Hooligan]. Directed by A. Zappulla and R. Camolino. Italy: Lazio Irriducibili Video, 2005.

Kennedy, D., and P. Kennedy. 'Introduction: Reflections on the Context of 'Left Wing' Fan Cultures'. *Soccer & Society* 14, no. 2 (2013): 117–31.

Kohn, M. *Brave New Neighborhoods: The Privatization of Public Space.* New York: Routledge, 2004.

Laurel, J.T.A. 'Why We Shouldn't Support the Africa Cup of Nations'. *The Guardian*, February 8, 2015. theguardian.com/world/2015/feb/08/Africa-cup-of-nations-equitorial-guinea (accessed January 22, 2015).

Manufacturing Consent: Noam Chomsky and the Media. DVD. Directed by M. Achbar and P. Wintonick. Zeitgeist Video, 1992.

Mariottini, D. *Ultraviolenza: Storie di Sangue del Tifo Italiano* [Ultraviolence: Stories of Blood in Italian Fandom]. Turin: Bradipolibri, 2004.

Öztürkmen, A. 'The Park, the Penguin, and the Gas: Performance in Progress in Gezi Park'. *TDR/The Drama Review* 58, no. 3 (2014): 39–68.

Parks, T. *A Season with Verona: Travels Around Italy in Search of Illusion, National Character and ... Goals!* New York: Arcade, 2002.

Podaliri, C., and C. Balestri. 'The Ultràs, Racism and Football Culture in Italy'. In *Fanatics!: Power, Identity and Fandom in Football*, ed. A. Brown, 88–100. London: Routledge, 1998.

Roversi, A. *Calcio, Tifo e Violenza: Il Teppismo Calcistico in Italia* [Football, Fandom and Violence: Football Hooliganism in Italy]. Milan: Il Mulino, (1992) 1994.

Roversi, A. *Hate on the Net: Extremist Sites, Neo-fascism On-line, Electronic Jihad.* Burlington, VT: Ashgate, 2008.

Sansonetti, A. 'Ultras Verona: Non solo Lampedusa'. *Blitz Quotidiano*, October 7, 2013. www.blitzquotidiano.it/sport/verona-sport/ultras-verona-lampedusa (accessed April 11, 2015).

Straus, B. 'American Pallotta out to Turn AS Roma into a 21st-century Empire'. *Sports Illustrated*, August 12, 2013. http://www.si.com/ (accessed March 21, 2015).

Testa, A., and G. Armstrong. *Football, Fascism and Fandom: The UltraS of Italian Football.* London: Black Publishers, 2010.

Ultrà. Directed by R. Tognazzi. Numero Uno International, 1991.

Conclusion

Contemporary life is structured, to a large extent, by media and by the consumption of goods. Innumerable media messages compete to enter our thoughts on a daily basis while the market economy attempts to provide a product to solve every problem and alleviate every concern. In fandom we see the convergence, and often a celebration of media and consumerism combined in a social context that encourages ferocious passion. Fans confer to and derive great meaning from the sporting contests that they enjoy. As a result, they often become avid and loyal consumers. But they are also discriminating and demanding. They want their 'product' to be better than before, and to achieve greatness. They can be impatient and unreasonable and they can also add great value to the sporting enterprise.

In addition to the forces of consumption and media, in fandom, we can see some of the primary tensions of our times. The desire for local community competes with the desire for mobility and the allure of a higher standard of living elsewhere. Fandom illustrates the tensions between local affiliation and global culture, between loyalty and choice. Fandom embraces the deep desire to belong to something bigger than the self without the limits of binding, long-term obligations. The desire to be part of the group competes with the desire to be a distinct individual. The anthropologist Victor Turner characterized the difference between pre-industrialized and post-industrialized societies through his concepts of liminal and liminoid.[1] Liminal experiences are intense experiences where one is temporarily cast outside of one's culture. As part of the ritual structure, the disorienting experience of liminality serves to give one a new perspective on their society. When the initiate is reintegrated into society, the person is in some way changed and is prepared to assume a new role, such as adulthood, in the society. The intensity of the liminal experience is due, in part, to the fact that one's immediate society is all encompassing. There are no other options. Industrialized societies offer liminal-like, *liminoid* experiences that may be intense and transformative, but are always optional. One may reject the ritual and find the means for survival elsewhere – in a different town or a different country. The stakes are simply not as high.

Football fandom, I would argue, offers liminoid experiences of great emotional intensity and of identity affirming power. Fandom is one ritualized solution to our desire for identity and sociality that can no longer necessarily be satisfied through birth and kinship. One has the opportunity and the burden to carve out one's identity in the place of one's choosing. Fandom is a choice, even if our fandom was bestowed upon us by our parents or grandparents. We can always turn our backs on the fandom of our family in pursuit of other experiences. With like-minded fans, we can gather and form an identity every Sunday in the terrace. We can relieve our stresses, and become pre-occupied with something that, in the face of real-life incursions, can be dropped instantly. The legendary Italian football coach, Arrigo Sachi, once commented that 'Football is the most important of the things that are not important'.[2] Perhaps the great strength of football is that however big the match, it is still, always a game meant to be played. Fans and players recover from mistakes and losses.

This volume has focused on how media glues fans together. From the stadium to the internet, media is central to the project of fandom. Media allows fans to support the team, express one's identity, and to connect with other like-minded fans for support and friendly competition in the ever-evolving process of becoming a fan. At the outset of this volume, I defined media in a broad way to consider how the faculties of the human body are media as well as mass media. This approach de-emphasizes the role of technology in communication, and instead rehumanizes communication. The sender of a message (a fan) chooses from a variety of expressive tools to express an idea or provoke a response. It matters less in my view if a medium is 'natural' such as the gesture of a hand, or a technologically advanced 'tweet' sent from a mobile phone. The art of gesturing, after all, has millennia of development behind it, and remains a semantically rich form of communication. It's my wish to avoid a media-deterministic approach that would treat mass media as having trajectories independent of the producers or consumers (audiences) of specific media texts. The medium is only part of the message. The ways in which media circulates and recirculates affects the meaning of the text. This volume has considered the lifespan of media from production to consumption. An image seen in a newspaper is treated differently than the one encountered on the clubhouse wall. The meaning of a text is a negotiation between the creator and the reader, and context conditions the ways in which a text can be received.

This volume begins with face-to-face communication in the spaces where fans can learn to become fans. Football fandom is a social project rooted, to some extent, in the face-to-face experience in the stadium and in the more intimate circumstances of daily life. I suspect that this will always be the case, but the neighbourhood sociality of Testaccio, and similar places, is threatened. The rhythms of modern life go against the traditional *dopolavoro* (after-work) social club that was a typical *male* place to unwind from the demands of labour. With the geographical expansion of 'the city', the daily commute by car or train becomes the after-work ritual. With hands on the steering wheel, mobile phone earpiece in place, the car seat becomes the place to unwind with friends. New telecommunications technologies can facilitate the coordination of time and place to congregate offline. The Core de Roma fan club stands as an example of a club that encompasses vibrant virtual and 'real-life' communities. For them, technology facilitates the daily interaction that forms strong bonds, but it replaces neither the energy of the stadium nor the fun of gathering together to dine.

Will the endless chatter of handheld electronic devices kill football? Italians love cell phones and they love football, but can these two passions co-exist in the stadium? The immediacy of the stadium and the unity of thousands of fans acting as one is the major appeal of the stadium. The NFL stadium or NBA arena in the US is a place where one might go to chat, drink beer, watch a bit of a game, and continuously tweet one's particular feelings of the moment, and take a "selfie" to authenticate the senders' whereabouts at a cool place. The stereotyped modern fan has their head down on the screen while the performers that they ostensibly paid to see are engaged in their competition. In short, the US arena expresses the telos of the market economy: a wired site of celebrity sighting, high energy sound and bright lights; a space of endless distraction, pseudo community and high calorie food with consumer choices in seating section and logo-ed memorabilia designed to separate fans from their discretionary income. Of course, one could argue that the changes to the NBA arena are simply a reflection of the times and the response to consumer demand. There is growing concern that sport will lose young participants,[3] (and ultimately, fans) because, unlike video games, there is no reset button. Sport stadiums in the US view themselves as entertainment arcades with dancers, huge video screens, halftime shows, t-shirt giveaways, and extensive eating and drinking options.

Contemporary life is lived through media. We have always used our bodies as media to present to the world. Gradually, we, as a species, have expanded our repertoire of media. The growing influence of asynchronous, and long-distance media has undeniably changed social life and fandom. Is physical presence too limiting in an age of long-distance connection? While attendance figures at Italian stadiums have been declining in recent years, the numbers have been steady and growing in the other parts of Europe. Due to the comparatively few interruptions, football does not lend itself to the constant distraction of social media. The modes of fan participation performed by the ultràs require continual attention to the ebb and flow of the match, and to the emerging chants initiated by *fans*, not marketers. Italian stadiums are remarkably bare. The Olympic Stadium in Rome has little advertising. There is a green pitch and blue seats, a roof over the stands. The large screens at either end of the stadium are underutilized by American standards – during the match, they show the score, and that is about it. Can the stadium become a refuge from the world of social media? Will it become a casualty of the instant gratification of video games and endless chatter offered on a screen?

There must be many people who crave the togetherness of the stadium and will forgo the pull of the phone to in order to participate in the match. Many hardcore fan groups shun social media altogether because it goes against their ethos of resistance. They believe (rightly) that it is far easier to be confrontational behind a screen. It takes more courage to show up and confront your rivals. The ultras in Istanbul and Cairo drew upon their experience in the stadium to confront police. I also see encouraging signs in the US. While I portray the NFL and NBA arenas as shopping malls with entertainment, there are vibrant fan cultures in Major League Soccer (MLS) and in college sports that demonstrate strong community. Others have pointed out to me that the tailgate culture that is an established tradition outside of the stadium at many professional and collegiate American football games is an analogue or substitute for the European or South American way of doing things. I would not want to diminish the experience of camaraderie that tailgaters feel, but I must point out that these temporary carnivals of fan culture must occur outside of the official boundaries of the stadium.

There is an opportunity for more work to be done on the lively fan culture that gathers around sport around the world. Though marketers know it exists, what really accounts for the depth of bonds that fans feel? What cultural forms will best suit the coming generations of fans? Doubtless, media will be part of the new forms of fandom, but the face-to-face connection of fans in the stadium must be retained.

Community will find a time and place to form. Of that I am certain. I am less certain of the future of the stadium as a site of fan singing and chanting, political dissent, biting humour and sentimental memorials. I fear that the voice of the fan at the stadium might prove too inconvenient to those who are in line to profit. I fear the idea of the stadium as an apolitical space is merely a guise for a different types of politics – a politics of hierarchy and control. Football run solely for profit, and not for fans and by fans is not football. May this volume stand as a documentation of the power of fans and the power of media to enable a fan voice that can joke, exalt, mourn, and if necessary, dissent.

Notes
1. Turner, *From Ritual to Theater*.
2. Original quote, 'Il calcio è la cosa più importante delle cose non importanti'.
3. Wallerson, 'Youth Participation Weakens in Basketball, Football, Baseball, Soccer'.

References

Turner, V. *From Ritual to Theatre: The Human Seriousness of Play.* New York: PAJ Publications, 1982.

Wallerson, R. 'Youth Participation Weakens in Basketball, Football, Baseball, Soccer'. *Wall Street Journal*, January 31, 2014. Wsj.com/articles/SB100014240.

Index

Note: Page number followed by n denote endnotes.

AC Milan football team 73–4
Albania and Serbia 124
America, Arsenal fan in 81
American football league 68
Anderson, Benedict 89
Andrews, David 72
Arkan 119n33, 133
A.S. Roma football team 54, 55, 88, 90, 95–7
Autogrill 15

Balotelli, Mario 129
Basso, Keith 19
Bauman, Richard 9, 26, 29
Beckham, David 109–10
Berlusconi, Silvio 73–5
brand(s) 6; communities 111; iconic 107; overview of 106–7; sport team 108–12; ultràs *see* ultràs
broadcast media 5; American fans 81; economics and fandom 75; fan diaspora 79–81; and fandom 69–70; political economy of 82; pub football 75, 79; radio sport 70–2; Roma Club Testaccio 77–9; social viewing 75–7; television *see* television broadcast media
Bromberger, Christian 128–9
BskyB (Murdoch) 73, 74
burrini 99

Cairo's Tahrir Square 125
Calderoli, Roberto 61
Chinaglia, Giorgio 116
chronotope 56
Commando Ultràs Curva Sud, (C.U.C.S) 35
Conflitto di Civiltà: Un Inganno Pericoloso (Conflict of civilizations: A Dangerous Deception) 60
Core de Roma: charitable initiatives 92; chat room 97; fan club history 90–3; online and offline communities 88–90; rival 99–100; Romanesco 98–9; website, evolution of 93–4, 99
Core de Roma Gens Romana 96
Core de Roma nel mondo 94
Coubertin, Pierre De 125
Cuban, Mark 68
cugini (cousins) 57
Curva Nord (North Curve) 27, 39, 47, 57
Curva Sud 27, 30, 32, 35–7

daily newspaper *see* print media
D'Azeglio, Marquis 18
Defour, Steven 123
De Rossi, Daniele 80
Di Canio, Paolo 58–61, 98, 100
digital information technology 87
digital media 85
Digos 131, 135n39
Donadoni, Roberto 116
Duncan, Carol 55

English Premier League (EPL) 87; NFL and 73; schedules 69; for 2016–2019 seasons 72
Evviva La Sparuta Minoranza 61

face-to-face interaction 3–5, 89; Autogrill 15; clubhouse 18, 22n27; football fandom and food 17–18; overview of 8–9; performance 9–10; public safety 14; regionalism in Italy 18–19; Roma Club Testaccio 19–20; Roman identity 20; in training ground 10–11; ultràs groups 11–13
fan club history 90–3
fan diaspora 79–81
fans performance at stadium 5; anniversary/memorial banners 36; banners 34–6; clothing 33–4; cultural performance 26–7; gestures 34; globalization 46–7; 'Il derby' 48; Olympic stadium 27–8; overview of 24–6; political banners 36–7; protest 37–8, 47–8; scarves 32–3; songs 39–46; symbols 31–2; timeline 28–31; voice 38–9
free newspaper 54

INDEX

Galliani, Adriano 74
Ginsborg, Paul 25, 73
Giulianotti, Richard 4
globalization 87
global media 87
'Grazie Roma' song 42–4

Hoeness, Uli 118
Holt, Douglas 107, 117

iconic brands 107
Il Romanista 54–5, 63
information technology 85
Inno della Lazio song 44–5
Irriducibili 57, 61–2, 113, 117–18, 119n40, 120n46
Italian football media politics 73
Ivy League hockey 68

James Dorsey's Middle East Football Blog 134
Jenkins, Henry 93, 111–12
jerseys, advertising and branding 109–10
Jeter, Derek 111
Jordan, Michael 109
Juventus football team 99–100

Keita, Seydou 112
Kohn, Margaret 125–6
Kraszewski, Jon 79, 82, 82n8
Kuper, Simon 10

L'amor per te mi fa teppista 115
'La Roma in vantaggio' 71
La Terra in Piazza (Dundes and Falassi) 27
La Voce Della Nord 57–9, 61–2, 72, 114–15
Lazio's ultras *see* ultràs
Lotito, Claudio 45–6, 57, 112, 115–17

Major League Soccer (MLS) 68
Manchester City, 'Our City' campaign 110
mass media 70
Mavericks, Dallas 68
media criticism 3–6
Mediaset 74
Merkel, U. 71
MLS *see* Major League Soccer
Monte di Cocci 19
multimedia 94–5
Murdoch, Rupert 72–3, 75

new media: A.S. Roma football team 95–7; consumer–producer 86–8; Core de Roma *see* Core de Roma; fan club history 90–3; multimedia 94–5; overview of 85–6; Romanità 95; Rome *vs.* Italy 101–2; Totti, Francesco 100–1
News Corporation (Murdoch) 72–4

No al Calcio Moderno 69, 113, 132
Non Mollare Mai song 41–2, 45

Obiang Nguema, Teodoro 124
Olympic Stadium in Rome 54
online media 6, 85
Original Fans 115–17
Özen, Saadet 133

Panini sticker booklets 54
participatory culture 111
pay-per-view satellite television 78
'people's team' (1927) 96
Pisanu Decree 130
politics 6; direct political action 132–3; distrust of state 129–30; Italian ultràs 127–9; militarization of stadium 130–2; overview of 122–5; public sphere 125–7; ultràs against commercialism 132
print media 5, 78; Anti-Lotito 61–2; circulation and identity 55–7; Di Canio *vs.* Totti 59–61; free newspapers 54; history of 52–4; *Il Romanista* 54–5, 63; *Irriducibili* 57, 61–2; *La Voce Della Nord* 57–9, 61–2; overview of 51–2
pub football 75, 79

Raciti, Fillippo 130
radio sport broadcast, history of 70–2
Ražnatoviæ, Željko *see* Arkan
regionalism in Italy 18–19
Roma Club Testaccio 19–20, 75–7; clubhouse of 55–6, 88–9; elaborate decorations of 66–7; operates 78; preference for 'old' technology 78
Romanesco 98–9
Roman fandom 3
Roman football stadium 68
Romanisti nel Mondo section 99
'Roma, Roma' song 40–1
Roversi, Antonio 87
Ruth, Babe 110–11

Sandri, Gabriele 130
satellite television 77–8
Search of Tottigol, In 2
Seattle fan culture 69
Sergio Rosi 56, 76
Singer, Milton 26
SkyItalia 74
social media 52
social project, football fandom as 1
Sordi, Alberto 98–9
Spain, sports journalism in 53
sparuta minoranza 61
'sport-media complex' 108–9

INDEX

sports journalism, in Spain 53
sport team brands 108–12
Stadio Olimpico 27, 32
stadium: militarization of 130–2; as political space 125–7
Super Bowl 70

Taksim protest 132–3
television broadcast media 71–2; impact of 72–3; sky satellite 77–8; soccer, in Italy 73–7
Tessera del Tifoso 131
Testa, Alberto 21n14
Thompson, Dondrea 55
Toffolo, Fabrizio 71–2, 115, 132
Totti, Francesco 47, 56, 59–61, 80, 85, 100–1
'true mass entertainment industry' in Spain 53
Turkle, Sherry 87
Turner, Victor 7n4
'Tutto il calcio Minuto per Minuto' 71

UEFA Cup 78
ultràs 119n24; against commercialism 132; history of 112–13; Irriducibili Inc. and 113, 117–18, 119n40, 120n46; *La Voce Della Nord* 114–15; *No al calcio moderno* 113; Original Fans 115–17; politics in 127–9
Un Americano a Roma 98
Unione Radiofonica Italiana (URI) 71

Venditti, A. 40–4
virtual communities 89

Weed, Michael 75, 79, 81, 82
World Cup Final (1954), radio broadcast of 71

Zanotti, Angela 18
Zawisza Bydogoszcz 123
Zoff, Dino 74

For Product Safety Concerns and Information please contact our EU
representative GPSR@taylorandfrancis.com
Taylor & Francis Verlag GmbH, Kaufingerstraße 24, 80331 München, Germany

www.ingramcontent.com/pod-product-compliance
Lightning Source LLC
Chambersburg PA
CBHW080939300426
44115CB00017B/2880